Accessible Elections

Accessible Elections

How the States Can Help Americans Vote

MICHAEL RITTER AND CAROLINE J. TOLBERT

OXFORD
UNIVERSITY PRESS

OXFORD
UNIVERSITY PRESS

Oxford University Press is a department of the University of Oxford. It furthers
the University's objective of excellence in research, scholarship, and education
by publishing worldwide. Oxford is a registered trade mark of Oxford University
Press in the UK and certain other countries.

Published in the United States of America by Oxford University Press
198 Madison Avenue, New York, NY 10016, United States of America.

Library of Congress Cataloging-in-Publication Data
Names: Ritter, Michael, author. | Tolbert, Caroline J., author.
Title: Accessible elections : how the states can help Americans vote /
Michael Ritter, Caroline J. Tolbert.
Description: New York : Oxford University Press, 2020. |
Includes bibliographical references and index.
Identifiers: LCCN 2020022211 (print) | LCCN 2020022212 (ebook) |
ISBN 9780197537251 (hardback) | ISBN 9780197537275 (epub) |
ISBN 9780197537282 (online) | ISBN 9780197537268 (updf)
Subjects: LCSH: Voting—United States. | Elections—United States. |
Voter turnout—United States.
Classification: LCC JK1967 .R57 2020 (print) | LCC JK1967 (ebook) |
DDC 324.6/5—dc23
LC record available at https://lccn.loc.gov/2020022211
LC ebook record available at https://lccn.loc.gov/2020022212

1 3 5 7 9 8 6 4 2

Printed by Integrated Books International, United States of America

Dedicated to Laura Kuhlman

Bert and Anne Tolbert

Contents

Contents

Figures

Tables

Preface

In the wake of the 2020 Covid-19 public health crisis, U.S. governors have taken on a new leadership role. Under federalism, state governments led the fight to limit the spread of the disease with policies ranging from banning large gatherings, to closing schools, restaurants and bars, and non-essential businesses—profoundly changing daily routines and the economy. But before the health crisis state governments were leading the way in making it easier to vote in elections in an effort to strengthen democratic government. *Accessible Elections* underscores how state governments can modernize their electoral systems to increase voter turnout and influence campaign and party mobilization strategies. Many scholars have dismissed state election reform laws—commonly referred to as convenience methods—as failing to significantly increase turnout or address inequality in who votes. As a recent FiveThirtyEight headline reads, "early voting laws probably don't boost turnout" (Rakich 2019).

Rather than focus on individual laws in isolation, this book develops the concept of accessible elections, defined as the combination of each state's voting and registration laws and past performance in administering elections in order to ensure that all eligible voters are able to participate. Election administration includes the registration of voters, counting of ballots, polling place access for disabled citizens, vote waiting time, online information on polling places, variation in voting machines, difference between ballots cast and votes counted, and more (Pew 2016; Burden and Stewart 2014). The existing research has not measured electoral features that include the laws and election administration. This study re-evaluates what state governments can do to increase participation rates for the American people, with additional emphasis given to the poor and racial and ethnic minorities. Using a data driven approach to measure electoral practices and voter turnout, our results suggest state election reform efforts do make a positive difference.

Reform of America's election rules is long overdue. Use of alternative or convenience methods to in-person election day voting reached a high point in 2018, with 40% of election ballots cast.

The 2020 election promises to be higher. Yet much of the core research in the field of voting rights and state voting/registration laws in the U.S. has not been updated to reflect current realities.

The last few decades have witnessed widespread changes in state election laws. In many states new technology has given individuals the ability to use the internet or their cell phones to become registered voters, request absentee ballots, and identify polling locations, changing the process of how people vote. Adding to these changes are recent state adoptions of same day registration, automatic voter registration, early voting, mail voting, and no-excuse absentee voting. Much of the published research was conducted when these laws were nascent. More than a decade later this study re-examines the effects of state voting laws, combined with election administration, to understand how state governments can make voting more or less accessible for the American people.

The message from much of the published literature is that state voting reform laws—especially early voting, and mail and no excuse absentee voting—generally benefit educated, older and more affluent people rather than disadvantaged demographic groups, as our research shows. Although same day registration has been shown to have positive benefits, one cannot understand the real effects of these laws without consideration of the implementation of the laws. The research design used here helps account for possible selection bias in why some states adopt voting reforms in the first place, by controlling for states with historically high or low turnout and their past performance in administering elections.

Much of the earlier work was based on more limited data, did not control for election administration (how well the states conduct elections) and did not include vote histories from the same people over time. Without vote histories, these earlier studies could not isolate whether state election laws were linked to changes in individual voting rates. With improved data, research design and statistical methods, we are able to learn more about how these new state laws effect voter turnout, and turnout by historically disadvantaged groups.

The current study uses national voter files with millions of cases and vote histories of the same individuals to detect change in political participation over time. Use of state voter rolls and panel data helps improve the study election reform by making the results more reliable. Panel designs with repeated measurements of voting over time are used to evaluate the effects of the state voting laws and develop improved predictive models. When measuring change in turnout over time for individuals, the results tell us a different story than much of the published research.

Empirical results show that how well state governments run elections matters, a factor generally overlooked in the voting literature. State election administration performance is a strong predictor of voter turnout in both midterm and presidential elections, and uniquely benefits the voting decisions of racial and ethnic minorities, and even the poorest of citizens. Of the voting laws, same day registration has the greatest effect in increasing overall turnout as well as turnout of the poor and racial minorities in both midterm and presidential elections. The effects are larger than reported in previous research. No-excuse absentee voting and mail voting also helps convert non-voters into voters in presidential elections. Early voting, largely dismissed in the election sciences literature, increases turnout in midterm elections, and even enables higher participation by racial minorities. Changing the rules of game is an important tool in addressing inequality.

This study takes advantage of institutional variation in election laws and electoral practices across the fifty states—registration laws, voting laws, and implementation of the laws—to isolate their effects on voting decisions, and campaign and party mobilization. Results show that convenience voting methods and quality election administration can improve voter turnout and campaign mobilization, even among America's most disadvantaged citizens.

State governments play an important role in making voting accessible for all Americans. Election rules and practices can be designed to increase overall voter turnout, and create more equality in participation across demographic groups. In the spirit of helping to inform policy debates using empirical research, we argue the American states are the true laboratories of democracy. State governments can choose to increase voter turnout, and reduce demographic inequalities in who votes. Future innovations in modernizing U.S. elections are likely to come from the states, seeking to preserve and strengthen democracy from the bottom up.

Acknowledgments

This project would not have been possible without generous funding provided by a grant from the National Science Foundation, Building Community and Capacity for Data-Intensive Research in the Social, Behavioral, and Economic Sciences and in Education and Human Resources (BCC-SBE/EHR). (NSF Proposal# 1338471). It enabled us to purchase the Catalist national voter file data used in this book. We are also indebted to our colleagues at the University of Iowa and Washington State University that provided critical feedback and support, including Julianna Pacheco, Rene Rocha, Cornell Clayton, Travis Ridout, and Steven Stehr, and to members of American Political Science Association's State Politics and Policy Section. We are especially indebted to our colleagues in the field of election reform and election sciences that have been pathbreakers in conducting rigorous, empirical studies of election rules in the United States.

1
The Problem with Voting in America

Since the controversial 2016 presidential election, new substantial divisions among the mass public have emerged over many aspects of American democracy and public policy. For example, only 49% of supporters of President Donald Trump believe that freedom of the press—defined as "news organizations [being] free to criticize political leaders"—is very important to maintaining a strong democracy, compared to 72% of people who voted for Hillary Clinton. But on core components of American democracy, there remains high support across the ideological spectrum. Nearly 70% of Trump supporters and 86% of Clinton voters believe that the right to non-violent protest is a very important part of a strong democracy. Protecting the rights of people with unpopular views is considered necessary for democracy among 71% of Trump supporters and 82% of Clinton supporters. The highest consensus occurs around the use of elections in democracies (Pew Research Center 2016). Ninety-one percent of Trump voters and 93% of Clinton voters believe that open and fair national elections are necessary for maintaining a strong democracy.

However, the systematic study of how elections are conducted in the U.S. does not have a long history. Elections require widespread citizen participation for legitimacy. Voter turnout in U.S. elections remains low in comparative perspective, with just over 60% of eligible citizens casting a ballot in presidential elections and 40% in most congressional elections (2018 was an exception, where turnout was similar to a presidential election). One explanation for the disconnect between the ideal of elections expressed in the Pew survey just mentioned as central to American democracy, and the decision to actually vote, involves the process of how elections are administered. Place, defined as where one lives, can play a significant role in whether someone participates in politics, as state and county governments wield much of the power to administer elections.

This study is about how elections are actually conducted across the fifty states, where average turnout swings more than 25 percentage points over

Accessible Elections. Michael Ritter and Caroline J. Tolbert, Oxford University Press (2021). © Oxford University Press.
DOI: 10.1093/oso/9780197537251.001.0001.

the past four decades, from an average low of 40% to a high of 66% (combining presidential and congressional elections) (United States Elections Project 2018b, 2018c). What explains this variation? The states vary in demographic composition, as well as in their wealth, economic profile, partisanship, diversity, historical development, and many other factors.

But one direct and systematic factor driving divergent participation rates is the bevy of state laws governing voting and elections, as the U.S. Constitution designates that the states are responsible for overseeing elections. Administering elections is a decentralized process, run by thousands of counties, the fifty states, and local jurisdictions. Some states have adopted a kaleidoscope of laws to encourage citizens to register to vote (or to register them automatically), cast a ballot on election day, and administer elections to facilitate participation of its citizens. Over the past few decades these states have modernized their election systems, developing *accessible election systems*. On the other end of the spectrum, some states have done little to modernize their election systems beyond the federal minimum standards. Some problems leading to poor administration of elections include voter ID laws that can act as barriers to voting, a dearth of polling locations, long waiting lines to vote, voting machines that don't work properly, and the omission of names from voter rolls (purging) for intermittent participation.

Leveraging millions of individual vote histories drawn from voter rolls from the fifty states, this study casts a fresh look at the effects of state voter and registration laws, and the administration of these laws, on voter turnout. Rarely has the published literature in political science measured both state election laws and administration of the laws simultaneously to predict voter turnout, as is done here. Emphasis is placed not only on predicting change in overall participation rates but also on turnout decisions for the poorest Americans—a disadvantaged population regardless of gender, race, ethnicity, region, age, or religion—and racial and ethnic minorities.

Do convenience voting—defined as in-person early voting, no excuse absentee/mail voting and same day registration—laws fail to meet expectations, as is commonly understood in the political science literature? Or are some states and local governments fulfilling the promise of accessible elections, actively seeking to encourage participation by all of their citizens? And if the latter holds true, can these states serve as models for future reform in American elections?

Inequality and Voting in America

In a landmark study comparing the U.S. to twenty other advanced industrial democracies, Powell (1986) reveals that the requirement to register to vote before casting a ballot significantly inhibits turnout in the U.S. The requirement to register before casting a ballot also explains why education and income are so strongly associated with voting in the U.S. but not in other democracies. The registration requirement has been found to reduce participation rates of disadvantaged demographic groups based on income, education, race, ethnicity, age, and English language proficiency.

In this spirit, President Barack Obama's Presidential Commission on Election Administration (2013) was tasked with finding ways "to promote the efficient administration of elections in order to ensure that all eligible voters have the opportunity to cast their ballots without undue delay, and to improve the experience of voters facing. . . obstacles in casting their ballots, such as members of the military, overseas volunteers, voters with disabilities, and voters with limited English proficiency" (Epstein 2013). Like the Help America Vote Act (2002) which compelled the states to improve election administration, including use of computerized voting systems, the goal of Obama's commission to make elections more "accessible" has a long history. This study picks up where the commission left off in terms of providing an empirical evaluation of the state of elections in the U.S.

For nearly half a century, proponents have argued that reforming voting and registration laws can boost participation rates and decrease inequality in the electorate based on demographic factors. The problem is that most published research to date has failed to show that state election reform—especially in-person early voting and no-excuse absentee or mail voting—significantly increases turnout, especially among disadvantaged demographic groups. This study re-examines the effects of voting and registration reforms on turnout and political inequality across the American states.

Election participation is highly unequal, when measured by demographic characteristics of the American electorate, revealing that the aggregate act of voting in U.S. elections is less than fully egalitarian. During the early years of America's democracy only white, male land-owners who were free citizens could vote and/or run for public office. Over the past 250 years, suffrage has expanded to include citizens of all races and genders, those at or above the age of 18, and non–land-owners. Yet the legacies of historical barriers to the ballot live on. In the 21st century, non-Hispanic whites, affluent individuals, and the college educated vote at much higher rates than their demographic counterparts who are non-white, less affluent, or less educated. Racial and ethnic minorities and others have encountered substantial institutional barriers to voting that have limited their participation in elections.

Inequality in political participation is a manifestation of America's history of economic inequality (Bartels 2008; Gilens 2012; Hacker and Pierson 2011; Franko and Witko 2017), ascriptive hierarchy (Smith 1993, 1997), and legacies of slavery and Jim Crow laws (Springer 2014). Hero (1992, 29) defines two-tiered pluralism as a societal phenomenon in which some groups occupy a higher "social and political arena or tier," while other groups are relegated to a lower tier, with this division being due to "historical, socioeconomic, or other factors." Applying this concept to voting means non-voters as well as the poor and working classes are less likely to be represented by government policy nationally (Griffin and Newman 2008; Bartels 2008) and by state lawmakers (Franko and Witko 2017). This two-tiered pattern of American voting has been reinforced by exclusionary voting laws and norms, including voter ID laws and unreformed state election systems. Can changes to state voting and registration laws make a dent in this problem, improving representation of all citizens?

State election practices can pose barriers to disadvantaged groups based on race or ethnicity as well as economic class. From poll taxes to today's photo ID laws, state voting requirements that necessitate individuals to spend money to be able to cast a ballot have long created barriers to participation that depress turnout of the poor relative to the middle class and affluent (Hajnal, Lajevardi, and Nielson 2017; Keyssar 2009; Kousser 1974; Walker et al. 2017; Springer 2014). While some laws can depress voter participation rates, other laws are innovations in the administration of elections, encouraging people to participate at higher rates.

Indeed, over the past fifty years, massive changes to state electoral rules represent a quiet transformation in the body politic. Starting largely in the 1970s, state governments began to adopt voting reform laws—including motor voter laws that allowed people to register to vote when getting a driver's license, as well as in-person early voting, home voting (no-excuse absentee or mail-in voting), and same day registration—to reduce obstacles to voting. The number of these convenience voting laws (early voting, no-excuse absentee/mail voting, and same day registration) has expanded exponentially across the states, as more states have sought to ease the process of casting ballots for their citizens. In 2000, only twenty-six states had at least one election reform law; by 2018, forty states had at least one of these laws (Larocca and Klemanski 2011; National Conference of State Legislatures 2018a, 2018b).

The sheer number of citizens using these new convenience voting laws has also expanded. According to the U.S. Census, among eligible voters only 11% used one of these alternative methods to cast a ballot in the 2000 election, compared to more than one in three (38%) in 2016 and 40% in 2018. In the wake of coronavirus public health pandemic, mail-in voting is expected to be widespread nationwide in the 2020 presidential election. Over this time period, the percentages of votes cast in person on election day (excluding same day registration voters) dropped from 89% to 60% (Current Population Survey [CPS] 2000–2016).[1] Given this significant transformation in how people engage in a core responsibility of democratic self-government— casting ballots in elections—it is time to re-evaluate whether state voting laws make a positive difference. Much of the existing literature is based on studies conducted when state convenience voting laws were nascent.

While the study of electoral systems is common in cross-national studies, it is rare in subnational politics in the U.S. (Carter and Farrell 2010; Gerken 2009; Massicotte, Blais, and Yoshinaka 2004). In this study a state's set of registration and voting laws, and overall administration of election, can be conceptualized as electoral practices. Unlike most of the previous research, our focus in the preparation of this book was not only on the effect of these laws on overall turnout, but especially on turnout of disadvantaged groups such as low-income citizens and racial and ethnic minorities. And unlike most previous studies, the effects of the state voting laws are compared side by side with the quality of election administration. *This study seeks to re-evaluate the effects of state electoral practices—convenience voting laws in addition to administration of elections—on voter mobilization and political participation.*

The Covid-19 public health pandemic of 2020 ignited a controversy over the widespread and seemingly benign practice of absentee or mail voting. Leading up to the 2020 presidential election, absentee or mail-in voting became a controversial topic. Since mail voting is consistent with social distancing practices used across the states to fight the pandemic, numerous

---

[1] All Current Population Survey descriptive estimates are voter validated following coding and weighting procedures detailed in Hur and Achen (2013) and the United States Elections Project (2018a).

Republican and Democratic controlled state governments mailed forms to all registered voters allowing them to request an absentee mail ballot for upcoming presidential election. President Trump strongly opposed the expansion of mail voting. In a May 26th tweet Trump said "There is NO WAY (ZERO?) that Mail-In Ballots will be anything less than substantially fraudulent. Mail boxes will be robbed, ballots will be forced and even illegally printed out & fraudulently signed." In response to the President's tweet, for the first time Twitter (one of the giant U.S. technology firms) fact-checked his posts, applying warning labels to two tweets that made misleading claims about mail-in voting. The warning labels said, "get the facts about mail-in ballots." The labels, when clicked, led users to a page describing Trump's claims as "unsubstantiated." "Trump falsely claimed that mail-in ballots would lead to 'a Rigged Election.' However, fact-checkers say there is no evidence that mail-in ballots are linked to voter fraud." This study does not focus on voter fraud per se but contributes to this debate by providing empirical support for the beneficial effects of mail voting on voter turnout.

From Convenience Voting to Accessible Elections

Election laws in the realm of voting are often referred to by scholars working in political science by the nebulous term "convenience voting" laws. Convenience voting laws—specifically in-person early voting (voting before election day at a polling place), no-excuse absentee or mail voting (receiving and submitting a ballot before election day via mail), and same day registration (registering and casting a ballot on a single day before or on election day)—are intended to make voting easier by reducing the cost of voting (Berinsky 2005). Rooted within an individual-level incentives and rational choice framework, convenience voting predicts that if the costs of voting are lowered sufficiently, the benefits will outweigh the costs, and participation will increase (Downs 1957).

Yet many studies have found the new state laws to have a minimal impact on voter turnout, and, if they do have an effect, they tend to exacerbate existing demographic biases in the American electorate (Berinsky 2005; Fortier 2006; Gronke et al. 2008a; Karp and Banducci 2001; Neely and Richardson 2001; Stein 1998). That is, they operate to increase voting among those individuals already predisposed to participate, including the educated, older, and affluent. By focusing on a cost-benefit analysis calculus, much of the previous research has neglected to take into account differences in state election practices in which the individual act of voting occurs (see Springer 2014 for a related criticism), including administration of the laws (Alvarez, Atkeson, and Hall 2013; Gerken 2009; Burden and Stewart 2014). Election administration—consisting of vote counting procedures, election review laws, poll workers, and other characteristics—is a major component of how states conduct elections, and is often missed by scholars focusing on the costs and benefits of individual voting laws.

State governments should make elections accessible, and thus it makes sense that political elites may seek to mobilize voters using these new laws. We would not expect ordinary citizens to be aware of changes to state election laws, so if we see behavior changing, other factors are likely the cause. One of these mechanisms, which is presented in Chapter 7, shows that candidates, parties, and campaigns are more likely to mobilize and contact people in states with convenience voter laws. This suggests that elites are playing a key role in making individuals aware of alternative voting laws and how they can participate. An indicator of this causal process would be change in political elite behavior after adoption of new voting laws, which can be seen in the mobilization of new voters. Convenience voting laws may make voting easier and less costly, which could modestly boost participation. We believe elite political mobilization is more important than simply reducing the costs of voting alone. By measuring how convenience voting laws affect voter mobilization, rather than just turnout, we may find a larger effect of these new voting rules.

This study reframes convenience voting laws as bundles of state voting and registration laws and election administration—policy choices that state governments make regarding ballot box access. By "bundle" we mean estimating statistical models to predict individual voter turnout in varying state contexts that measure availability of three state convenience methods and also measure how well the state does in administering elections. Some states may have one of the three voting laws, while another will have all three. Some states may be high on the election administration index (doing well), while others are low. In this way the states have different bundles of laws and different track records of election administration. From these models, we estimate the independent effects of these three laws, except in cases where we measure the interactive effects of the voting laws and how well the state does in administering elections.

The existing research on convenience methods has focused on the effects of individual laws largely in isolation, rather than on how various election laws combine with the administration of the laws. In contrast, our research nests individual decision making within a neo-institutional perspective; individuals' voting decisions occur within state electoral contexts. Gerken (2009), Alvarez, Atkeson, and Hall (2013), Burden and Stewart (2014), and other scholars argue that election administration is increasingly important, although they do not directly link election administration to voter turnout. Karp and Brockington (2005) find that individuals are more likely to claim they voted in countries with higher turnout rates, suggesting that voting decisions are structured by the voting norms embedded in electoral systems (also see Green and Gerber 2015; Gerber, Green, and Larimer 2008). Building on this, accessible election systems are measured empirically by bundles of state election laws and election administration performance.

Making State-to-State Comparisons Clearer

In seeking to measure the cumulative effects of convenience voting methods, our study measures policy choices state governments can make. Accessible elections take the form of different bundles of electoral laws, rules, and practices. A concern is that early voting and no-excuse absentee/mail voting vary from state to state. Walker, Herron, and Smith (2018), for example, examined the impact of in-person early voting in North Carolina in 2012 and 2016. They made use of North Carolina voter file data and cross-county variation in the implementation of early voting in the state. Their study measures county-level differences in overall early voting hours, evening hours, Saturday hours, Sunday hours, and the number of early voting site changes from 2012 to 2016. They ultimately found no consistent patterns associated with early voting.

In our study, state electoral practices are measured using the Election Performance Index (EPI) developed by MIT/Pew Research Center (see also Burden and Stewart 2014; Gerken 2009; Stewart 2006, 2008, 2014). The fifty state EPI measure is constructed in part from data that is specific to election jurisdictions within a state (e.g., component measures such as provisional ballots accepted or rejected are derived from local election officials in counties or precincts). It measures the average quality of election administration performance within a state for a given year, across townships, cities, precincts, and counties. While election administration of early voting can vary within a state, a key implication of the Walker et al. (2018) study is that controlling for within-state election administration variation is a prerequisite for any study that aims to identify the independent effects of state election laws on political participation. Since the EPI represents the average quality of election administration within a state, including this measure helps isolate the independent effects of state election laws on voter turnout. Controlling for election administration in the states is important in its own right, and we show that this has independent effects on political participation. Taking account of within- and across-state variation in the conduct of elections also enables a better comparison of election laws across states. We argue that scholars of election laws should control for election administration.

National Voter Files

A contribution of this research is the data used to measure individual voting decisions. Most research on political participation has relied on two general types of data: public opinion election surveys and government data from the Census. Public opinion surveys, such as the American National Election Survey (ANES) and the Cooperative Comparative Election Study (CCES) merged with state election law data have been used extensively to evaluate state voting laws (Hajnal, Lajevardi, and Nielson 2017). With surveys the sample sizes are generally smaller, yet questions can be designed to measure a wide range of phenomena associated with political behavior. A limitation is that these datasets tend to over-report voter turnout because the samples are more likely to include registered voters and because of social desirability effects, when people report that they voted but did not. A Pew Research study by Igielnik et al. (2018) found that one in ten people who reported voting in their surveys were not found in the state voter rolls. But unlike the ANES, the CCES matches respondents to the state voter rolls to verify self-reported voter turnout.

Extensive research has also relied on the micro data from the Current Population Survey Voting and Elections Supplement from the U.S. Census (Leighley and Nagler 2013; Hanmer 2009). These data includes large samples, and while the data is self-reported, aggregate turnout rates tend to be more accurate. This data also provides excellent trends over time. But government data lacks information on partisanship, political interest, voter mobilization and other factors known to predict turnout. While the Census survey is conducted every two years, the data is cross-sectional and does not re-interview the same people over time.

The present study draws on a fundamentally different type of data—national voter files—to understand the effects of state voting laws and election administration on political participation that includes repeated measures of voting for the same individuals over time. The data is based on official voter rolls from each of the fifty states (180 million people) combined with data on 60 million unregistered voters (all U.S. adults, or 240 million people). The remaining roughly 80 million people in the U.S. are age 17 and under, and are not eligible to vote. It is not survey data, but rather population election data. Our strategy of using voter histories and panel data from state voter rolls goes well beyond much of the published literature in this area. We use the 1% sample available to academics for a total of 2.4 million individuals.

Although such files have been employed by political campaigns for many years, and pollsters use voter files to draw samples for their surveys, their use by journalists and academics has increased recently as access to the data files is more widely available (Hersh 2015). There is growing use of state voter rolls with very large sample sizes by academics to study campaigns, voting, and elections (Hersh 2015; Fraga 2018; Hersh and Nall 2016; Rogers and Aida 2014; Hersh and Ghitza 2018; Nickerson and Rogers 2014; Herron and Smith 2012).

The data used in this study includes vote histories for individuals over time; state voter rolls are panel data with repeated observations for individuals over time. Since turnout data is not self-reported, the data more closely matches actual turnout rates. Our data, drawn from December 2015, finds that 65% of the sample voted in 2008, 58% in 2012, 43% in 2010, and 35% in 2014. The election statistics with millions of individuals' vote histories makes our data fundamentally different from most previous research.

Because so much of the variability in whether someone votes in an election is a function of whether they voted in the previous election, voter histories create a within-subjects experiment (pre- and post-test), allowing the researcher to strip out much of the variability in explaining turnout from year to year. The Pew Research Center estimates that among their respondents in the American Trends Panel who appeared in five different national commercial voter files, 75% voted in every election and 10% never vote (so 85% didn't change their voting behaviors) (Igielnik et al. 2018). Statistical models are designed to measure the demographic and state electoral practices factors for people who changed their voting decisions—who didn't vote in one election but did in the next, or vice versa. While most predictive power in voting decisions is based on prior voting decisions, does living in one state with convenience voting laws (early, mail/absentee, same day registration) make a difference?

In a perfect experiment, researchers would assign people to live in different states with different election laws to study if they will be more or less likely to vote. We cannot do that. But the panel data/vote histories sheds new light in this research area, even if it is not a randomized experiment. When the state laws change over the period of study, so does the coding. We are interested in what combination of state election laws and election administration are associated with a higher probability of becoming mobilized to vote. Lagged panel models measure the change in the probability of voting from midterm to midterm election, or presidential to presidential election. Panel data to measure change over time for the same individuals is considered one of the best methods to develop causal arguments (Angrist and Pischke 2008).

The data is from Catalist, one of a number of firms that manages a national database of voting-aged people. Catalist's commercial voter files includes regularly updated voter registration records from every state for 180 million people combined with data on sixty million unregistered voters. The core component of the file is the official state lists of registered voters, supplemented with data from commercial databases—such as credit rating agencies—to locate people missing from state voter rolls (Igielnik et al. 2018). To identify unregistered individuals, Catalist employs three methods: flagging voters present in past voter files who are not present in the most recent ones; relying on U.S. Postal Service National Change of Address data to find individuals who have moved to a new state without registering; and using customer files of retailers and direct marketing companies (Cantoni and Pons 2019, 6). Because of the comprehensive voter data, numerous scholars have used Catalist for studies of political participation in the U.S. (Hersh 2015; Fraga 2016; Hersh and Nall 2016; Rogers and Masahiko 2014; Hersh and Ghitza 2018; Nickerson and Rogers, 2014).

In the aftermath of the contested 2000 presidential election, Congress adopted the Help America Vote Act of 2002 (HAVA) to create a single, uniform, centralized, interactive computerized statewide voter registration list administered at the state level. The digital databases made it possible for candidates, parties, and commercial organizations to collect and compile national files of voters by combining the digital files from each state. The political parties took advantage of this new source of data for voter mobiliza-tion (Hersh 2015). In 2006 Democratic Party leaders set up Catalist, which offered one of the most comprehensive databases of voting age Americans at the time.

Beyond voter registration information, these figures include other public records as well as commercial data, with each individual entry containing hundreds of pieces of information, from casting a ballot to having a home internet subscription. The registered voter lists are combined with data from other public sources, such as the National Change of Address data-base run by the U.S. Postal Service, death records from the Social Security Administration, and lists from marketing firms and commercial data aggregators. For some variables (age, gender, political party in the thirty states with partisan registration, voter registration, and in some states race/ethnicity) the data is hard and is based on state voter files.

Other variables, such as education, income, residential mobility, and news consumption, are indirectly estimated using a statistical matching process to analyze data to verify or update records of voters and non-voters. The Pew Research Center reports that the national voter files are able to accurately categorize 79% of panelists (on average) by race and ethnicity, including an average of 93% for non-Hispanic whites, 72% for Hispanics, and 67% for blacks. They are also highly accurate in terms of partisanship and turnout, when matching respondents to their Pew survey respondents. In general, Hersh (2015) has found Catalist data and imputations to have high predic-tive validity. In this study the individual-level voter file data is combined with state-level variables measuring voting and registration laws, and election administration.

A limitation is that the voter files do better in including registered voters than the unregistered. Pew comparing five different national voter roll files found that unregistered individuals generally are included in the commercial files, and that unregistered voters that didn't appear were similar to all unreg-istered individuals (Igielnik et al. 2018). It found that a very high percentage of individuals (91%) from Pew nationally representative surveys could be matched to at least one of the five national voter files, suggesting that the files cover a large share of the U.S. population. Unregistered people who are younger (18–24), who frequently change residences, or who are Hispanic are less likely to appear in the commercial voter files (Igielnik et al. 2018). These demographic groups are also less likely to appear in standard surveys or gov-ernment surveys. This means that if there is a bias in the results reported in this study, it is that the effect sizes may be smaller than they should be. While not perfect, these large-sample datasets go far beyond standard surveys in measuring registered voters in the American states. It should be noted that no other surveys perfectly represent the adult population of the U.S. either. The advantages of the national voter files appear to outweigh their costs.

Value Added—Framework, Data, and Results

A distinguishing feature of American politics is not only the decentralized electoral system with significant variation in electoral laws across the states, but also wide gaps in turnout rates between states (as discussed earlier in the chapter). By seeking to measure state accessible elections we may be able to understand whether changes to the laws have the intended effect in boosting participation.

Five meaningful contributions are made that move beyond existing research. First, convenience voting laws and administration of the laws are used to predict individual voting decisions over time in both presidential and midterm elections. Studying the effects of registration and voting laws and administration of elections over time in predicting voter turnout is a new and significant contribution of this study. Second, national voter files (Catalist), large-sample survey data (CCES), and advanced statistical modeling are leveraged to more accurately estimate the effects of state voting laws on individual-level voting decisions using panel models (see Ashok et al. 2016). Third, building on Burden et al. (2014), the study considers a combination of state election laws to isolate independent effects of each one on voting. While most of the published literature focuses on overall turnout rates (see Rigby and Springer 2011 for an exception), an important contribution to this study emphasizes turnout for the poor versus the non-poor, for varying racial and ethnic groups, as well as overall turnout rates (see Franko and Witko 2017). Fifth, accessible elections (laws and administration of elections) are used to help understand elite behavior, such as campaign mobilization, which is necessary for bringing new voters into the electorate.

Accessible election systems can be evaluated by how well they meet the needs of the most disadvantaged members of society. Disadvantage is represented in this research by citizens living at or below the federal poverty rate. Poverty is positively correlated with race, ethnicity, youth, and other demographic factors of interest to scholars of American politics.

Disadvantage is also measured by the race and ethnicity of the respondent. Our inquiry is not only whether electoral laws increase overall turnout, but whether the laws also help equalize voting rates between more and less advantaged members of the population.

In sum, this project contends that state election systems can influence voter turnout and change the probability of people voting from one election to the next, even in disadvantaged groups like the poor and racial and ethnic minorities. Previous research has not measured state election systems (alternative voting laws + election administration), so we offer a new framework of accessible elections. New data in the form of national commercial voter files with vote histories for the same individual is used to create change models. This new data is being used increasingly by political science scholars.

With the new theory and data, we also present new results. Despite much previous research that found limited effects of alternative voting laws conducted nearly two decades ago, today 40% of all votes are cast using these methods. Modeling change in the probability of voting using vote histories exposes a significant effect of voting laws and election administration on political participation—up to a 10% increase in the probability of becoming a voter if living in a state with these laws, all else equal.

We believe state governments can play a positive role in creating accessible and modernized electoral systems that encourage people to vote. Candidates, parties, and campaigns do the heavy lifting of getting voters to use these alternative voting laws as they seek to win elections. This book provides the empirical evidence for how this works. Despite the conflict within contemporary U.S. politics, the findings reported here show progress for democratic governments.

2
Measuring Accessible Elections

Do states with accessible electoral systems, defined by adoption of voting and registration reforms and quality administration of elections, increase voter turnout and benefit racial and ethnic groups and the less affluent? Do they encourage parties and candidates to bring new individuals into the electorate who would not otherwise vote? These are central questions we ask when examining the impact of convenience voting laws and election administration on voter turnout.

Voting rights and election law took center stage in 2018, not only in Florida and Georgia, where controversy made headline news, but nationwide. Georgia voters seeking to support Stacy Abrams as the first black female major-party gubernatorial nominee in U.S. history experienced the dark side of how state governments administer elections. Headlines revealed large voter purges, blocked absentee ballots because of mismatched signatures, voting machine breakdowns in high-minority districts, long lines, and voters disenfranchised by Georgia's strict photo ID law (Rubin 2019). Over 1.4 million voter registrations were purged since 2012 in the state. Yet voter turnout in 2018 soared as Democrat Abrams ran against Republican Brian Kemp, who was also secretary of state at the time. Because voting is a more complicated process today with early voting, home voting (mail/absentee), and same day registration, how state governments administer elections plays an outsized role.

The problem for political science research is that election administration is rarely included in models predicting voter turnout, despite the authority of state and local governments to administer the process. While most research in political science has focused on state voting and registration laws, election administration may be equally or more important. As Abrams argues, "it has so many pieces, and that's the architecture" (Rubin 2019). Abrams argues that some states have moved from Jim Crow laws and practices that blocked nonwhites and poor whites from voting (Springer 2014) to more sophisticated systems of election administration that have similar outcomes. Chapter 6 of this book contributes to this debate with empirical data.

Accessible Elections. Michael Ritter and Caroline J. Tolbert, Oxford University Press (2021). © Oxford University Press. DOI: 10.1093/oso/9780197537251.001.0001.

In contrast to Stacy Abrams' remarks, previous studies in political science have found that state reforms to make voting and registration easier have generally had a limited effect in boosting turnout. Existing research has focused on state adoption of new voting laws, but has generally not considered how state government's administration of election may effect participation rates.

Inequality in who participates in American politics has drawn the attention of many scholars dating back to E. E. Schattschneider (1960). In *The Semi-Sovereign People*, Schattschneider argued for expanding the electorate and increasing voter turnout for citizens who are not regular voters (see Franko and Witko 2017 for an update to Schattschneider's argument). In the realm of voting, scholars have traced inequalities in turnout to restrictive voting laws (Keyssar 2009; Springer 2014). Over the past several decades, states have experimented with convenience methods for voter registration and casting a ballot to improve participation in U.S. elections. Much of the research points to the limitations of the laws in boosting turnout (Berinsky 2005; Burden et al. 2014; Gronke, Galanes-Rosenbaum, and Miller 2008a). But these studies generally do not take into account implementation of the laws in predicting turnout (see Walker, Herron, and Smith 2018 for an exception).

Two separate bodies of literature exist: One focuses on voting and registration laws and voter turnout, and the other on election administration, including its effect on public opinion or political parties and candidates. Research on the effects of the election reform laws rarely considers how the administration of elections affects turnout. Those who study election administration focus on quality of state registration and election data, accuracy of vote counts, density of polling stations, post-election audits, poll worker training, trust in the election system, and more much—all valuable components of election systems—but rarely link these processes to voter turnout. With a few exceptions, most existing research has not brought together the two literatures, as we do here.

Only by measuring election administration directly and empirically can scholars understand the true effects of state voting reforms on participation rates, as the effectiveness of the laws is a function of how well they are administered by state and local governments (Gerkin 2009). Few published studies have considered how election reform laws and administration of elections work together. Since political participation rates may be attributable to the laws as well as their implementation, not controlling for election administration may mask the true effects of the laws on turnout.

This study borrows data used in the study of election administration to study voter turnout. It develops a holistic approach to the study of voting in U.S. elections, which we call "accessible elections," that evaluates the performance of state voting laws while simultaneously measuring government implementation of these laws. In so doing, it helps paint a more realistic picture of state electoral practices that better match current political realities. Beyond individual demographic and partisan factors, state electoral rules may be critical to whether people decide to participate in American democracy. Quantifying the quality of each state's election administration over time also captures each state's historical legacy of promoting or hindering turnout (Keyssar 2009; Kousser 1974). Some states have significantly modernized systems for facilitating participation in elections, while other state have not.

State electoral practices are measured using the Election Performance Index (EPI) developed by the MIT Election Data and Science Lab (2016) and the Pew Charitable Trusts (2016) (see also Burden and Stewart 2014; Gerken 2009; Stewart 2005, 2008, 2014) alongside multiple convenience voting laws, such as same day registration, mail and absentee voting laws, and early voting. These factors are used to predict individual level voting decisions, turnout for different income and racial groups (inequality), and campaign/ party mobilization. The research design measures whether state electoral rules affect individual voting decisions and changes in turnout from election to election for the overall U.S. population and for poor people, defined as citizens living at or below the federal poverty rate.

Building on Hersh's (2015) book *Hacking the Electorate*, the study uses election data based on the voter rolls from all fifty states combined with commercial and government data. The study's results are made possible with a comparative research design that helps protect against selection bias that has hampered previous studies. Using the 2016 Catalist dataset's 1% sample of the U.S. population (2.4 million observations), and the 2010–2014 CCES over time survey dataset (165,000 observations), statistical models are developed to predict voter turnout with panel data (repeated observations) based on individual voting histories. The idea is to determine if living in a state with accessible elections affects whether an individual will convert from a nonvoter to a voter. The focus is on measuring change over time for the same individuals, and comparing the voting behaviors of people living in states with and without reform election systems.

The large-sample election data facilitates drilling down to state electorates, and analyzing demographic subsamples in the population. Almost no previous work has explored how convenience voting laws affect turnout among individuals living at or below the federal poverty rate because of the difficulty of obtaining representative samples of this demographic (but see Hanmer 2009 showing that same day registration boosts participation for the young and the lower educated). While Chapter 5 explores the poor, Chapter 6 explores the effect of state electoral systems on change in turnout for racial and ethnic groups.

A number of unique findings are drawn from this research. First, while same day registration is shown to increase turnout in both presidential and midterm elections (a finding echoed in other research), the size of the effect is much larger than identified in previous research. States with early voting and mail/absentee voting are also associated with higher turnout in contrast to many previous studies, though the effects are not as consistent compared to same day registration. Most importantly, state election administration quality is found to positively shape individual voting decisions in both midterm and presidential elections, as well as among the poor and for racial and ethnic minorities. Absentee/mail voting and same day registration are found to boost turnout among the poor in presidential elections, while early voting and same day registration lead to this outcome in midterm elections. Different racial and ethnic groups benefit from different bundles of convenience voting laws.

Accessible elections also increase individual participation rates through voter mobilization drives. Individuals are more likely to be contacted to vote by campaigns or parties in presidential elections when their state has absentee/mail, early, or same day registration voting laws; same day registration also increases campaign contact in midterm elections (see Chapter 7). This study provides strong evidence that convenience voting laws can increase turnout and reduce voting inequality. But the effect of state voting and registration laws must be examined in conjunction with state election administration.

The accessible elections framework emphasizes how state governors and legislatures can modernize their electoral practices to increase political participation as well as campaign and party mobilization strategies. Future innovations in modernizing U.S. elections are likely to come from the states, which are the true laboratories of democracy.

Convenience Voting Laws

An assumption in the convenience voting literature is that the effects of election laws are uniform across the states. A number of scholars have shown that it is important to control for state contextual factors and over time effects in order to understand the true impact of election reform laws on political participation (Hanmer 2009; Leighley and Nagler 2013; Springer 2014). Leighley and Nagler (2013), for example, find that no-excuse absentee/mail voting laws and same day registration have positive over time effects on aggregate turnout, and Springer (2014) demonstrates this same outcome with same day registration going back over a century of aggregate turnout rates across the fifty states.

The fifty states vary in the restrictiveness of their voting laws—an important component of the accessibility of a state's electoral system—as shown in Figure 2.1. The figure follows a pyramid format, with the most restrictive election reform laws at the top and the least restrictive at the bottom. In-person early voting gives individuals the convenience of being able to cast a ballot during a period of days or weeks before election day. However, this law still requires people to register to vote, and submission of ballots

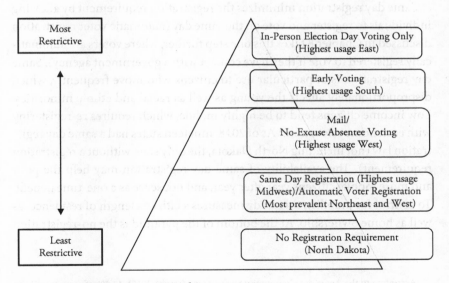

Figure 2.1. Convenience voting laws.
Data from Current Population Survey (2016); National Conference of State Legislatures (2020, 2018a, 2018b).

must be supervised by poll workers and must occur at the polls. As of 2018, thirty-four states had in-person early voting (National Conference of State Legislatures [NCSL] 2018a). In the early 2010s, several Southern states (such as Florida and North Carolina) made their early voting provisions more restrictive by lowering the number of days during which an individual could vote early (Herron and Smith 2014). This may be in part because Southern states have adopted fewer election reform laws than other regions of the nation, likely reflecting a political history of slavery and Jim Crow laws that did not encourage voting by all members of society (Keyssar 2009).

Home voting (mail or no-excuse absentee voting), which was present in thirty states as of 2018, is less restrictive because it allows an individual to vote early before an election, and to do so from the convenience of their own home or another location besides a polling place without direct government supervision. No-excuse absentee or mail voting states, which allow individuals to request to vote via postage for any reason, are different from the twenty other states that have absentee voting but which require a specific excuse for an individual to vote in this way (NCSL 2018a). However, mail and absentee voting laws are still more restrictive than same day registration because of their registration requirement; one must be registered to cast a ballot following these methods.

Same day registration minimizes the registration requirement by allowing individuals to register and vote on the same day (automatic voter registration discussed in Chapter 8 takes this one step further, where voters are automatically registered to vote if they have contact with a government agency). Same day registration is of particular use to citizens who move frequently, which disproportionately affects the young as well as racial and ethnic minorities. Low income citizens tend to be highly mobile, which requires re-registering with each home relocation.[1] As of 2018, nineteen states had a same day registration law (not including North Dakota, the only state without a registration requirement). The availability of same day registration may help the poor and more mobile citizens year after year, and not serve as a one-time benefit. To control for mobility, this study measures a citizen's length of residence, as well as home ownership. At the bottom of the pyramid is the no-registration

---

[1] According to the American Community Survey (see Mateyka 2015), 14.3% of movers are individuals earning less than $25,000 per year. This is compared to 9.9% earning between $25,000 and $49,999, 8.2% earning between $50,000 and $74,999, 6.6% earning between $75,000 and $99,999, and 5.6% earning $100,000 or more.

requirement, which is the least restrictive form of voting and present only in North Dakota (NCSL 2018b).[2]

This study also looks forward to recent adoption of state automatic voter registration laws. What began in Oregon as automatic voter registration (AVR) in 2015 has spread across the states, expanding motor voter laws (passed in 1993) that allowed people to register to vote when getting a driver's license. Prior research has found that young people and low-educated people are more likely to vote when same day registration laws are present, and this study finds that poor people and minorities benefit from same day registration. AVR is an extension of same day registration. In 2018, seventeen states had enacted AVR laws (see Figure 2.2), and, as of 2020, nineteen states and the District of Columbia have approved AVR, making voter registration "opt-out" instead of "opt-in" (NCSL 2020). Yet only six states used it in 2018, when six million people were automatically registered to vote or had their registrations updated. Eligible citizens who interact with government agencies, such as the DMV, are registered to vote or have their existing registration information updated, unless they decline. Accessible voting laws continue to change the composition of state electorates by increasing voting rates of disadvantaged groups—racial and ethnic minorities, young people, and poor people.

Regional patterns are evident in Figure 2.2, which displays state adoption of these reform laws effective in 2018. Early voting is the most common, and it is located in every region of the country. There are a few states in the Northeast and the South without this law. No-excuse absentee or mail voting laws are present in all Western and most Midwestern states; only a few states in the Northeast and in the South have these laws. Only three states—Washington, Oregon, and Colorado—use all-mail elections for every election (Utah recently moved toward this voting method). For this study, however, no-excuse absentee voting and mail voting are measured by the same indicator variable, as they each effectively allow citizens to vote from home. Same day registration states tend to be in the Midwest or West, although a few Northeastern states have adopted same day registration. Since 2010, there has been rapid expansion of same day registration, with nine states adopting the law in this period (NCSL 2018b). As of 2018, AVR is most common in the Northeast and the West, but the law is also present in a handful of states in the Midwest

---

[2] In our analyses, North Dakota is coded as a same day registration state. This reflects coding conventions in prior election reform law research.

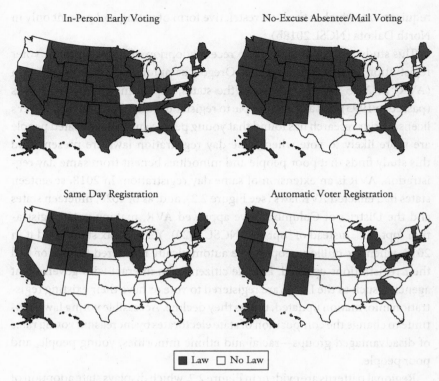

Figure 2.2. Election reform laws by state (2018).
Note: Alaska and Rhode Island are same day registration states during presidential years. Colorado, Oregon, and Washington are all-mail voting states. However, Colorado is also a same day registration state and technically an in-person early voting state because polls are open from fifteen days to election day itself for individuals to submit ballots (Ballotpedia 2016). North Dakota, in this study, is also considered a same day registration state because having this law is akin to having no separate registration requirement. By 2020, eighteen states plus Washington, D.C., had adopted AVR.

and the Southeast. There is considerable variation across the states in terms of the presence of these laws. AVR laws are shown for comparison, but are not analyzed in the later chapters since they are so new.

Another way to understand these patterns is the substantial variation in how individuals cast ballots depending on where they live. The ways Americans vote differ significantly across the states, in which nearly half of all ballots were cast using convenience methods in 2018. Reflecting the increasing popularity of alternative modes of voting, according to the Current Population Survey in 2016 only 62% of ballots were cast in the traditional manner on election day, with 18% voting via mail or absentee ballot, 17% voting early, and 3% by same day registration.

Regional patterns were particularly evident. Among voters, in-person election day voting was the lowest in the Western states (33%), followed by the South (59%) and the Midwest (70%), and was the highest in the Northeast (93%). Comparing traditional election day voting in the West and East resulted in a 60% difference. All-mail ballot election can reduce the cost of voting by making it easier for individuals to vote through the elimination of needing to travel to the polls and the potential loss of wages from taking time off of work to vote. In 2018, four in ten ballots were cast using convenience voting, which includes any method other than voting in person on election day (Misra 2019; U.S. Census) (see Figure 2.3). The rate of early voting and voting via mail in 2018 was not significantly different from the rate of the same in the 2016 presidential election.

Convenience voting was used in the historic 2018 midterm elections with the highest turnout in four decades. Between the 2014 and 2018 midterm elections, three states had dramatic increases in alternative voting—36 percentage points in Utah, 25 points in Texas, and 21 points in Georgia (U.S. Census 2019). Utah's increase was the result of legislation that expanded mail voting, while highly contested elections in Texas (Beto O'Rourke, Senate) and Georgia (Stacy Abrams, Governor) may help explain the latter with their large voter mobilization drives. These trends illustrate that state context matters in shaping how votes are cast in contemporary elections.

In-person early voting is the highest in the South, with 34% of voters casting ballots before election day—significantly higher than the 11% in

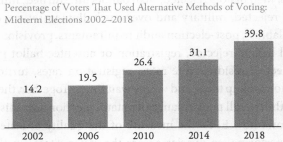

Percentage of Voters That Used Alternative Methods of Voting:
Midterm Elections 2002–2018

Note: Alternative methods of voting include early voting and voting by mail.
Source: U.S. Census Bureau; Current Population Survey Voting and Registration Supplements: Midterm Elections 2002–2018.

Figure 2.3. Percent of voters using convenience methods in midterm elections.

the Midwest, 6% in the West, and just 4% in the Northeast (2016 election). Absentee or mail voting is most typical in the West (with all-mail voting states like Colorado, Oregon, and Washington), where 59% of all ballots were submitted via the mail or absentee in 2016. This compares to 9% in the Midwest, 6% in the South, and only 2% in the Northeast. Use of same day registration was the highest in the Midwest at 10% of the voting electorate, 2% in the West, and only 1% in both the Northeast and the South. Finally, nonvoting was most common in the South and West (both 41%), followed by the Northeast (38%), and lowest in the Midwest (36%) (Current Population Survey 2000–2016).

Quality Election Administration and Convenience Voting Go Together (but Are Different)

A state's electoral practices can be measured as the combination of voting reform laws and election administration. As mentioned earlier, the election administration performance index (EPI) used here was developed by the MIT Election Data and Science Lab (2016) and Pew Charitable Trust (2016). The EPI was developed to quantify how election administration varies across the fifty states, seeking measures that captured the concepts of convenience (accessibility to voters), integrity (protecting against voter fraud), and accuracy (maximizing vote count precision) (see Gerken 2009). The seventeen-component summary index takes accounts of various aspects of a state's electoral system, including data completeness, disability- or illness-related voting problems, mail ballots rejected, mail ballots unreturned, military and overseas ballots rejected, military and overseas ballots unreturned, online registration availability, post-election audit requirements, provisional ballots cast, provisional ballots rejected, registration or absentee ballot problems, registrations rejected, residual vote rates, registration rates, turnout rates, voting information lookup tools, and voting wait times. Together, these measures control for the overall performance of a state's election administration.

Figure 2.4 shows how EPI—the measure of the quality of state election administration performance—varies across the states. States in the upper Northeast, upper Midwest, and Pacific Northwest do better, compared to those in the South and the lower Northeast.

To measure if convenience voting laws are related to election administration, Table 2.1 reports Pearson correlations between each state's EPI and

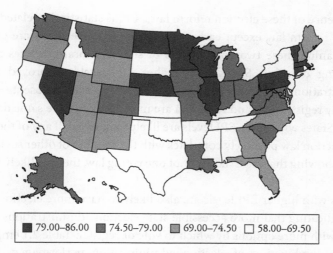

| ■ 79.00–86.00 | ■ 74.50–79.00 | ■ 69.00–74.50 | □ 58.00–69.50 |

Figure 2.4. Election Performance Index by state (2016).

Note: Data from MIT Election Data and Science Lab (2016) and Pew Charitable Trusts (2016). EPI data also available for every two-year interval from 2008 to 2016.

Table 2.1 Correlations between Convenience Voting Laws and Election Performance Index American States (2008–2018)

	EPI	Early Voting	Mail/ No- Excuse Absentee Voting	Same Day Registration	Automatic Voter Registration	Count of Election Reform Laws
EPI	1					
Early Voting	0.09	1				
Mail/No- Excuse Absentee Voting	0.11**	0.62***	1			
Same Day Registration	0.26***	0.12***	0.27***	1		
Automatic Voter Registration	0.18***	0.05***	0.09	0.06	1	
Count of Election Reform Laws	0.22***	0.75***	0.83***	0.61***	0.25***	1

Note: Data from MIT Election Data and Science Lab (2016), Pew Charitable Trusts (2016), and National Conference of State Legislatures (2020, 2018a, 2018b). Pearson *r* correlations.

* $p < 0.10$, ** $p < 0.05$, *** $p < 0.001$.

the presence of these election reform laws. EPI is statistically related to each election reform law except early voting, but the correlations are generally low, meaning these two components of state electoral practices measure something different. States with higher EPI levels—improved election administration—are more likely to have mail/no-excuse absentee voting, same day registration, and AVR, but are most likely to have same day registration. States with lower EPI levels are likely to have few if any of these laws. Each election law positively correlates with the number of other such laws in a state, showing that once states adopt one voting law, they are likely to adopt others.

States with higher EPI levels are also likely to have more election reform laws, indicating that more accessible state election administrations are correlated with more options by which to vote or register. Table 2.1 emphasizes that the combination of election administration performance (the EPI measure) and election reform laws together can help create accessible election systems. The implication for researchers is the need to control for state election administration to identify the independent effects of each law on turnout.

Yet the argument that states with higher quality election administration (EPI) and convenience voting laws "go together but are different" is not compelling. Rather, the EPI acts as a surrogate for increased access to elections in some manner not picked up by the three convenience voting laws.[3]

Accessible Election Model

The components of a state's electoral practices can be used to build an accessible elections framework. The framework predicts that state voting laws and election administration will impact voter turnout rates and mobilization patterns at the individual level, as well as for disadvantaged groups. Figure 2.5

[3] Critics might argue that the election administration index (EPI) includes a couple of components that may overlap with the convenience voting laws. We have checked the robustness of our results by including a variable for EPI that doesn't include these overlapping components. The results reported in this study do not change when this stripped down EPI is used (robustness check results are available upon request). Conceptually, and this is described in Chapter 2 of Burden and Stewart's (2014) *The Measure of American Elections*, voter registration and historical voter turnout are considered by elections scholars to be global indicators for the overall performance of a state's election administration (i.e., state registration/turnout rates can be signs for other features of a state's voting system, like waiting times, poor poll worker training, uneven administration of voter ID laws, etc.). This is why these two components are included in the MIT/Pew index in the first place.

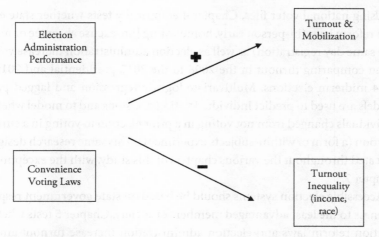

Figure 2.5. Model of accessible elections.

outlines the model. States with more convenience voting laws and quality election administration are expected to have higher rates of voter mobilization and turnout, and lower levels of turnout inequality.

From this model, several research hypotheses are generated. States with voting laws and high-performing election administration are predicted to have (a) citizens who are more likely to vote; (b) poor people and racial and ethnic minorities who are more likely to vote; and (c) political parties that are more likely to recruit broad segments of the populace to vote. Each of these hypotheses is evaluated in a separate chapter.

Overview of the Chapters Ahead

Chapter 3 pays attention to where this research fits in compared to previous literature. This includes variation in state election administration, measuring the cumulative effects of numerous voting laws, identifying the impacts of these laws and election administration on turnout inequality, examining how these factors shape campaign and party mobilization, and making use of a new data source to improve the study of voter turnout. Accessible elections are defined as different combinations of state election laws and election administration that promote or hinder voter turnout and turnout equality.

Using national voter files, Chapter 4 empirically tests whether state election reform laws (in-person early, home voting [no-excuse absentee or mail], and same day registration) as well as election administration increase voting when comparing turnout in the 2008 to the 2012 presidential and 2010 to 2014 midterm elections. Multivariate logistic regression and lagged panel models are used to predict individual voting decisions and to model whether individuals changed from not voting in a prior election to voting in a current election (a form of within-subjects experiment). This same research design is repeated throughout the various chapters of this study, with the exception of Chapter 7.

Accessible election systems should be based on state government responsiveness to the least advantaged members of society. Chapter 5 tests whether election reform laws and election administration increase turnout among the poor, a historically marginalized voting group. The voting records of several hundred thousand poor people and unregistered poor are drawn from the national voter files, representing previously unavailable data from all fifty states. This places the emphasis on how accessible elections may benefit the most disadvantaged of citizens. Again, lagged panels are utilized to measure if convenience laws and election administration bring citizens from this underrepresented voting bloc more actively into the electorate.

Most published research has focused on overall voting rates, not turnout broken down for minorities vs. non-Hispanic whites. Why would changes in the costs of voting differentially affect racial/ethnic minorities? That is, why should we expect to get something different examining these subgroups other than the average voting law effects previous works have identified? After the Supreme Court's majority decision in *Shelby County v. Holder* (2013) weakened Department of Justice (DOJ) protections against possibly discriminatory voting laws, the number of states imposing voting law restrictions has grown considerably. Recent literature has emphasized the negative impact such restrictive voting laws have had on voter participation among African Americans and Hispanics (Anderson 2018; Berman 2015; Hasen 2012; Walker, Sanchez, Nuno, and Barreto 2018).

Yet we don't understand the cumulative effect of state electoral practices on political participation for different racial and ethnic groups. Given demographic change in the U.S. where one in four voters is a racial/ethnic minority (2018), are these groups differentially affected by state voting laws, and by the implementation of these laws? Have campaigns and candidates (especially these affiliated with the Democratic Party) been able to modify their mobilization strategies for minorities depending on the election laws available in different states? Chapter 6 sheds light on the differential effects of alternative voting laws on different racial and ethnic groups.

Chapter 7 examines whether the mobilization strategies of political parties and candidate campaigns are structured by election administration performance and election reform laws. First, this chapter considers the impact of the accessible electoral system components on an individual's likelihood of being contacted by a campaign. Data for this chapter comes from the 2010, 2012, and 2014 CCES. There are two dependent variables: campaign contact and turnout. The analysis sheds light on how an individual's likelihood of being contacted by campaigns and candidates changes when a state's election reform laws and election administration change.

The conclusion summarizes the empirical support for the accessible election model to illustrate that election reform laws and quality election administration lead to higher voting rates in elections, more balanced turnout between the poor and the affluent and minorities and non-Hispanics whites, and more active campaigns and parties to bring new voters into the electorate. Accessible electoral practices appear to make a difference in positively shaping voter turnout in the American states.

3

Why Studying State Voting Laws
Is Not Enough

The costs associated with voting are real. According to a subsample of 127,709 non-voters from the 2000–2016 U.S. Census's Voter and Registration Supplement (Current Population Survey), 36% of non-voters did not vote because of transportation problems, 13% for personal or family medical reasons, and almost 12% because they were too busy or were out of town. Additionally, 6% cited registration problems, 4% reported forgetting to vote, and 2% emphasized inconvenient hours of polling places. Nearly 12% said they were not interested in the election, felt their vote would not count, or did not like the candidates.[1] Convenience voting laws—such as early voting, mail or absentee voting, or same day registration—and well-run elections can reduce the time and transportation costs associated with voting, or essentially eliminate the registration requirement. Paradoxically, a number of studies have found that all of these laws, except for same day registration, often fail to boost political participation rates and do not bring new voters into the electorate (Berinsky 2005; Burden et al. 2014; Gronke et al. 2008a; Hanmer 2009; Karp and Banducci 2001; Springer 2014; Walker et al. 2018; and others).

Berinsky (2005), Bowler and Donovan (2008), and Burden et al. (2014) have argued that identifying the effects of election reform laws on voter turnout is conditional on many factors, including political interest, electoral competition, and campaign mobilization. To more accurately estimate the effects of these laws, researchers must control for not only the state laws themselves, but also these mobilization factors. This study argues that one cannot measure the effect of state voting laws independently of the administration of elections.

Election administration is a key missing component in many studies of voter turnout and election reform in the states.

---

[1] The remaining respondents cited bad weather or an unspecified reason for not voting.

Accessible Elections. Michael Ritter and Caroline J. Tolbert, Oxford University Press (2021). © Oxford University Press.
DOI: 10.1093/oso/9780197537251.001.0001.

An additional limitation of some previous research on U.S. election reform is the lack of a comparative research design, where cases are selected for inclusion in the sample without significant variation in type of electoral system in use (single case studies). By necessity, much of the existing research is also non-experimental, drawing on observational government data and placing significant weight on the attitudes or behaviors of citizens residing in jurisdictions adopting the election reform or using a particular election rule. The lack of a comparative framework can lead to selection bias and potentially distort the empirical results. For example, states that adopt laws making it easier to register and to vote may also have higher turnout rates in the first place (Hanmer 2009). This makes it challenging to isolate the effects of the laws on political behavior. It is worthwhile to review some of the most important contributions to our understanding of the effects of state election reforms on political participation.

Four Key Studies

Four highly cited recent studies deserve attention for their use of careful research designs to tease apart cause and effect (Angrist and Pischke 2008). Springer (2014) builds an impressive time-series dataset of aggregate state turnout rates over nearly a century (1920–2000) to study the impact of early voting, absentee voting, and same day registration on turnout, comparing the effects of these more recent laws to Jim Crow voting laws decades earlier.

Springer examines the simultaneous effects of various election reform laws to identify each law's unique impact, and the longitudinal data allows measurement of change in state voting rates over nearly a century of US history. She finds that modern voting laws have a non-constant impact across the states, with election reform laws typically having less of an effect in Southern states than non-southern states. Only same day registration stands out for significantly increasing turnout among the contemporary state election laws, and this beneficial effect pales in comparison to the negative effect of Jim Crow laws (literacy tests, poll taxes) used historically. Using a century-long time series, Springer (2014) is able to render more precise estimates of the effects of modern voting reforms, especially the relative importance of same day registration.

While Springer's (2014) contributions are admirable, the data used in her study is nearly twenty years old, with the most recent data from 2000. Seismic changes in the number of states with absentee/mail, early, and same day registration laws have occurred since this time. In addition, her study draws on aggregate turnout data from the fifty states that does not allow inferences about individual voting decisions; it also does not permit one to test alternate hypotheses—based on partisanship or political interest—pertaining to turnout or voter mobilization. These other confounding factors may be important in understanding the effects of the laws.

Another landmark study by Leighley and Nagler (2013, Chapter 4) also uses Current Population Survey longitudinal-data statistical models to measure effects of early, absentee/mail, and same day registration laws across the states from 1972 to 2008 to predict individual-level voting decisions and aggregate state turnout. Time-series and difference-in-differences methods reveal that both same day registration and no-excuse absentee voting are associated with higher turnout but not early voting. Between Springer and Leighley and Nagler and others there is fairly robust evidence that same day registration does increase voter turnout.

One limitation of their study is the omission of critical control variables in the Census data such as partisanship and political interest, which are known to predict voting decisions. Another is the lack of panel data that would allow the authors to take repeated measurements of an individual's voting decisions over time. Such over-time designs can be used to create stronger causal models than the models from cross-sectional datasets. Nevertheless, Leighley and Nagler, known for their very important contributions to research on voting and turnout, find more positive outcomes associated with state election reform laws than most previous research.

Another landmark contribution to our understanding of election reform laws is that of Hanmer (2009), who uses a difference-in-differences approach and Census Current Population Survey data to predict individual voting decisions. He compares the probability of individual voting in early-adopting same day registration states (Maine, Minnesota, and Wisconsin) to later-adopting ones (Idaho, New Hampshire, and Wyoming), and to non–same day registration states to examine any changes in turnout over time. The pre-post design controls for state factors that explain adoption of same day registration in the first place. He finds that while same day registration has a more minimal effect in increasing turnout than previously found (but still significant), the law boosts turnout among less educated and young voters. This focus on disadvantaged voters is especially important, and is developed more in this study.

Hanmer also explores (although more descriptively) whether government elites and party leaders create incentives for citizens to vote because of the law. An example he cites is the motivation among government elites in the first set of states to adopt same day registration to enhance turnout through eased voting requirements, a motivating factor not present among the elites in the second set of states. Party elites in the second set of same day registration states advocated adoption of the law to avoid federal requirements that their states implement the "motor voter" provision the National Voter Registration Act. These different elite motivations affected both state government implementation of the law and citizen behavior in response to the law. Hanmer (2009) finds same day registration to have the highest impact in early adoption states.

While Hanmer's study has significantly contributed to our understanding of state voting laws, it too has a few shortcomings. Like much of the previous research, the data is now more than a decade old. Reliance on Census data means that important control variables such as partisanship and political interest are omitted; would inclusion of these factors change the findings? Focusing on same day registration, he does not control for the presence of early voting, mail voting, or absentee voting laws in the state. Another concern is that his research design depends on the quality of matches between same day registration treatment and control states. For instance, his first comparison consists of Minnesota and Wisconsin as treatment states, and Iowa and South Dakota as control states. While these states are certainly contiguous, they are substantially different in terms of population (5 million to 6 million people in treatment states, versus under 1 million to 3 million in control states) and other factors. The author considers population to be one of his matching criteria, and if this difference in state populations affects the quality of his matches, it may affect the study's inferences.

Finally, Burden and colleagues (2017, 2014) make significant strides in improving our understanding of these election reform laws by measuring state combinations of early voting and Election Day Registration (EDR) to account for the simultaneous existence of these laws at the state level. Their study also controls for the presence of voter identification laws and registration closing dates. Drawing on Current Population Survey data, the researchers use statistical matching and difference-in-differences to model individual- and county-level turnout. The result show that more citizens vote in states with same day registration (the combination of early voting and EDR), but early voting alone reduces turnout. While they do not directly model the mobilization of voters, they theorize that states with combinations of early voting and EDR have longer voter periods, and because of this campaigns and parties have longer mobilization periods during which to bring voters to the polls. By demonstrating that combinations of these laws have unique effects on turnout, this study has been profoundly important in election reform literature.

Because of the use of Census data, the authors cannot measure partisanship, interest, or voter mobilization. Moreover, their study focuses on higher turnout presidential elections, omitting midterm elections. Same day registration has been found to have larger effects in midterm elections (see Tolbert et al. 2008), and excluding those elections may mask potential effects of these laws. Convenience voting methods may have their largest effect in lower information midterm elections when presidential campaigns are absent. This study utilizes a dataset that is not subject to these constraints, and also examines the effects of the laws in both presidential and midterm elections.

Many Other Studies Find Minimal Effects of Convenience Voting Laws

Beyond the four recent studies discussed so far, there is a large field devoted to the study of voting laws dating back half a century. While the more recent studies have found some positive effects, much of the earlier research found more limited boosts in participation from the laws. Neeley and Richardson (2001, 387) evaluate two competing hypotheses—the mobilization voting thesis and the convenience voting thesis. The mobilization hypothesis predicts that election reform laws bring new individuals from low-propensity turnout groups (e.g., low socio-economic status, less partisan, and younger) into the electorate, whereas the convenience voting hypothesis predicts that election reform laws primarily advantage individuals who are already likely to vote (e.g., high socio-economic status, partisan, and older). An implication of the former hypothesis is that lowered administrative barriers to voting will motivate new individuals to vote, while the latter hypothesis suggests that the laws have a minimal effect on turnout since they merely provide an alternate way to vote for individuals who would have participated regardless. Studying early voting within a Tennessee county, Neeley and Richardson (2001, 386–387) find that the convenience voting hypothesis is a more accurate thesis regarding early voting—it is used primarily by demographic groups that are likely to vote anyway.

In a highly cited article, Berinksy (2005) discusses the logic behind the inference that convenience voting laws have a minimal effect on turnout. Addressing the effects of absentee, in-person early, and mail voting laws, he notes that individuals who use these laws tend to be of higher socio-economic status, with higher levels of political engagement and knowledge—the same groups of people are more likely to cast a ballot in-person on election day. Rather than bring new voters into the electorate, the laws simply change how existing voters participate. Echoing this point, several other researchers emphasize that convenience voting laws by themselves are not the main drivers of turnout (Arceneaux, Kousser, and Mullin 2012; Burden et al. 2014; Karp and Banducci 2001; Neely and Richardson 2001; Oliver 1996). Rather, political interest, electoral competitiveness between candidates, and mobilization campaigns are key factors that stimulate turnout and motivate individuals to make use of these laws (Bowler and Donovan 2008; Donovan 2008; Karp and Banducci 2001).

These studies generally find that early voting (whether in-person or absentee/mail) has minimal effects on voter turnout, and tends to exacerbate existing demographic inequalities in the electorate. An estimated 27% of non-voters from the 1996–2014 Current Population Survey cited a lack of political interest and disconnect from campaigns as main reasons for not casting ballots. Same day registration is an exception to these results, likely because this law does not penalize individuals who only become motivated to register and vote on the day of an election or immediately before an election—individuals who, on average, tend to be low socio-economic status, young, and not very partisan (Ashok et al. 2016; Hanmer 2009).

Many other studies corroborate this minimal-effects thesis. Some early studies found that mail voting in Oregon increased turnout by 10 percentage points (Southwell 2016; Southwell and Burchett 2000), but Gronke and Miller (2012) fail to replicate these findings using later elections, and they characterize any increase in turnout as a limited novelty effect. Using a natural experiment in Californians, Kousser and Mullin (2007, 428) find that mail voting does not result in greater political participation. Other work indicates that mail voting mainly advantages individuals who are already predisposed to vote regardless of format (Alvarez, Levin, and Sinclair 2012; Berinsky, Burns, and Traugott 2001; Karp and Banducci 2000).

Regarding absentee mail voting, Patterson and Caldeira (1985, 766) find a large turnout impact in California and Iowa districts "where partisan candidates are likely to harvest absentee votes in the very localities where their party is otherwise strong." This suggests that absentee voting advantages partisan rather than non-partisan voters. Echoing this finding, Oliver (1996, 498) reports that overall turnout is increased with absentee voting, but only "when [the] liberalization of absentee voter eligibility is combined with party mobilization efforts." Karp and Banducci (2000, 191), similarly, find that "self-selection plays a greater role in determining who votes absentee than does party mobilization," with partisans, those active in politics, and those of higher socio-economic status more likely to vote absentee. These findings comport with a broad array of studies on this mode of voting (Barreto, Streb, and Guerra 2006; Hall, Gregorowicz, and Alley 2016; Gronke, Galanes-Rosenbaum, Miller, and Toffey 2008a). However, more recent research by Leighley and Nagler (2013) using time-series data suggests that no-excuse absentee voting laws can boost voter turnout. Even so, there is a lack of consensus on the impact of this law on participation.

Mixed findings are especially evident regarding the impact of in-person early voting on voter turnout. Using state-level data from 1980 to 2006, Gronke, Galanes-Rosenbaum, and Miller (2007) show that the law has no impact on turnout (also see Burden et al. 2017, 2014 for similar findings). Other research shows that turnout gaps between advantaged and disadvantaged voting groups is greater with early voting (Gimpel, Dyck, and Shaw 2006; Knopf 2012; Neeley and Richardson 2001; Stein 1998), between the poor and the better-off, and the young and the old.

Some evidence, though, suggests that early voting may enhance turnout among historically marginalized voting groups. Stein and Garcia-Monet (1997, 668–669), to this point, examine 1992 presidential election turnout in Texas counties and find that not only do counties with higher total participation have higher proportions of votes cast early, but that Clinton's vote was higher in counties "where the proportion of votes cast early and the percentage change in new voter registration were high." This suggests, to Stein and Garcia-Monet (1997, 668), that "Democratic Party efforts to turn out core supporters" such as Hispanic voters "through early voting appears to have been efficacious." In the wake of recent early voting restrictions in Florida in 2011, Herron and Smith (2014, 2012) corroborate Stein and Garcia-Monet's finding that racial and ethnic minorities, registered Democrats, and those with no party affiliation benefit from early voting laws, as these groups had the largest declines in early voting in the 2012 presidential election compared to the 2008 election (after the early voting restrictions went into effect). Yet in a later study comparing early voting across counties in North Carolina, the authors find a null effect (Walker, Herron, and Smith 2018).

Other recent studies together present an inconclusive portrait regarding the impact of convenience voting laws. Using 1998 to 2012 Current Population Survey data, Miller and Powell (2016) find that early voting, no-excuse absentee voting, and permanent absentee voting are positively related to voting among the disabled. Wass et al. (2017), using six rounds of the European Social Survey, find that countries with more individuals with impaired health or functional ability are also more likely to adopt voting methods such as mail voting, early voting, proxy voting, and vote casting outside of polling locations. These findings are important because they demonstrate that convenience methods can be used to make voting more accessible. Other studies, though, examine the impact of early voting in a number of different countries and find that early voting has less of an effect on increasing turnout, and has more of an impact on retaining likely voters in the electorate (Garnett 2019; Laing, Miragliotta, and Thorton-Smith 2018; Sheppard and Beauregard 2018).

These findings are similar to much of the research in the United States, which generally shows that early voting has a limited impact on stimulating new voter turnout (Berinsky 2005; Burden et al. 2014; Gronke et al. 2008a). Importantly, our study adds to this literature by measuring election administration simultaneously with three modes of convenience voting (in-person early voting, no-excuse absentee or mail voting, and same day registration) providing more positive results. All in all, these findings are divided over whether early voting exacerbates or mitigates the participatory bias in the electorate, a question that is especially relevant in light of recent early voting restrictions in the states.

Compared to the other laws, same day registration has been found to benefit citizens from disadvantaged demographic groups as it removes the need for voters to complete two separate actions: registering before an election, and then casting a ballot on a later day (Burden et al. 2014, 96; Hanmer 2009; Springer 2014; Wolfinger, Highton, and Mullin 2005, 3; Wolfinger and Rosenstone 1980; Fitzgerald 2005). Individuals are not penalized for neglecting or forgetting to register, reducing the informational threshold needed to understand how to register to vote. One merely needs to be aware of the date of the election and the location of the polling place. This lower information cost suggests that same day registration might be a preferred voting option for the poor. Hanmer (2009) finds that young and less educated citizens are most likely to benefit from same day registration. Many studies have found that same day registration leads to higher turnout (Brians and Grofman 2001; Burden, Canon, Mayer, and Moynihan 2014; Fenster 1994; Fitzgerald 2005; Hanmer 2009; Knack 2001; Neiheisel and Burden 2012; Leighley and Nagler 2013; Rigby and Springer 2011; Springer 2014; Tolbert et al. 2008).

Research design limitations may hamper evaluations of how these laws shape participation rates. A number of studies examine only a handful states or counties within a single state (Barreto et al. 2006; Gronke and Miller 2012; Hanmer 2009; Karp and Banducci 2001; Kousser and Mullin 2007; Neely and Richardson 2001; Southwell and Burchett 2000). Several studies rely on a single year to analyze the impact of these laws, rather than measuring changes in turnout over time (Highton and Wolfinger 1998; Huang and Shields 2000; Timpone 2002; Wolfinger and Rosenstone 1980; but see Springer 2014). Some of the most cited articles rely only on descriptive or correlational statistics to formulate conclusions about their effects (Berinksy 2005; Gronke et. al. 2008a; Stein 1998).

As alluded to at the beginning of the chapter, more recent analyses draw on large-sample over-time survey data from the U.S. Census with representative state samples (Burden et al. 2014; Hanmer 2009; Leighley and Nagler 2013; Springer 2014) and the very large sample Cooperative Comparative Election Survey (CCES). This information is incorporated into research designs that includes time-series cross-sectional (Leighley and Nagler 2013; Springer 2014), difference-in-differences (Hanmer 2009; Burden et al. 2014), and statistical matching (Burden et al. 2014), as well as models that control for multiple laws simultaneously (Burden et al. 2014; Spring 2014). These studies have made important inroads into our understanding of state election reform laws, especially the positive effect of same day registration.

Why Studying the Laws Is Not Enough—State Election Administration

However, even these more recent contributions have limitations. Few election reform law studies have controlled for state election administration, despite how important implementation is for the effectiveness of laws (Bardach

1977). Above and beyond the effects of convenience methods, variations in election administration across the fifty states may impact voter registration and turnout. According to Justice John Paul Stevens, quoted from the majority opinion in *Crawford v. Marion County Election Board*, "public confidence in the integrity of the electoral process has independent significance, because it encourages citizen participation in the democratic process (Lowenstein et al. 2008, 315–329). A state's electoral practices are structured by its administration (Burden and Stewart 2014). Broadly, Alvarez et al. (2013, 31) describe a state's election administration as an *electoral ecosystem*, a holistic set of rules, procedures, technologies, and local election officials that shape individual-level registration and turnout in fifty states.

Election administration practices have real impacts on how individuals cast ballots. Across states, for instance, there is considerable variation in the number of polling stations per precinct (density of polling places), the length of polling lines, and the existence of online information sources people can use to find out where to vote in their precinct (Pew 2016; Stein and Vonnahme 2014). Such "how to vote" factors can directly influence turnout. Having more polling stations, shorter lines, and more readily available election information makes it easier for citizens to vote, independent of the effect of election reform laws.

Other examples of administration include cross-state variations in the quality of voting machines that affect residual vote rates, or the difference between ballots cast and votes counted in an election (Ansolabehere and Stewart 2005; Stewart 2014); the existence of post-election audit laws that can catch problems and authenticate election results (Stewart 2008; Alvarez et al. 2013, 25–26); the lenience of state provisional ballot policies allowing citizens to cast a preliminary ballot if they are not registered or do not show up in a precinct's voter database (Hanmer and Herrnson 2014); and the degree of professionalism and training among poll workers which affects how voter ballots are processed (Alvarez et al. 2013, 29). In these myriad of ways, the administration of election laws may influence an individual's likelihood of voting.

While there is a growing literature on election reform and administration, it rarely applied to understanding voter turnout or political participation. For example, Alvarez and Grofman's (2014) edited book is directed toward an academic audience interested in election administration efforts that have changed over a decade-and-a-half following *Bush v. Gore* (2000). The contributions within the volume examine various elements of election administration—including registration laws (Alvarez and Hall 2014), ballot design (Kropf 2014), poll worker training (Hall and Moore 2014)—and how these factors structure political participation. The chapters show that absentee and early voting laws have grown in usage since the 2000 election recount in Florida. Gronke (2014a) suggests that the waves of election reform efforts spurred by this event prompted increased diffusion of early voting laws across the states. Kropf (2014) shows that subpar ballot design can lead voters to improperly submit their votes, leading to disparities between the number of votes cast versus counted at the county level. This research applies Alvarez and Grofman's (2014) logic to the study of individual-level turnout decisions.

In a related study, Hasen (2012) uses case studies to examine the 2000 election dilemma in Florida, as well as a host of other election administration issues in the states in the aftermath of *Bush v. Gore*. Writing for an audience of academics and laypersons seeking a better understanding of the "black box" of electoral practices in the United States, Hasen hypothesizes that many problems of U.S. elections can be attributed to two features of election regulations: local administration of elections and partisan control of elections (see Gerken 2009 for a related argument). In the U.S., counties are given extensive authority in administering elections. Hasen argues that negative vote outcomes are traceable to county disparities in resources (e.g., quality of election machines, poll worker training, etc.), a lack of uniformity regarding the procedures counties follow to count votes, and differences in how they adjudicate election disputes. Another problem is that most high-ranking election officials—such as state secretaries of state—serve in elected or appointed positions that are contingent on an administrator's party affiliation. This means that party goals sometimes come into conflict with administering fair elections. The author corroborates these hypotheses with numerous examples including cases of voter suppression, vote counting and recounting issues in contested elections, poor-quality voting machines leading to lost votes, and confusing ballot designs resulting in invalid votes being cast.

Burden and Stewart's (2014) important edited volume uses a data-driven approach to understand and evaluate multiple aspects of U.S. election administration, although none of the authors address voter turnout or inequality in turnout per se. Chapters within the volume focus on provisional ballots (Hanmer and Herrnson 2014), polling place experiences (Stein and Vonnahme 2014), quality of voter registration lists (Ansolabehere and Hersh

2014), residual vote rates (Stewart 2014), and voter confidence in accurate ballot counting after absentee or early voting compared to in-person election day voting (Gronke 2014b), among other elements of election administration. Findings indicate that each of these elements is an important factor in structuring the voting experience of citizens.

Measuring public confidence in election results (i.e., public opinion) is a common outcome variable in studies of election administration. Paul Gronke (2014b, 261–268), using data from the Survey of the Performance of American Elections and the Cooperative Congressional Election Study (CCES), measures citizen confidence in election processes. He finds that voters are more confident that their votes will be counted in states with post-election audits, more professional poll workers, and high-quality voting machines. More confidence in elections may lead to higher voter turnout. Moreover, in-person election day voters, in-person early voters, and mail voters are more likely to report confidence that their ballots were counted when they trusted local election officials (Gronke 2014b, 264). In similar research, Atkeson and Saunders (2008, 27) study absentee and early voters in Colorado and New Mexico, and they find that residents of these states were less confident that their ballots were accurately counted because of how these modes of voting "disconnect voters from election day activities." This lower sense of efficacy—or belief that a ballot has been tallied in an election—likely affects an individual's inclination to use one of these vote methods rather than in-person election day voting.

A few studies have linked the density of early voting sites to voter turnout. Using Election Assistance Commission data to measure the density of early voting sites per county in the 2008 and 2012 elections, Fullmer (2015a) finds this factor to have a positive and significant impact on turnout. A key implication, drawn from these works, is the importance of measuring elements of state's election administration to understand voter turnout.

Alvarez, Atkeson, and Hall (2013), in a groundbreaking study, seek to understand standards and methods used to evaluate elections and electoral practices. While they do not examine registration and voting laws or political participation, they show how multiple features of election administration can be assessed to determine how accessible it is for voters: vote counting accuracy (residual votes), postelection audits, poll worker training, and voter confidence surveys.

One study does connect election administration to political participation. Ewald (2009) examines the localized and partisan nature of American election administration. He uses process tracing and case studies to examine how variations in county-based election administration, with occasional state- and federal-level interventions, have shaped political participation over the course of American history. His data includes legal, legislative, and historical records stretching from the founding period in America to *Bush v. Gore* (2000) and the Help America Vote Act (2002). While the research focuses on state- and locally based election rules, and how they influence political participation, it does not use systematic data and statistics to draw generalizable conclusions of the effects of election reform laws (institutions) on voter turnout.

New measures have been developed to quantify state election administration, expanding empirical research in this field. Gerken (2009) first proposed and Stewart (2008) developed the Election Performance Index (EPI) measure to assess and rank the performance of fifty state election administrations with the idea of shaming under-performing states into improving how they conduct elections. By making this information publicly available through Pew Charitable Trusts and the MIT Election Data and Science Lab, the intention was to spur improvements in registration and voting procedures used by state and local governments.

The current study uses the comprehensive election performance index from Pew and MIT, building on the research just discussed, alongside state convenience voting laws to predict individual-level turnout decisions, something that has not been done previously. The idea of accessible elections is that both the laws and their administration may structure political participation for voters.

Electoral Practices & Design Improvements

Studying State Voting Laws in Isolation

The research designs used in many previous studies examines the effect of a single state election law, such as early voting, on voter turnout rates without accounting for a state's other voting reform laws. That is, these studies neglect to control for the joint effect that election laws and administration have on individual and aggregate-level turnout. Building on Burden et al. (2014) and other recent studies (Leighley and Nagler 2013; Springer 2014), this study contends that both convenience voting laws and administration of election are important in understanding micro-level voting decisions.

Threats of Selection Bias when Studying Convenience Voting Laws

As discussed earlier, much of the published work on election laws and voter turnout has not carefully controlled for selection bias in the set of states that have adopted convenience voting laws. Some studies move us closer by arguing that scholars need to control for endogenous factors as well as state convenience methods to avoid biased conclusions using observational data. Michael Hanmer (2009) convincingly illustrates that overall turnout boosts from same day registration are more modest than previously thought, using matched treatment and control cases and difference-in-differences statistical methods. He also accounts for factors (e.g., pro-voting state cultures proxied by state legislative records that he measures with case studies but not quantitatively) that may make certain states more likely than others to adopt same day registration and motor voter laws in the first place. Hanmer's (2009) work sets a standard for studying the effects of state election reform laws by controlling for factors that makes some states more likely to adopt election reform laws in the first place. The use of panel survey data and voter histories are used in this study to help control against selection bias threats.

Focusing on Overall Turnout Rates Rather than Turnout for Disadvantaged Groups

Much of the existing research in political science has focused on predicting overall voter turnout resulting from adoption of voting and registration laws, rather than voting rates for disadvantaged demographic citizens (but see Brians and Grofman 2001; Franko, Kelly, and Witko 2016; Oliver 1996; Patterson and Caldeira 1985; Springer 2014; Rhine 1995; Southwell and Burchett 2000; Stein and Garcia-Monet 1997). Studying overall participation rates—or statewide averages—may mask important variation across demographic subgroups. A priority of this study is whether disadvantaged voters, such as the poor, are more likely to vote in states with more accessible elections. Previous research on poor people's movements (Piven and

Cloward 1977) contends that only when the poor participate in mass protests can their voices be heard. Can convenience voting methods directly increase the political voice of the poor and racial and ethnic minorities?

Modeling Turnout, not Political Contact and Mobilization

Finally, although much prior research has examined voting and turnout (see Berinsky 2005), there has not been much attention paid to how these laws and state electoral practices impact the likelihood of political campaigns and parties contacting and mobilizing citizens to vote in elections (see Rosenstone and Hansen 2002 for the landmark study on voter mobilization). Burden et al. (2014) suggest that different mobilization strategies surround the laws, but the authors do not directly measure mobilization or campaign contact. They also do not examine how these laws differentially impact the likelihood that different socio-economic status individuals will be contacted by a campaign. In states with more accessible electoral systems, the expectation is that political campaigns and parties will work to ensure that more citizens are targeted to vote. Individuals from historically marginalized voting groups (e.g., low socio-economic status) will also be mobilized at higher rates.

Data Quality

Another limitation of existing research is that the U.S. Census data used in many prior studies does not include measures of political interest, partisanship, and campaign contact. Yet decades of research confirms that individuals who are interested in politics, are partisan, and have been contacted are more likely to vote (Parry et al. 2008). These confounding factors are related to turnout decisions, and thus they need to be included in statistical models estimating the effects of election reform laws.

Survey-based datasets, such as the American National Election Study, can be vulnerable to sample bias, as discussed in Chapter 1. While the sample sizes in the Current Population Survey are relatively large compared to standard surveys, until recently few previous studies made use of public records (voter rolls) of citizen registration and turnout (but see Herron and Smith 2014; Hersh 2015). Recent research has made use of national voter files based on precinct, county, and state registration and voting records to produce findings not possible with survey research. Ansolabehere and Hersh (2014), for example, identify sex- and race-based interactive effects associated with turnout, finding that among Hispanics and African Americans women are more likely to vote than men. In another study, Hersh and Nall (2016) show that this data—combined with disaggregation or multilevel modeling and poststratification techniques—facilitates more precise measurements of sub-state variations in political behavior.

In the area of election administration, Ansolabehere and Hersh (2014) are able to assess the overall quality of state voter registration databases, including whether states have correct voter mailing addresses, reliably remove dead voters from the rolls, and list voters' correct birthdates to determine eligibility based on Catalist data. These data are also used by Ashok et al. (2016) to identify the day during an early voting period when individuals cast their ballots, with a further finding showing that when individuals cast their ballots is related to age, partisanship, and socio-economic status.

Despite the advanced research designs used in many recent studies, advances in data quality and data science may be leveraged to retest the effects of state electoral laws, rules and practices on political participation. This study uses national voter files, as discussed in more detail in Chapter 1. Catalist data helps protect against the response and sample bias associated with survey datasets, and is even used to create the vote validated turnout measure commonly used in CCES. Voter histories are used to construct models where turnout for the same individual can be modeled over time; measuring change in participate rates for the same individual over time reduces bias in making inferences. These factors help parse out the influence of these confounding factors related to voting.

Panel Data and Change Models

Overreliance on cross-sectional data, even time-series cross-sectional data, to draw conclusions can be misleading, as other factors may be driving the patterns in the data. To understand whether state election laws or the administration of the laws affects voter turnout and for different demographic groups, we need data over time. Since our focus is individual voting decisions, the gold standard is panel survey data where the same individuals are measured across elections (a form of within-subjects experiment). In this study we use change models (what are called lagged "panel models") to predict voting in the 2012 presidential and 2014 midterm elections, controlling for the individual's turnout decision in the previous presidential (2008) or midterm (2010) election. Voter histories are the strongest predictor of turnout decisions. But some individuals become mobilized and others choose not to vote. Panel survey research designs allows us to hone in on the effects of state election laws and administration of the laws on changes in turnout rates over time, and for different demographic groups, controlling for other factors.

Accessible Elections

The adoption and administration of election laws is a constitutionally protected prerogative of the states (Article 1, Section 4 of the U.S. Constitution), leading to fifty different types of accessible state elections across the states (Keyssar 2009; McDonald 2010). States not only have adopted different voting and registration laws (Burden et al. 2014) but have adopted different registration laws, polling location provisions, and historical legacies of promoting or hindering turnout that, over time, impact voting. These factors play an interactive role in shaping voting behavior.

Electoral laws and practices are created and altered by political actors to impact political behavior, and over time these laws give rise to new participatory cultures that prompt further additions or alternations to these laws. Citizens' political behavior may be influenced by historically embedded configurations of political institutions; political participation in turn facilitates the design of future institutions. A neo-institutional perspective, as defined by Orren and Skowronek (2004, 78; see also Steinmo, Thelen, and Longstreth 1992) recognizes that institutions shape behavior, but that citizen behavior can reform political institutions. This school of thought combines history with the notion that "institutions participate actively in politics: they shape interests and motives, configure social and economic relationships, [and] promote as well as inhibit political change" (see Putnam 1993; Tocqueville 1835).

This argument is consistent with policy feedback. According to Mettler and SoRelle 2014, 168), "political actors are keenly aware of policy benefits' capacity to alter participatory dynamics. . . . They have the ability to exacerbate or mitigate existing inequalities by providing resources to some groups rather than others." By creating laws favorable to certain groups rather than others, state governments signal to individuals within these groups whether or not their behaviors are endorsed by the state. Over the past fifteen years, a growing body of policy feedback research has found that government policy affects opinion and behavior in several areas, including the environment, health care, welfare reform, smoking bans, and same-sex marriage (Gusmano, Schlesinger, and Thomas 2002; Hetling and McDermott; Johnson, Brace, and Arceneaux 2005; Kreitzer, Hamiltion, and Tolbert 2014; Pacheco 2012, 2013; Pacheco and Fletcher 2015).

A policy feedback link may also exist between state electoral practices and individual voting behavior. State government rules and procedures impact who is able to vote, and which groups are targeted by political campaigns and parties for mobilization (Burden et al. 2014). They affect the amount of resources (e.g., canvassing, advertising, direct mail) that campaigns devote to voter recruitment, and the symbolic importance that a state government attaches to the participation of particular groups (Mettler and SoRelle 2014; Waldman 2016). State legislatures and political elites have a long history of adopting or annulling voting laws in order to affect turnout in ways that are advantageous to political parties rather than state citizenries (Keyssar 2009; Keys 1949; Schattschneider 1942). Using voting laws, state governments signal to citizens whose participation is valued, and this affects who takes part in elections.

While same day registration has been used by the Democratic Party to mobilize college students who are unregistered to vote (Hanmer 2009, Chapter 7), states with strong historical voting norms, such as Maine, Minnesota, and Wisconsin, also have party elites who are more likely to endorse adoption of laws that improve turnout. While some states advocate for laws to increase turnout, others actively legislate to reduce it. Herron and Smith (2014) reveal that Florida restrictions on early voting (reducing the number of days allowed for early voting, especially Sundays used in Souls to the Polls minority voting drives) depressed the turnout levels of racial minorities and other Democratically aligned population groups, which was to the distinct advantage of the Republican Party. Restrictive voting laws signal to these groups that they are symbolically less valued members of the electorate, depressing their participation, while expansive voting laws signal the opposite (Soss and Schram 2007).

Looking Ahead

This chapter has summarized the election reform literature relating to voting and registration laws and the election administration literature, suggesting a new way to weave together these two fields. Understanding the performance of state voting laws and election administration performance is the goal of this study's research design. In the next chapter, the first empirical test of this accessible elections framework is evaluated. Do state election reform laws and election administration performance shape change in individual-level turnout?

4

Accessible Elections
and Voter Turnout

Low voter turnout and inequality in who votes across demographic groups are two significant problems facing American democracy over the past century. Only one in three (33%) individuals eligible to vote cast a ballot in the 2014 midterm election, a low point, while 58% and 59% did so in the 2012 and 2016 presidential elections (United States Elections Project 2018c). These highly competitive elections, along with 2008 and 2018, mark the highest turnout levels in modern times (United States Elections Project 2018c). But this pales in comparison to voting rates in the most recent national elections in other democracies: 87.2% in Belgium, 85.8% in Sweden, and 71.2% in France (Desilver 2016). Participation in U.S. elections is heavily skewed toward the more educated and affluent citizens. Voter turnout in the 2012 presidential election, for example, was over 10 percentage points higher for individuals earning more than $50,000 per year than those earning $30,000 to $39,000 (Current Population Survey 2012).

Relatively low participation in elections and unequal voting rates can result in negative outcomes (Lijphart 1997; Brown, Jackson, and Wright 1999; Jackson, Brown, and Wright 1998), including the election of candidates who do not reflect the interests of a majority of the population (Bartels 2008; Key 1949), policy outcomes skewed toward wealthy voters (Hill and Leighley 1992; Lijphart 1997; Franko and Witko 2017), and lower trust in government and government legitimacy (Keyssar 2009). Do convenience voting laws—early voting, home voting (mail/absentee), and same day registration—increase turnout and increase participation rates among individuals from lower social status groups? Or, rather, do they have only minimal effects, as found by a number of scholars (see Chapter 3)?

While the challenges of inequality in who votes remains constant, the legal landscape for voting and registration laws across the states continues to change. Recent reforms in the areas of voting and registration aim to address this problem. In the wake of the controversial 2000 election, where the

Accessible Elections. Michael Ritter and Caroline J. Tolbert, Oxford University Press (2021). © Oxford University Press.
DOI: 10.1093/oso/9780197537251.001.0001.

presidential candidate with the most popular votes was not elected, and the Help America Vote Act (2002), federal and state governments moved toward making election administration procedures more accessible for citizens (Alvarez, Atkeson, and Hall 2013; Gerken 2009; Stewart 2008; Stewart 2006). Use of in-person early voting and home voting (mail/absentee) has steadily increased. In the swing state of Florida, 75% of votes were cast before election day in 2016, compared to 50% in 2012. Early voting among Latinos in Florida increased by 100% from 2012 to 2016 (Florida Secretary of State 2016a, 2016b; McDonald 2016b). But these elections also experienced a backlash, where the time window to vote early was reduced and restricted in many states, including Florida and North Carolina. The result was a significant decrease in minority turnout rates (Brennan Center for Justice 2016; Herron and Smith 2014).

With the growing number of Americans casting a ballot using these new laws, what are the cumulative effects on voting rates? Although several recent studies (Burden et al. 2014; Hanmer 2009; Leighley and Nagler 2013; Springer 2014) have found same day registration to have a positive effect on overall turnout rates, same day registration may not be the only voting reform that matters.

National voter files based on fifty state voter rolls and panel models (where the same individuals are measured over time) are used to examine the effect of the laws on turnout among the general populace, updating the previous literature based on earlier elections. Previous research often had much smaller sample sizes and lacked panel data. Like an experiment, panel data provides a pre- and post-test within individuals, reducing the number of factors that can lead to a change in behavior for respondents. Most previous research also did not measure implementation of the laws, or election administration, focusing primarily on adoption of convenience voting laws. The accessible elections framework takes account of the combination of election laws and election administration performance in shaping individual voting decisions. The goal is to measure the effect of electoral practices in changing the probability that a non-voter will cast a ballot in a future election.

Guiding Research Questions

Drawing on the discussion in the previous chapters, here we develop two testable research hypotheses predicting individual turnout decisions.

H1: Election reform laws (early, no-excuse absentee or mail voting, and same day registration) and better election administration will increase individual-level voter turnout.

Individuals are more likely to vote in states with election administration practices that reduce the difficulties associated with the voting process (Alvarez, Atkeson, and Hall 2013; Burden and Stewart 2014; Gerken 2009). Evaluating the laws in this context, this study re-evaluates their effects on political participation.

More active campaigns and mass media coverage make it more likely that individuals will vote during presidential elections, whether or not a state has any one of these election laws. In low-salience midterm elections, convenience voting laws have been found to be more critical in determining whether individuals cast a ballot. Some studies (Tolbert and Smith 2005; Tolbert, Grummel, and Smith 2001; Tolbert, McNeal, and Smith 2003) have noted similar differential turnout effects of ballot initiatives, with initiatives having a larger effect on turnout in lower information midterm elections. Election reform laws are expected to have a similar effect.

H2: Convenience voting laws and state election administration will have their largest impact on turnout in midterm elections.

Research Design

This study's research design employs several techniques to reduce error in evaluating the effects of convenience methods on turnout decisions, as discussed in the previous chapters. Burden et al. (2014, 100) argue that the states are so heterogeneous in their sets of election reform laws that it is reasonable to assume that the impacts of the laws are exogenous, "at least in terms of unobserved variables that are correlated with turnout" (Burden et al. 2014, 100). Building on the work of Burden and colleagues, the design includes the cumulative set of alternative voting laws present in each state: in-person early voting, home voting (no-excuse absentee or mail voting), and same day registration with three binary variables. Much research has often measured the presence of only one of these laws at a time.

Some states have stronger traditions of promoting participation in elections and government than others (Hanmer 2009; Elazar 1972, 1994). To isolate the effect of these laws on participation, it is necessary to control for the propensity of the state to encourage voter turnout in general. The risk of endogeneity is that state-level factors that lead to a state's adoption of election reform laws also motivate individuals to vote, independently of the effect of the laws (Hanmer 2009). To control for this potential selection bias, or confounding factor, election administration performance is measured for each state every two years (see Chapter 2). States with higher performing election administration tend to have higher turnout rates overall, so this factor serves as an important control variable. Election administration performance captures both the accessibility of a state's voting system and a state's legacy of promoting or hindering turnout. This makes comparisons across the states easier by soaking up a significant component of variation in state electoral systems—a factor missing from most previous research focusing on the laws and not election administration.

A third design component to isolate the effects of the voting reform laws on turnout is the use of national voter files with vote histories (panel data) for the same individuals over time. Catalist offers sample sizes many times larger than the Census's Current Population Survey or Cooperative Congressional Election Study (CCES), data used by previous scholars, providing more precision in evaluating the effects of the laws. Few previous studies have used these very large samples to evaluate the effects of states' election reform laws, as done here.

Panel data provides repeat measurements for the same individual over time, and offers a significant improvement in modeling compared to earlier research. Most of the variation in voting decisions across individuals is absorbed by knowing someone's voting history. If an individual voted in the 2010 congressional elections, they were likely to vote in 2014. Does living in a state with election reform laws change the probability that an individual who did not vote in 2010 would cast a ballot in 2014? Because we have voting histories, these types of models allow the researcher to isolate the effect of contextual factors (such as state residence and voting laws) on turnout decisions with more precision. We call our use of lagged panel models "change models."

Here panel models are used to predict the change in the probability of voting, simulations focusing on what it takes to convert a non-voter into a voter. The dependent variable is dichotomous (1 = voted and 0 = non-voting), but the models include a lagged term (independent variable) for voting in the previous election (again coded 1 = voted and 0 = non-voting). Turnout in the 2010 midterm election is used to predict turnout in the 2014 midterms, and turnout in the 2008 presidential election is used to predict turnout in the 2012 election. We compare change in midterm–midterm election turnout, and presidential–presidential election turnout. Lagged panel models (i.e., controlling for turnout in the previous election) means that an individual's having voted in 2008 will perfectly predict the score for that same person if they voted in 2012. Similarly, a non-voter in 2008 will perfectly predict a continued non-voter in 2012. Explanatory variables—such as demographic factors and state election features—will only have an impact on people who changed their voting behavior—non-voter in 2008 to voting in 2012, or vice versa. By using lagged panel models, we are focusing on predicting who changed their voting behavior.

Lastly, model statistical outcomes are checked for robustness using a number of alternative specifications such as multilevel modeling to evaluate the stability of the empirical results.

Data

This study measures the impact of a state's set of voting laws and election administration on political participation. We seek to test whether state convenience voting laws and election administration are bringing voters into the electorate, or whether restrictive state election systems are reducing turnout. As discussed in Chapter 1, the analysis uses national voter files and vote histories of the same individuals to detect changes in individual-level turnout over time. The Catalist data includes all 240 million adults based on fifty state voter rolls—180 million people, combined with data on 60 million people who are not registered to vote. We analyze a random 1% sample draw from this population, or approximately 2.4 million people which includes registered and unregistered voters. The election data compiles individual voting data from county and state voting records and select demographic data (such as age, race, partisanship, and sex) from these records, merging this information with commercial data available from other sources (see Chapter 1). Catalist imputes other individual-level variables, such as income, home ownership, education, and employment, using algorithms based on information from commercial and public records (Ansolabehere and Hersh 2014; Hersh 2015).[1]

---

[1] Catalist data includes a number of imputed variables, including news interest, home ownership, and employment. Hersh (2015, Chapter 4) notes that these simulated variables are less accurate

Variables

The primary explanatory variables measure an individual's residence in a state with the convenience voting methods (early, home voting [no-excuse absentee/mail], and same day registration), as well as the election administration performance (National Conference of State Legislatures 2018a, 2018b). The Appendix lists the state voting and registration laws, and their changes over time. Pew/MIT Election Data and Science Lab's election administration index is not static but is compiled every two years from 2008 to 2016 (see Appendix). The measure takes account of changes in a state's election administration, such as average wait times, provisional ballot use, voting information lookup tools, ballot design quality, and election machine performance, among other variables. The dynamic index reflects changes in these and other electoral system factors every two years.

As discussed earlier, the primary outcome variable is whether the individual cast a ballot in the election, according to the state voter rolls. Registered and unregistered voters are included in the 2.4-million-person sample, which measures turnout histories across four elections (2008, 2010, 2012, and 2014). Voting in an election is coded 1 and non-voting is coded 0. Registered voters who didn't vote are assigned a 0 for each election year. Unregistered voters who didn't vote are also coded 0. A lagged term for voting in the previous election, discussed previously, allows us to model the change in the probability of voting over time.

At the individual and state levels, a number of control variables are included to account for other factors that may increase the probability that an individual votes. At the state level, an important control is the competitiveness of state-level elections, since more competitive elections are associated with more active campaigns and higher turnout (Leip 2015; Rosenstone and Hansen 2002).[2] The vote margin variable captures a winning candidate's

---

predictors than the variables based on actual voter roll records. When these variables are excluded, the results of the statistical analysis remain unchanged. The study's sample includes 2,321,638 individuals for the 2012 presidential election and 2,218,389 individuals for the 2014 midterm election across the fifty states. The data was also cleaned to remove individuals who were too young to have voted, or who had an unlisted age or gender. Again, the sample includes both registered and unregistered voters.

[2] Individuals may be more likely to vote in elections in which they have a greater probability of casting the deciding vote (Blais 2000), and because campaigns and parties are more likely to mobilize citizens in these contexts (Rosenstone and Hansen 2002; Cox and Munger 1989).

margin of victory in presidential election years, or the margin in the closest statewide election in midterm years (gubernatorial, senatorial, or average across all House districts if neither of the other seats is subject to election). It represents the margin separating the election victor in a state from the second-place candidate. The number of ballot initiatives appearing on state election ballots is also included (Ballotpedia 2008–2014). At the individual level, covariates are measured that have been associated with a higher probability of voting, including a respondent's gender (binary variable for male coded 1, and female 0), race (binary variables for African American, Hispanic, Asian, or other race[3] coded 1, and non-Hispanic whites coded 0), and partisan status (Republican or Democrat). The statistical models also measure whether an individual owns a home or is employed (measured with binary indictor variables), as both factors have been linked to higher participation rates. Additional variables include age (in years), education (propensity score measure of an individual's likelihood of having a bachelor's degree), income (propensity score ordinal scale divided into twenty categories ranging from "$0 to $10,000" to "$141,000 or greater"), length of residence (in years), and news interest (propensity score measure of an individual's likelihood of having a subscription to a news publication).

For individuals without information available on income, a binary variable measures missing information on income, allowing us to account for the omitted data without deleting the case from the sample (which can lead to bias). Lists of these individual-level variables and their coding are included in Appendix B. In general, the variables Catalist directly measures, including partisanship (thirty states), turnout, age, gender, and in some states race, are more accurate than the indirect measures. But as discussed in Chapter 1, these figures have been found to have a general high degree of accuracy.

Recap on Panel Models

As discussed in the Research Design section, we develop change models to predict whether a person voted in the 2012 presidential election, controlling for whether they voted in 2008. The setup allows us to measure the change in the probability of an individual voting from the 2008 to the following

---

[3] The "other race" category encapsulates individuals who did not locate themselves in the white non-Hispanic, African American, Hispanic, or Asian racial categories.

2012 presidential election. We also model turnout in the 2014 midterm election, controlling for turnout in the 2010 midterm election. These lagged panel models mean that most of the variation in predicting voting in 2012, for example, can be explained by whether an individual voted in 2008 (once someone becomes a voter, they tend to vote over their lifetime) (Plutzer 2002; Pacheco and Plutzer 2008). But some people are mobilized. For this group of people, we want to know what state they lived in, and whether state election laws and administration of the laws affected their voting decision, controlling for other standard predictors of voting.

Panel designs with repeated measurements of voting over time are used to evaluate the effects of state laws and administration of the laws in order to develop improved predictive models and help to develop models that show causation rather than correlation.

Results

Do Alternative Voting Laws Increase Turnout in Midterm Election?

Summary patterns of descriptive data can help provide a preliminary answer to this question. Table 4.1 presents a cross-tab, showing the number of voters and non-voters, and associated percentages, in states with and without convenience voting methods in the 2014 midterm election. As is the case with most other midterm elections (2018 being an exception), the national turnout rate was low, with just 37.14% of eligible voters casting a ballot. Beyond this general finding, there is noticeable variation in turnout based on whether the state had one of the three election reform laws. Indeed, in states without any election reform laws, just 34.62% of citizens cast a ballot, lower than the national baseline average. Conversely, using the same national turnout benchmark, voting rates are slightly higher in absentee/mail states (39.26%) and early voting states (37.55%), and substantially higher in same day registration states (48.59%). These preliminary statistics suggest that while same day registration has a large effect on voter turnout, absentee/mail voting and in-person early voting may have only minimal effects on overall participation in elections (Gronke et al. 2008a).

But these descriptive results may be misleading, attributing turnout effects to election laws when in fact other factors may play a greater explanatory role

Table 4.1 Voter Turnout in the 2014 Midterm Election, Varying Convenience
Voting Laws

	No Election Reform Law	In-Person Early Voting	No-Excuse Absentee/Mail Voting	Same Day Registration	Overall Total
Non-Vote	65.38% (391,365)	62.45% (1,005,856)	60.74% (833,297)	51.41% (126,600)	62.86% (1,459,196)
Vote	34.62% (207,238	37.55% (604,693)	39.26% (538,633)	48.59% (119,664)	37.14% (862,270)
Total	100.00% 598,603	100.00% (1,610,549)	100.00% (1,371,930)	100.00% (246,264)	100.00% (2,321,466)

Note: Data from Catalist (2016).

(see Hanmer 2009; Springer 2014). Multivariate regression models, controlling for other factors associated with turnout, are necessary to understand
the true effects of the laws on voting decisions.

Table 4.2 reports lagged panel models, predicting the probability of an individual voting in the 2014 midterm election, controlling for whether they
voted in 2010. This is the first model of a series of models to evaluate the
effect of state election reform laws and election administration on turnout
decisions. Because so much of the variation in voting in 2014 is soaked up by
including a covariate for previous voting history, the model allows a measure
of what factors are statistically significant in changing the probability of an
individual voting in 2010 and not voting in 2014, or vice versa.

An additive modeling design is used where column 1 includes the
covariates for the election reform laws and the control variables. Column 2
adds in the variable for election administration performance to see how implementation of the laws effects turnout decisions. Models reported in the
third, fourth, and fifth columns add in interaction effects between each state
voting law and election administration index to measure if the quality of a
state's election administration structures the influence of these laws on voting
decisions. Although only key results are depicted in Table 4.2, estimates are
produced while controlling for the full slate of individual- and state-level
variables mentioned earlier in the chapter (full table results are also available
in Appendix C).

According to the baseline model (column 1) of Table 4.2, only same day
registration has a positive and statistically significant effect on changing the

Table 4.2 Effects of Convenience Voting Laws on Changing Probability of Voting from 2010 to 2014, Varying Election Performance Index (Lagged Panel Models)

	Election Reform Laws	Election Reform Laws + EPI	In-Person Early Voting × EPI	No-Excuse Absentee/ Mail Voting × EPI	Same Day Registration × EPI
Vote 2010	2.05***	2.05***	2.05***	2.05***	2.05***
	(0.072)	(0.070)	(0.069)	(0.068)	(0.069)
In-Person Early Voting	0.10	0.19*	−0.60	0.15	0.20*
	(0.112)	(0.106)	(0.616)	(0.096)	(0.108)
Absentee/ Mail Voting	−0.07	−0.11	−0.12	−1.51**	−0.12
	(0.108)	(0.093)	(0.093)	(0.477)	(0.091)
SDR	0.43***	0.28**	0.23*	0.20*	1.38*
	(0.119)	(0.122)	(0.122)	(0.119)	(0.716)
EPI		0.01**	0.01	0.03×10^{-1}	0.02**
		(0.005)	(0.007)	(0.006)	(0.005)
Early Voting × EPI			0.01		
			(0.009)		
Absentee/ Mail Voting × EPI				0.02**	
				(0.007)	
SDR × EPI					−0.01
					(0.010)
Pseudo R^2	0.267	0.268	0.268	0.269	0.268
N	2,321,466	2,321,466	2,321,466	2,321,466	2,321,466

Note: Based on Catalist data (2016) measuring voting behavior of same eligible voters in the 2010 and 2014 elections. Vote 2010 variable is included to control for turnout in past election. To conserve space, only the primary covariates are reported here. Full regression models are reported in Appendix Table C1.1. The estimates are unstandardized logistic regression coefficients. Robust standard errors in parentheses are clustered by state. Multilevel models reveal similar results. *P*-values are based on two-tailed tests.

$^*p < 0.10$, $^{**} p < 0.05$, $^{***} p < 0.001$.

likelihood of voting in 2014 midterm election. This means that individuals residing in states with same day registration are more likely to become voters in 2014, when they did not vote in 2010, controlling for all other factors included in the statistical model.

The results remain stable in Table 4.2, even after controlling for a state's election administration performance (the EPI measure), which is shown in the second model to have a direct, positive, and significant effect on turnout. Individuals living in states with better administration of election are more likely to become voters, even if they did not vote in the past. Controlling for

EPI also reveals that in-person early voting has a positive and significant impact on turnout in the midterm, indicating that the impact of early voting on turnout is strongly shaped by the average quality of a state's election administration; this is linked to new research on early voting (also see Walker, Herron, and Smith 2018).

Additionally, the results suggests that election administration performance has a moderating influence on the effect of same day registration on turnout. Specifically, after controlling for a state's EPI, the magnitude of same day registration's positive effect on turnout is reduced. This suggests that it is important to control for election administration when evaluating the effect of state voting laws on turnout.

Of the latter three models, only the fourth model has a noteworthy result. In this model, election administration performance (the EPI measure) has a positive and statistically significant interactive effect with absentee/mail voting. This suggests that absentee and mail voting have their largest effects on increasing turnout when they operate within states with a high-quality level of election administration. The results support the hypotheses that election reform laws can enhance turnout, that election administration shapes this outcome, and that performance of a state's election administration structures the impact of each law.

Since the findings reported in Table 4.2 are logistic regression coefficients, which are difficult to interpret in terms of substantive magnitude, the effect sizes were converted to predicted probabilities to make them more readily interpretable, holding all other control variables constant at their mean values. Predicted probabilities were estimated to show in percentage terms the likelihood of an individual voting in 2014 if they were a non-voter in 2010. This simulation strategy is used to show how much of an impact a state's election reform laws and election administration performance had on an individual's likelihood of voting.

Figure 4.1 illustrates how the probability that an individual voted varied depending on whether they lived in a state with same day registration (whether or not they used the law to register on election day). This figure also shows how the influence of these laws on turnout changed after controlling for a state's EPI or election administration performance. The left side of Figure 4.1 displays a typical individual's probability of voting when residing in a state with same day registration versus living in a state without same day registration. The figure on the left does not include the control for the EPI variable, while the right side model includes the EPI control variable. Without the moderating influence of a state's election administration, same

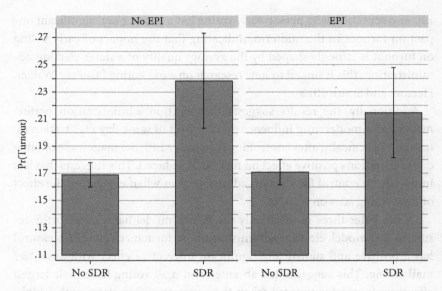

Figure 4.1. Probability that a non-voter in 2010 votes in the 2014 midterm election in states with and without same day registration, varying Election Performance Index.

Note: Bars in the left panel report the probability of voting in 2014 for Model 1 in Table 4.2 that does not include the EPI covariate. The bars on the right report the same relationship, but based on Model 2 that includes this covariate. All other variables held at mean values. Ninety percent confidence intervals included.

day registration is associated with a 7% higher likelihood of voting in 2014 for individuals who did not vote in 2010. After controlling for state election administration, the effect of living in a state with same day registration on turnout is estimated to be a still substantively significant 4.4%. This effect size is similar to that reported by Hanmer (2009).

This shows that same day registration has a strong and significant impact on increasing voting for individuals who did not vote in the previous mid-term election, with the effect also being structured by the overall quality of a state's election administration. Same day registration increases turnout in midterm elections more so than is commonly understood in previous research, which often focuses on presidential elections.

Figure 4.2 shows how election administration (the EPI measure) influenced an individual's decision to vote in 2014 if they did not vote in 2010, holding the laws and other factors constant. The results are substantively significant. Ranging from the lowest to the highest performing state

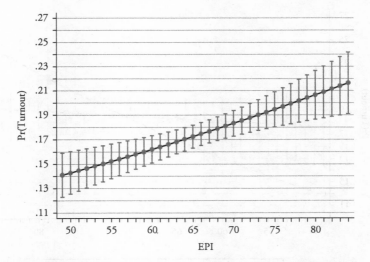

Figure 4.2. Probability that a non-voter in 2010 votes in the 2014 midterm election, varying Election Performance Index.

Note: Line reports the probability of voting in 2014 for Model 2 results in Table 4.2. EPI varied from minimum to maximum values. All other variables held at mean values. Ninety percent confidence intervals included.

election administration, an individual is approximately 7.5% more likely to vote in midterm elections. Independent of the convenience voting laws, the quality of a state's election administration has a discernible effect on turnout in midterm elections. Scholars have generally not recognized the powerful and independent effects of state election administration on voter turnout.

To better understand the moderating influence of election administration performance, Figure 4.3 shows how no-excuse absentee/mail voting affected an individual's likelihood of voting in 2014 if they did not vote in 2010, varying EPI from minimum to maximum values. At the lowest level of election administration performance, an individual in a no-excuse absentee/mail voting state is about 6% less likely to vote than an individual in a state without this law. However, as a state's election administration performance increases, so too does an individual's probability of voting in an absentee/mail voting state. At the highest level of state election administration performance, an individual in an absentee or mail ballot voting state has a 24% probability of voting, compared to 19% probability for an individual in a non–mail ballot voting state (a 5% difference).

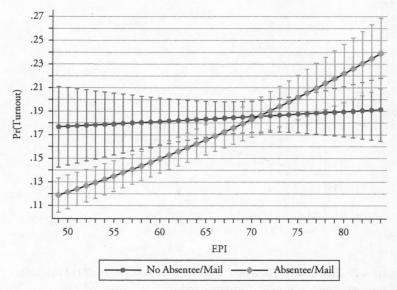

Figure 4.3. Probability that a non-voter in 2010 votes in the 2014 midterm election in states with and without no-excuse absentee/mail voting, varying Election Performance Index.

Note: Lines report probabilities of voting in states with and without absentee/mail voting in 2014 from Model 4 in Table 4.2. All other variables held at mean values. Ninety percent confidence intervals included.

Additionally, Figure 4.3 also illustrates that no-excuse absentee/mail voting has a larger substantive impact on turnout in states with the highest performing election administration (e.g., Minnesota and North Dakota), compared to the absentee/mail voting state with the lowest performing election administration (California). Indeed, an individual is 12% more likely to cast a ballot in an absentee/mail voting state with the highest, compared to lowest, EPI value. Importantly, Figure 4.3 adds substance to the argument that the performance of election reform laws is conditioned by the overall quality of a state's election administration.

The results reported in these figures show state election reform laws and election administration performance can have powerful and positive effects on turnout in a midterm elections. But do these factors also shape electoral participation in information-rich presidential elections, when voter turnout is generally much higher?

Presidential Election

Descriptive statistics, again, are first reported for turnout in the 2012 presidential election for states with and without each voting reform law (see Table 4.3). According to the Catalist data, the national baseline average turnout level was 60.42%. However, turnout levels were below this baseline in states with no election reform laws (58.94%). Turnout levels were approximately the same in states with in-person early voting (60.38%). On the other hand, 62.1% of people voted in states with no-excuse absentee/mail voting, and 68.76% for states with same day registration. These numbers might be masking the true effects of these laws on turnout behind other individual- and state-level factors. For this reason, multivariate logistic regression is again used.

Following the same design as in Table 4.2, Table 4.4 reports how an individual's likelihood of voting changed from 2008 to 2012. As expected, fewer convenience voting laws have a direct role in promoting turnout in presidential compared to midterm elections, as more individuals are motivated to cast ballots in these high-salience contests, independent of election laws and administration. Still, same day registration has a consistently positive and significant effect on turnout across most models, even after controlling for election administration performance. Individuals who did not vote in 2008 are more likely to become voters in 2012 if living in a state with same day voter registration, controlling for all other factors. This is powerful evidence that same day registration does increase participation in

Table 4.3 Voter Turnout in the 2012 Presidential Election, Varying Convenience Voting Laws

	No Election Reform Law	In-Person Early Voting	No-Excuse Absentee/Mail Voting	Same Day Registration	Overall Total
Non-Vote	41.06%	39.62%	37.9%	31.24%	39.58%
	(243,160)	(594,174)	(466,517)	(65,739)	(878,043)
Vote	58.94%	60.38%	62.1%	68.76%	60.42%
	(349,035)	(905,463)	(764,328)	(144,682)	(1,340,346)
Total	100.00%	100.00%	100.00%	100.00%	100.00%
	(592,195)	(1,499,637)	(1,230,845)	(210,421)	(2,218,389)

Note: Data from Catalist (2016).

elections, and its effect is not conditional on how well the state implements elections (interaction term is not significant in column 5 of the table).

To understand the substantive effects shown in Table 4.4, we convert the same day registration coefficient from Model 2 in Table 4.4 to predicted probabilities. This graph models the likelihood that a non-voter in 2008 submitted a ballot in 2012, holding all other variables at their mean values. According to Figure 4.4, same day registration enhances the probability of a non-voter in 2008 casting a ballot in 2012 by nearly 10%. This is a large positive impact of the state voting law on turnout, controlling for election administration.

Table 4.4 Effects of Convenience Voting Laws on Changing Probability of Voting from 2008 to 2012, Varying Election Performance Index (Lagged Panel Models)

	Election Reform Laws	Election Reform Laws + EPI	In-Person Early Voting × EPI	No-Excuse Absentee/ Mail Voting × EPI	Same Day Registration × EPI
Vote 2008	1.88***	1.88***	1.88***	1.88***	1.88***
	(0.071)	(0.071)	(0.070)	(0.071)	(0.071)
Early Voting	0.02	0.04	0.43	0.03	0.04
	(0.096)	(0.090)	(0.653)	(0.090)	(0.091)
Absentee/Mail Voting	−0.05	−0.06	−0.06	0.47	−0.06
	(0.093)	(0.093)	(0.095)	(0.694)	(0.092)
SDR	0.41***	0.38***	0.39***	0.39***	−0.98
	(0.113)	(0.112)	(0.107)	(0.105)	(1.183)
EPI		0.00	0.01	0.01	0.004
		(0.006)	(0.009)	(0.009)	(0.006)
Early Voting × EPI			−0.01		
			(0.010)		
Absentee/Mail Voting × EPI				−0.01	
				(0.010)	
SDR × EPI					0.02
					(0.016)
Pseudo R^2	0.248	0.248	0.248	0.248	0.248
N	2,218,389	2,218,389	2,218,389	2,218,389	2,218,389

Note: Based on Catalist data (2016) measuring voting behavior of same eligible voters in the 2008 and 2012 elections. Vote 2008 variable is included to control for turnout in past election. To conserve space, only the primary covariates are reported here. Full regression models are reported in Appendix Table C1.2. The estimates are unstandardized logistic regression coefficients. Robust standard errors in parentheses are clustered by state. Multilevel models reveal similar results. *P*-values are based on two-tailed tests.

* $p < 0.10$, ** $p < 0.05$, *** $p < 0.001$.

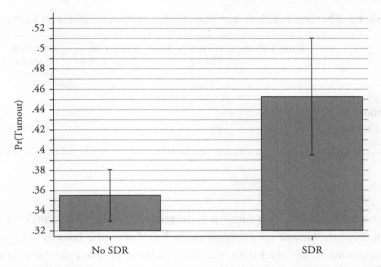

Figure 4.4. Probability that a non-voter in 2008 votes in the 2012 presidential election in states with and without same day registration.

Note: Bars report probabilities of voting in states with and without same day registration in 2012 for Model 2 in Table 4.4. All other variables held at mean values. Ninety percent confidence intervals included too.

Conclusion

This chapter re-evaluates the impact of in-person early voting, no-excuse absentee or mail voting, and same day registration voting alongside the performance of a state's election administration. Key findings are summarized in Table 4.5. In-person early voting (midterm elections), no-excuse absentee/ mail voting (in midterm elections conditional on quality EPI), and same day registration (midterm and presidential elections) enhance the probability that individuals are mobilized by these laws to vote, even if they were non-voters in previous elections. Individuals living in states with a history of better implementation of elections (i.e., election administration) are more likely to vote in midterm elections, independent of the effects of the reform laws. These results affirm parts of the accessible elections model presented in Chapter 2.

Combined, these findings suggest that some states have more accessible electoral practices, with both convenience voting laws and high-quality election administrations increasing the likelihood that citizens vote, even non-voters. The results also suggest that the prevailing consensus that these laws

Table 4.5 Electoral Practices with Statistically Significant Effects on Turnout

	Early Voting	Absentee/Mail Voting	Same Day Registration	Election Performance Index
2012 Presidential Election			✓ (+)	
2014 Midterm Election	✓ (+)	✓ (+)	✓ (+)	✓ (+)

have a minimal effect on turnout is overstated (see Berinsky 2005; Gronke et al. 2008a). Almost no previous study has shown the laws to change the composition of the electorate, that is, bring new people into the electorate and thereby enhance their representation. This chapter shows that early voting and same day registration have this effect. Uniquely, too, this chapter demonstrates that the average quality of a state's election administration has a significant and independent impact on turnout, and moderates the effect of election reform laws (particularly same day registration) on this outcome.

There are several implications for future research. First, a state's election administration is a central component in the assessment of voting reform laws (Alvarez, Atkeson, and Hall 2013; Gerken 2009). Second, simultaneously controlling for the concurrent presence of several election reform laws, as well as election administration, permits more precise estimation of the independent effects of these factors (see Burden et al. 2014, 2017; and Springer 2014). This accessible elections empirical framework opens new doors for future research on voting reform laws.

5

Accessible Elections to Help Poor People

Chapter 4 found that early voting, absentee and mail voting, and same day registration have a positive impact on overall turnout, after controlling for the accessibility of a state's electoral system. But do these laws increase turnout of one of the most marginalized voting groups in the United States—the poor? The true test of an accessible electoral system is if it benefits the most disadvantaged members of society. A more rigorous test of the theoretical framework focuses on turnout rates of poor people (a subsample) in relation to state election reform laws. By doing so, this chapter contributes to the growing literature on inequality and politics. The results suggest that convenience voting laws are more beneficial to the economically marginalized than previously understood. These reforms might even be used to re-shape the electorate to create more political equality.

Forty years ago, Piven and Cloward in *Poor People's Movement* (1977) argued that America's electoral system disadvantaged poor people's involvement in politics. Schattschneider (1960), in the landmark book *The Semi-Sovereign People*, frames his study around a thought experiment imagining the political system if all people voted, including the poor and disadvantaged. He believed responsible political parties would promote policies that were more representative of the poor and working classes, not just the business class and affluent.

Contemporary U.S. and global politics has experienced rapidly increasing economic inequality (Solt 2008, 2010; Franko and Witko 2017). Bartels (2008), in *Unequal Democracy*, uses roll call voting to show that U.S. senators from both political parties are moderately responsive to middle-class voters and very responsive to the upper classes, but not to the lowest class (represented by the bottom third of the income distribution). Senate representation principally benefits the middle and affluent classes. Gilens (2012) finds a similar pattern with policy representation, demonstrating that when the policy interests of the affluent and less well-off diverge, individuals at the 90th income percentile have a significant influence on policy change, but none for 10th percentile income earners. Elected officials most value the

Accessible Elections. Michael Ritter and Caroline J. Tolbert, Oxford University Press (2021). © Oxford University Press.
DOI: 10.1093/oso/9780197537251.001.0001.

input of those with property and capital (Keyssar 2009, 39–40; Hacker and Pierson 2011; Schattschneider 1960, 34–35).

Building on these studies on inequality in American politics, this chapter explores whether voting and registration reforms in the U.S. benefit economically disadvantaged citizens—a topic few previous scholars have explored, in part because of limited available data for poor Americans. While substantial literature has explored inequality and representation, few scholars have focused on poor people and political participation (see Brians and Grofman 2001; Franko and Witko 2017; and Rigby and Springer 2011 for exceptions). Today Millennials are more likely to be poor than any other generation.

Disparities in voter turnout rates based on wealth or income have been constant features of American politics. Figures 5.1 (2014 midterm election) and 5.2 (2016 presidential election) provide a snapshot of turnout rates across income groups in two recent elections, drawing on the U.S. Census's Current Population Survey. During the 2014 midterm election, just 24% of the poor (those living at or below the federal poverty level) voted, relative to 39% of the non-poor. In the 2016 presidential election, 42% of those at or below the federal poverty line cast a ballot, compared to 62% turnout of those above the poverty line, a 20% difference. Voter participation in elections sharply drops off for the poorest citizens.

Another way to measure inequality in participation in elections is the percentage of the electorate that falls into different income categories. In the 2016 election, 12% of the voting age population consisted of individuals

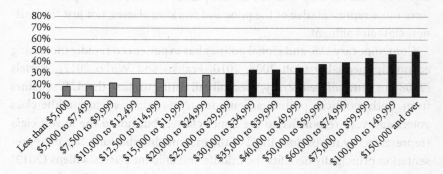

Figure 5.1. Voter turnout (%) across income groups in 2014 midterm election.
Note: Gray shaded lines are incomes at or below the federal poverty rate for a family of four (U.S. Dept. Health and Human Services 2016). These percentages calculated using validated vote calculation procedures (Hur and Achen 2013; United States Elections Project 2018a). Number of observations is 99,651.

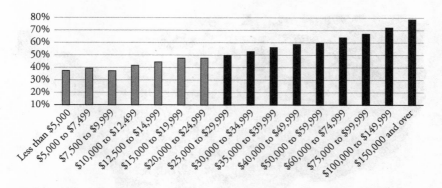

Figure 5.2. Voter turnout (%) across income groups in 2016 presidential election.

Note: Gray shaded lines are incomes at or below the federal poverty rate for a family of four (U.S. Dept. Health and Human Services 2016). These percentages calculated using validated vote calculation procedures (Hur and Achen 2013; United States Elections Project 2018a). Number of observations is 102,198.

below the federal poverty level. This compares to 25% of the voting age population that earned a household income of $100,000 or more (U.S. Census 2017), or were what we would call affluent. Past disparities in voting between the well-off and less well-off continue in the present era.

Poverty is a systemic feature across the states. It is neither geographically limited to a specific region of the country, associated with a single demographic group, nor a feature of recent historic vintage. Figure 5.3 shows that poverty is widespread in America, displaying the percentage of households in poverty across the nation's 3,000-plus counties. While the South has historically had the highest rates of overall poverty and children in poverty, the Southwest and the Northeast also have large disadvantaged populations. All states have some degree of poverty, and poverty affects both rural and urban counties. Recalling Figures 5.1 and 5.2, one can theorize that economic inequality tends to map onto political inequality.

A lack of political resources, including civic skills, time, and money, are recognized as key factors in lower political participation rates among the poor (Schlozman et al. 2013; Verba et al. 1995). Low political efficacy is also linked to decreased turnout rates (Gaventa 1980). Historically, some state electoral practices were designed to prevent poor whites and African Americans from voting through poll taxes, literacy tests, and residency requirements (Keyssar 2009; Springer 2014). Powell (1986, 31) notes that what distinguishes the

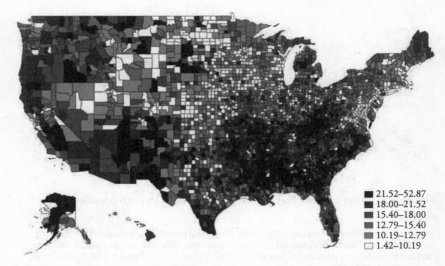

Legend:
■ 21.52–52.87
■ 18.00–21.52
■ 15.40–18.00
■ 12.79–15.40
■ 10.19–12.79
□ 1.42–10.19

Figure 5.3. How many adults in poverty (%) across American counties, 2011–2015.

Note: Data based on five-year average from American Community Survey (2011–2015)

U.S. electoral system from other developed democratic countries is the more pronounced impact of individual-level characteristics such as education and income on voter turnout. Most other established Western democracies have automatic voter registration laws, compulsory voting laws, or both, which place less importance on these individual-level factors in predicting whether one votes. While some states have very recently adopted automatic voter registration, in the U.S. education and income are key predictors of turnout (before 2016 no state had automatic registration, as of 2020, nineteen states plus Washington, DC do—see Chapter 8). In the absence of accessible election laws, the poor—who are also more likely to have lower levels of education, be young and to belong to racial minority groups—are thus particularly disadvantaged politically in the U.S.

Depressed political participation by the lower and working classes has detrimental consequences for many reasons. Lower turnout among the poor has limited their policy representation in Congress (Bartels 2008, Gilens 2012), state legislatures (Rigby and Wright 2013), and in policy areas such as more equitable taxation and social welfare benefits (Erickson 2015; Franko and Witko 2017; Franko, Kelly, and Witko 2016; Lijphart 1997). Key (1949, 319) summarizes the electoral fate suffered by the poor when he notes that "the blunt truth is that politicians and officials are under no compulsion to pay much heed to classes and groups of citizens that do not vote." Low turnout among the poor is a systemic problem with far-ranging consequences in the United States.

Poverty also affects other demographic groups, such as women and racial and ethnic minorities. Historically, poverty is woven together with race and gender in explaining disadvantage in American state political systems. Schlozman, Verba, and Brady (2012, 36) use multivariate analysis to control for many factors related to voting and find that race- and gender-based participatory inequalities have their origins in economic inequality. Although race and gender play a role in policy design, lower incomes among racial minorities and females (compared to non-Hispanic White males) have further disadvantaged them in state electoral systems. Hero's (1992) paradigm of two-tiered pluralism illustrates that minorities and the poor experience a lower tier of American politics, encountering substantial barriers to voting, including recently enacted voter identification laws to vote (Barreto, Nuno, and Sanchez 2009).

Election Laws and the Poor

Do convenience voting laws—absentee/mail, early, and same day registration voting—provide some counter for these historical trends? This is an active area of debate within election reform law research; interestingly, though, it is rarely empirically studied. As discussed in the preceding section the dominant perspective holds that, except for same day registration, convenience voting laws (specifically absentee, early, and mail voting) tend to retain active members of electorate (educated and affluent) rather than stimulating turnout among less active members of the electorate (Berinsky 2005; Brians and Grofman 2001; Gronke et al. 2008a; Karp and Banducci 2001). That is, these laws mainly benefit the middle class or well-to-do, rather than the economically marginalized. Turnout among the poor, according to this viewpoint, does not increase.

A second perspective holds that the effects of all these laws are structured by a host of factors, such as election administration (Stewart 2008), party mobilization, state political culture, and the existence of other reform laws (Burden et al. 2014; Donovan 2008; Hanmer 2009; Leighley and Nagler 2013). The previous chapter drew from this literature and demonstrated that early voting and same day registration have more beneficial impacts on political engagement than previously recognized. Few existing studies, however, have directly examined the effects of these laws on turnout of poor citizens (see Rigby and Springer 2011).

This study makes several new contributions to the larger debate on inequality and the political system. Large samples of individuals living at or below the federal poverty line are drawn from national voter files amounting to nearly 400,000 observations for the 2008, 2010, 2012, and 2014 federal elections. No previous study has examined samples of poor citizens this large, increasing our confidence in the empirical results. Subsampling the poor can be used to identify unique effects of state voting laws on participation rates.

While income is indirectly measured in the commercial voter files using credit scores and public records, poverty is at the extreme end of the distribution for the variable measuring income. Our models do not include the variable for income, reducing the potential for error, but rather subsample for individuals living at or below the poverty level. While certainly some individuals living at the poverty level are misclassified in our data and should be included, and others may be included that should be omitted, in general these data have been found to be quite accurate. Given problems with missing data on income questions in survey research, this sample provides an alternative way to identity this difficult-to-measure population.

While cross-national comparative politics regularly measures electoral systems, this concept is rarely measured in studies of voting behavior in the U.S. As noted in Chapter 4, covariates estimating the impact of multiple election reform laws and state election administration performance are included in statistical models, allowing for a more complete measure of state electoral practices.

As also discussed in Chapter 4, panel data over time are used to add causal leverage in calculating how state electoral practices relate to changing participation decisions by poor citizens. Measures of electoral competition are analyzed alongside the electoral system variables, capturing state variations in competitive campaign environments that may also drive turnout. The statistical models include individual-level partisanship and political interest variables, which are not readily available in Census data used by many previous scholars. Finally, both presidential and midterm elections are analyzed, to understand if the laws are more impactful in higher turnout presidential elections (Hill and Leighley 1994) or during low-stimulus midterm elections.

Many previous studies have focused on presidential elections, omitting mid-term elections.

Descriptive data indicates that the poor and non-poor use convenience voting at roughly similar rates. The U.S. Census Current Population Survey reports that in the 2016 presidential election 66% percent of poor citizens voted in person on election day, 15% percent voted early, 15% percent voted absentee or by mail, and 3% percent registered to vote and cast a ballot on the same day. The comparative rates for the non-poor for each mode of voting are 61% percent, 17%, 18%, and 3%. Of course, multiple causes of voting are not analyzed by the descriptive turnout data.

What we Know about Political Participation for Poor People?

What does the literature say about political participation for poor people, and why would we expect these laws to make a difference? As discussed previously, the civic voluntarism framework is helpful (Schlozman, Verba, and Brady's 2012; Verba, Schlozman, and Brady 1995), explaining how socio-economic inequalities are translated into biases in participation in politics. Using survey data with information on respondent demographic characteristics as well as engagement in multiple forms of political participation (e.g., voting, contacting politicians, making donations, writing a letter, etc.), the authors identify a socio-economic gradient linked to many forms of participation in politics. On this gradient, lower socio-economic class citizens are less likely to have the wealth that is necessary to make donations; to have the education that helps them develop the civic skills needed to cast a ballot; and to be active members of community organizations that nurture the development of civic skills (e.g., letter writing, public speaking, and planning) germane to public engagement. Similarly, Leighley and Nagler (2013) as well as Wolfinger and Rosenstone (1980) examine this phenomenon using Census data and multivariate regression, finding that socio-economic factors are critical predictors of voting over time—affluent individuals are significantly more likely to participate than the less well-off, controlling for all other factors (see also Brady, Verba, and Schlozman 1994; Campbell, Converse, Miller & Stoke 1960).

Schattschneider points out that lower turnout among the poor is an outcome of a political system that largely excludes their policy interests: "The flaw in the pluralist heaven [the competition between the interests of the non-poor and poor in society and government] is that the heavenly chorus sings with a strong upper-class accent. Probably about 90% of the people cannot get into the pressure system" (1960, 34–35). Compared to the poor, the affluent have greater levels of financial resources to command the atten- tion of political elites through political donations, business connections, and more. They also tend to vote at higher rates, and can disproportionately dic- tate the terms of discourse in politics, to the exclusion of the poor.

Additionally, Schattschneider also emphasizes that neither major polit- ical party offers policy platforms reflecting the interests of the poor. With no policy representation, the poor are given limited incentive to vote; however, because of this low participation, politicians have limited reason to be re- sponsive to their interests.

Other research buttresses the viewpoint that the choice not to vote among the poor may also be driven by a lack of policy representation. As mentioned earlier in the chapter, both Bartels (2008) and Gilens (2012) find that polit- ical elites in Congress are more likely to vote and design policy with the rich in mind, with little if any thought for the poor. Adding to this discussion, Rigby and Wright (2013) find that the policy positions taken by state parties are almost exclusively influenced by those with the highest incomes (Rigby and Wright 2013). Having little policy influence likely dampens the turnout incentive for citizens who are poor.

A lack of meaningful choices among candidates for public office may also reduce turnout of the poor (Leighley and Nagler 2013, Chapter 5). Using the 1972–2008 American National Election Studies (ANES), the authors measure how voters from different income quintiles view the policy positions of two competing candidates, and whether recognizing a difference predicts turnout. They find that low-income voters are far less likely than those of high income to detect a difference in candidate policy positions. If the poorest (first quintile) perceived as much of a difference between the two candidates as the affluent (fifth quintile), they predict turnout among the poorest would increase by 3.5 percentage points (Leighley and Nagler 2013, 139).

But government laws regulating elections may be able to help. Schattschneider (1960, 70, 96–97) notes that political power is mainly exercised through procedures, including "institutions" such as election laws and political parties. He argues that if election procedures were altered to bring more excluded voting groups into the fold and increase turnout, there would be significant changes in public policy. In a reciprocal relationship, higher turnout among the poor would lead to greater government elite support of social welfare and New Deal–type policies, while greater government support of these issues would reinforce higher turnout among the poor. There are two important implications to draw from Schattschneider's research. One, election rules can be changed that may bring new voters into the fold; and, two, more poor people would vote if the government were to give attention to their policy concerns.

The experiences of poor people interacting with government and government policy can affect incentives to participate. One area of research, for example, finds that welfare systems are linked to political efficacy and participation habits among the poor (Soss and Schram 2007, 2011). Similarly, Hersh (2015, 59–60) notes that political campaigns and candidates increasingly draw on data science and U.S. Census data to identify neighborhoods for canvassing individuals based on their socio-economic status, which may increase participation by the poor.[1] Some campaign mobilization drives may target individuals in areas that hold disproportionately high levels of poor people.

In another example of policy mobilizing the needy, Piven and Cloward (1977) use case studies to examine patterns of political participation by poor people in several different policy arenas (unemployment, union rights, civil rights, and welfare) over the course of the twentieth century. These are issue areas in which the poor have had a high stake, and have been motivated to vigorously engage in many forms of political participation (e.g., voting, protests, strikes) to impel government and corporate leaders to yield to their demands.[2] The authors find that the status quo of low participation by the poor can be broken during times of economic disruption, which prompts them to engage in politics and to vote. Political elites, seeking to placate the interests of the poor, recognize and enact into law some of their policy goals. The key point here is that policy—social welfare, data collection, campaign recruitment, and so forth—shapes participation among the poor.

If welfare social services, active campaigns, and other policies can shape turnout among the poor, then state election laws and election administration may also be able to influence participation by this demographic group.

---

[1] Although federal law prohibits the Census from disclosing to campaigns the income of individuals, this information is made available to campaigns at block group levels consisting of 200,000 people.

[2] However, Piven, and Cloward (1977, 15) note that a recurring clamp on poor participation has been "restraints on the ballot box" and other prohibitions on their political participation, which limited their gains in these policy areas.

Voter turnout among the poor has direct implications for the development of more egalitarian government policies. Many researchers (Hill, Leighley, and Hinton-Andersson 1995; Franko, Kelly, and Witko 2016; Franko and Witko 2017; Lijphart 1997; Pacek and Radcliff 1995) find that when there is higher turnout among the least wealthy, or when there are lower turnout disparities between the lowest and highest income groups, government policy becomes more aligned with the interests of the working and middle classes. Franko, Kelly, and Witko (2016), measuring class bias in turnout by taking the difference in turnout probabilities among the richest and poorest in each state, find that states with lower class bias in turnout are associated with more liberal state governments and economic policies, political outcomes favoring the poor.

In related research, Franko and Witko (2017) find that Americans in the aggregate since the 1980s have become increasingly aware of growing trends in economic inequality at the state and national levels. With this heightened awareness, citizens are more likely to elect left-leaning state legislatures, whose members in turn are more likely to adopt state-level policies such as higher minimum wage levels and earned income tax credit provisions that benefit the poor. They also find that when economic inequality is high in initiative states, citizens are more likely to use this lawmaking tool to enact higher taxes on the wealthy. Since poor citizens have different political preferences than middle class and rich citizens (see Leighley and Nagler 2013), promoting higher turnout among the poor may lead to better policy representation of their needs and interests. In sum, it is important to assess whether election reform laws facilitate increased political participation among the poor.

The Poor and Election Reform Laws

A gap in the literature on the poor and political participation is that almost no scholarly research has specifically focused on turnout of the poor (defined by the federal poverty threshold) related to convenience voting laws. For the scholars that do study how state election laws affect turnout inequality, the approaches include calculating voter turnout with an ordinal income measure, income quintiles, income quartiles in combination with education, neighborhood poverty, state per capita income as measures of socioeconomic status, or a ratio of voter turnout for low to high income groups

(Brians and Grofman 2001; Dyck and Gimpel 2005; Gronke et al. 2008b; Karp and Banducci 2000, 2001; Monroe and Sylvester 2011; Richey 2008; Rigby and Springer 2011). Previous studies have not been able to analyze a subsample of poor due to limited sample sizes.

While same day registration has been found to boost turnout,[3] previous research has not explored the potential interactive effects of the laws and administration of the laws for citizens from different income groups. Bowler and Donovan (2008), Donovan (2008), Burden et al. (2014), and Berinsky (2005) argue that citizens will take advantage of these voting laws if they are mobilized to do so, but measures of electoral competition are often omitted. Several studies (Karp and Banducci 2000; Richey 2008) use precinct, county, and state-level aggregate analyses, making it difficult to control for individual-level motivational factors associated with the use of election reform laws. Additionally, many studies are limited to single states (Karp and Banducci 2000; Dyck and Gimpel 2005; Monroe and Sylvester 2011; Richey 2008), are focused on only one state voting law (Brians and Grofman 2001; Monroe and Sylvester 2011; Richey 2008), or are limited to presidential elections (Brians and Grofman 2001; Richey 2008; Burden et al. 2014). Most of the research was conducted more than a decade ago, when the expansion of state voting and registration laws was not as widespread.

An exception is the work of Rigby and Wright (2011), who use aggregate 1988–2000 Census data from the Current Population Survey to examine how early voting, absentee voting, same day registration, and other election reform measures shape turnout ratios between the rich (family incomes four times the federal poverty threshold) and the working class (two times this threshold). Among these laws, they find that only early voting has an effect, and this takes the form of exacerbating turnout inequalities between the rich and the working class. Springer (2014), exploring aggregate turnout from 1920 to 2000 using cross-sectional time-series models, finds that more affluent states with higher per capita income have higher turnout in presidential elections, as well as states with same day registration. However, Rigby and Wright's (2011) and Springer's (2014) use of aggregate state level measures make it more difficult to understand what factors drive participation rates by the poor. These studies end in 2000, before many states adopted absentee/mail, early, and same day registration voting. Changes in

[3] A few pivotal studies (Karp and Banducci 2001; Fitzgerald 2005), which have tended to find that convenience voting laws benefit already likely voting groups, have not controlled for income.

the accessibility of state electoral systems since this time merit an update of their results.

More recent research using causal inference methods improve research findings in this area. As discussed in earlier chapters, Burden et al. (2014) use individual- and county-level data from all fifty states with multinomial statistical modeling to show that higher income citizens are more likely to cast a ballot using absentee and early voting in presidential elections than citizens with lower income. Hanmer (2009, Chapters 3 and 6) finds that same day registration increases turnout among the young and less educated, but does not directly measure participation by the poor. Although his study does not show an increase in turnout among the poor, his findings suggests that same day registration may hold promise for the poor as well.

Other encouraging research indicates that same day registration increases turnout among those of lower income in a broader range of states. Using temporal state adoptions as a treatment effect to study voter turnout by different demographic groups, including income quintiles, Leighley and Nagler (2013, Chapter 4) find that first wave (Maine, Minnesota, and Wisconsin) and third wave (Iowa, Montana, and North Carolina) same day registration states have the largest effect in boosting turnout among those in the second lowest income quintile (almost 6% for wave 1, and 2% for wave 3). This is the working poor, those who are just above the federal poverty mark. However, the most affluent voters (fifth quintile) benefit the most among the second wave same day registration states. These multivariate analyses do not provide any evidence that early or absentee/mail voting increases turnout of the poor.

The existing research provides mixed evidence about whether election reform laws can substantially increase turnout of the poor, and almost no existing research measures how election administration quality affects turnout. Given the increased presence of these laws in the states, the findings of previous research need to be updated. Most importantly, the existing research does not directly measure turnout decisions among poor citizens, missing opportunities to identify unique effects associated with various income groups.

The Poor and Election Administration

We know less about how election administration effects political participation for economically disadvantaged individuals. Research has found that poor citizens are more likely to participate in elections if voting machines are easier to use (Ansolabehere and Stewart 2005; Stewart 2014); if a state has flexible provisional voting laws that do not penalize citizens for casting ballots in the wrong precinct (Hanmer and Herrnson 2014); and if poll workers provide assistance needed by poor citizens to vote (Alvarez et al. 2013, 29). As discussed in Chapter 3, Gronke (2014b) finds citizens are more confident in early voting and mail voting if poll workers are well trained. Poor citizens may be more likely to cast ballots using election reform laws if they are confident that they can register to vote and know that their vote will be counted (Alvarez et al. 2013; Gerken 2009). This chapter evaluates the effects of state voting laws on turnout of the poor while taking account of a state's election administration.

Research Hypotheses

Four key hypotheses are tested in this chapter:

H1: Poor people will be more likely to become voters in states with a more highly performing election administration.

H2: Poor people will be more likely to become voters in states with early voting.

H3: Poor people will be more likely to become voters in states with home voting (no-excuse absentee or mail voting).

H4: Poor people will be more likely to become voters in states with same day registration.

Data and Methods

A similar modeling strategy to that employed in Chapter 4 is used here, and to avoid repetition just a few details will be repeated. Lagged panel logistic models are used to test if election reform laws and election administration positively shape the voting decisions of those at or below the federal poverty line. Predicted probabilities are used to help understand the substantive magnitude of the results. Catalist subsamples of poor citizens are merged with state aggregate variables measuring the presence of election reform laws and the average quality of a state's election administration. For both the midterm and presidential elections, the data consists of subsamples of the most economically disadvantaged citizens—the poor.

The subsamples of poor citizens are made up of those below the federal poverty threshold (U.S. Department of Health and Human Services 2016). The federal and state governments use this statistic to determine citizen eligibility for various government programs, such as welfare, Medicaid, and food stamps. For a family of four, this threshold ranged from $21,200 in 2008 to $23,850 in 2014 (U.S. Department of Health and Human Services 2016).[4] Due to the ordinal structure of the income variable in the original datasets, individuals with family incomes at or below $25,000 were counted as the poor to be consistent with the threshold set by the Department of Health and Human Services (2016). Catalist subsamples include 353,200 individuals for the 2012 presidential election and 369,517 individuals for the 2014 midterm election across the fifty states.

Results

Midterm Election

To establish basic patterns in turnout for poor people, Table 5.1 reports how this outcome varied in 2014 depending on whether a state had no election reform law, in-person early voting, no-excuse absentee/mail voting, or same day registration. In the midterm election, overall only 28.36% of the poor cast a ballot. While this is nearly 10% lower than the national turnout level for the same year (see Table 5.1), large variation exists when controlling for state election reform laws.

Relative to the national baseline, turnout for the poor was higher in early voting (29.52%), no-excuse absentee/mail voting (31.11), and same day registration (37.68%) states. Conversely, rates were noticeably lower in states without any election reform laws (24.91%). The accessibility of being able to cast a ballot from one's residence, workplace, or other location (as with absentee voting), to vote for an extended period of time beyond election day (as with early voting), or being able to register and vote for an extended period

---

[4] The federal poverty rate is identical in the contiguous forty-eight states, and is slightly higher in Alaska and Hawaii due to these states' higher costs of living. Even with this consideration, these states' poverty rates are similar to that of the other states, and therefore allow an identical measurement strategy to specify poor individuals in all fifty states.

Table 5.1 Voter Turnout among the Poor in 2014 Midterm Election, Varying Convenience Voting Laws

	No Election Reform Law	In-Person Early Voting	No-Excuse Absentee/ Mail Voting	Same Day Registration	Total
Non-Vote	75.09% (69,796)	70.48% (146,742)	68.89% (115,460)	62.32% (13,508)	71.64% (223,677)
Vote	24.91% (23,156)	29.52% (61,468)	31.11% (52,139)	37.68% (8,168)	28.36% (88,555)
Total	100.00% (92,952)	100.00% (208,210)	100.00% (167,599)	100.00% (21,676)	100.00% (312,232)

Note: Data from Catalist (2016).

Table 5.2 Effects of Convenience Voting Laws and Election Performance Index on Change in Probability of Voting among the Poor from 2010 to 2014, Varying Election Performance Index (Lagged Panel Models)

	Baseline	EPI
Vote 2010	1.98*** (0.069)	1.99*** (0.068)
Early Voting	0.08 (0.085)	0.11 (0.089)
Absentee/Mail Voting	0.02 (0.074)	0.01 (0.072)
SDR	0.30** (0.140)	0.25* (0.141)
Election Admin. Performance		0.005 (0.004)
Pseudo R^2	0.231	0.231
N	312,232	312,232

Note: Based on Catalist data (2016) measuring voting behavior of same eligible voters in the 2010 and 2014 elections. Vote 2010 variable is included to control for turnout in past election. To conserve space, only the primary covariates are reported here. Full regression models reported in Appendix Table C1.3. The estimates are unstandardized logistic regression coefficients. Robust standard errors in parentheses are clustered by state. Multilevel models reveal similar results. P-values are based on two-tailed tests.

* $p < 0.10$, ** $p < 0.05$, *** $p < 0.001$.

of time in addition to election day (as with same day registration), appears to enhance turnout among the most marginalized of voting groups.

To focus more uniquely on how these state electoral system variables impact the voting behavior of the poor, Table 5.2 displays the results from a multivariate logistic regression model predicting turnout of poor citizens in the 2014 election, including a control for their vote history in 2010. Following the setup for Chapter 4, the first model only includes the state election laws, while the second adds in state election administration.

The results presented in Tables 5.2 show that same day registration has a distinctly positive impact on changing the likelihood of voting among the poor from 2010 to 2014. Moreover, none of the convenience voting laws disadvantages the poor relative to the non-poor (i.e., there are no negatively signed coefficients). These null findings for mail/absentee voting and early voting are significant and important. Despite previous research suggesting these laws disadvantage the poor, there is no evidence of that when using state voter roll data for the analysis. Having illustrated how these factors shape turnout among the poor in a midterm election, the next step is to examine how they influence this outcome in a presidential election.

Presidential Election

In the 2012 election, the national turnout level for those with an income at or below the federal poverty threshold was 54.78% (see Table 5.3), approximately six percentage points lower than average turnout rates. But poor turnout was higher in early voting (55.61%), no-excuse absentee/mail voting (58.08%), and same day registration (63.78%) states. The same was not true of states without an election reform law (52.13%). Relative to average national turnout and turnout in states with none of these voting reform laws,

Table 5.3 Voter Turnout among the Poor across American States in 2012 Presidential Election, Varying Convenience Voting Laws

	No Election Reform Law	In-Person Early Voting	No-Excuse Absentee/ Mail Voting	Same Day Registration	Total
Non-Vote	47.87% (89,211)	44.39% (86,293)	41.92% (63,820)	36.22% (9,921)	45.22% (133,929)
Vote	52.13% (46,506)	55.61% (108,117)	58.08% (88,417)	63.78% (17,468)	54.78% (162,249)
Total	100.00% (89,211)	100.00% (194,410)	100.00% (152,237)	100.00% (27,389)	100.00% (296,178)

Note: Data from Catalist (2016).

these findings suggest that each of these convenience voting laws increases voter turnout among the poor in presidential elections.

Are the poor uniquely impacted by any of the state electoral system variables, after controlling for other factors related to voter turnout? Table 5.4 evaluates this proposition. A baseline model (column 1) shows that the poor are significantly more likely to vote in states with no-excuse absentee/mail voting and same day registration. These results persist in the second model, which controls for election administration. These findings indicate that the poor are distinctly benefited by these two election reform laws in presidential elections. While the coefficient for early voting is negatively signed, it is not significant. Again, there is no evidence that early voting works against poor people. However, the election performance index coefficient is negative and statistically significant, but the substantive effect is tiny, given the very small size of the coefficient. Predicted probabilities suggest the poor are not harmed or benefited by improved election administration in presidential elections, when controlling for the state voting and registration laws.

Table 5.4 Effects of Convenience Voting Laws on Change in Probability of Voting among the Poor from 2008 to 2012, Varying Election Performance Index (Lagged Panel Models)

	Baseline	EPI
Vote 2008	1.63***	1.63***
	(0.055)	(0.055)
In-Person Early Voting	−0.09	−0.11
	(0.078)	(0.068)
No-Excuse Absentee/Mail Voting	0.20**	0.21***
	(0.069)	(0.061)
Same Day Registration	0.37***	0.42***
	(0.085)	(0.092)
Election Admin. Performance		−0.01*
		(0.006)
Pseudo R^2	0.163	0.163
N	296,178	296,178

Note: Based on Catalist data (2016) measuring voting behavior of same eligible voters in the 2008 and 2012 elections. Vote 2008 variable is included to control for turnout in past election. To conserve space, only the primary covariates are reported here. Full regression models reported in Appendix Table C1.4. The estimates are unstandardized logistic regression coefficients. Robust standard errors in parentheses are clustered by state. Multilevel models reveal similar results. P-values are based on two-tailed tests.

* $p < 0.10$, ** $p < 0.05$, *** $p < 0.001$.

Figures 5.4 (absentee/mail) and 5.5 (same day registration) uses probability simulations to calculate the substantive effects of these laws on the probabilities of poor people voting in 2012 if they did not vote in 2008, holding other factors constant. According to Figure 5.4, no-excuse absentee/mail increased a poor person's probability of voting by 5% comparing 2008 to 2012, relative to a similar poor person in a state without this voting method (53% to 58%). Being able to request, mark up, and send in a ballot combined with the heighted salience of presidential elections significantly enhances a poor person's likelihood of voting. This is a substantive effect only present in presidential elections.

Figure 5.5 illustrates that same day registration advantages poor people in presidential elections. Overall, having same day registration in a state enhances a poor person's probability of changing from a non-voter in 2008 to a voter in 2012 by 9%. This is in comparison to the likelihood that a poor person in a non–same day registration state will change from a non-voter in 2008 to a voter in 2012 (34% vs. 43%). This law, essentially, makes a

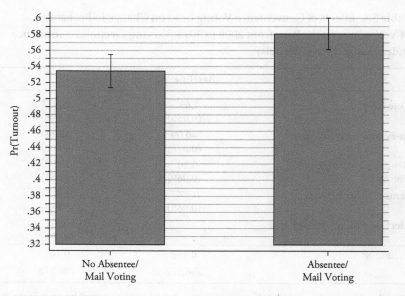

Figure 5.4. Probability that a poor non-voter in 2008 votes in the 2012 presidential election in states with and without no-excuse absentee/mail voting.

Note: Bars report probability of voting in states with and without absentee/mail voting in 2012 for Model 1 in Table 5.4. All other variables held at mean values. Ninety percent confidence intervals included.

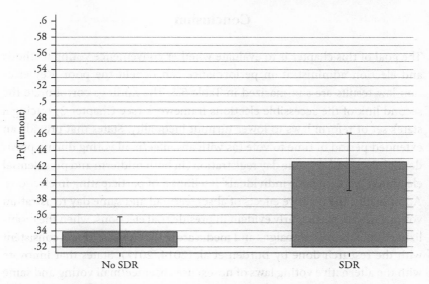

Figure 5.5. Probability that a poor non-voter in 2008 votes in the 2012 presidential election in states with and without same day registration.

Note: Bars report probability of voting in states with and without Same Day Registration in 2012 for Model 1 in Table 5.4. All other variables held at mean values. Ninety percent confidence intervals included too.

tremendous difference in motivating poor non-voters in 2008 to go out and cast a ballot in the 2012 election. Collapsing registration and voting into one action, and extending the period of time during which an individual can vote, substantially alters the level of electoral engagement among the poor.

As robustness checks we conducted subsample models comparing how convenience voting laws and election administration affect turnout of the poor versus all other income groups (non-poor and the affluent) in both the 2008 to 2012 and the 2010 to 2014 elections. The non-poor are defined as those above the federal poverty threshold for a family of four, whereas the poor are defined as those at or below the threshold for a family of four; an affluent individual is one with an income of $100,000 or more. The results suggest that both the poor and the non-poor and affluent tend to benefit from convenience voting laws, especially same day registration in presidential and midterm elections. The evidence shows that the poor do benefit to a similar extent (if not more in some cases, such as with mail/absentee voting in presidential elections) from convenience voting laws.

Conclusion

The goal of this chapter is to evaluate whether convenience voting methods and election administration performance can benefit the poor. Key election law results are summarized in Table 5.5. The findings corroborate the second link of the accessible elections framework (see Chapter 2) tracing a state's set of reform laws to lower turnout inequality. States that provide an extended period of time to vote (as with absentee/mail voting during presidential elections) or same day registration (in both midterm and presidential elections) increase poor individuals' likelihood of participating in elections. Additionally, the positive effects of absentee/mail and same day registration voting laws are particularly evident in presidential elections, when the mobilizing influences of campaigns and media are at their peaks. This is consistent with the research done by Burden et al. (2014, 2017). States that innovate with the alternative voting laws of no-excuse absentee/mail voting and same day registration can improve voter turnout among the poor.

These findings point to a need to re-evaluate prior election reform law research (Berinsky 2005) holding that absentee/mail voting disadvantages . lower socio-economic status relative to higher socio-economic status citizens. This prior research did not take account of the overall accessibility of state's election administration (Alvarez et al. 2013; Gerken 2009), a state's history of promoting or hindering turnout (Keyssar 2009; Hanmer 2009), or the competitiveness of a state's elections (Bowler and Donovan 2008). The results suggest that convenience voting laws may have beneficial effect on turnout of economically disadvantaged people.

The final implication is practical in terms of public policy. Two alternative voting laws—absentee/mail voting and same day registration—significantly

Table 5.5 Electoral Practices with Statistically Significant Effects on Turnout among the Poor

	Early Voting	Absentee/Mail Voting	Same Day Registration	Election Performance Index
2012 Presidential Election	✓ (+)		✓ (+)	(−)
2014 Midterm Election			✓ (+)	

shaped turnout among the poor from 2008 to 2012, and from 2010 to 2014. The results have cross-group relevance. Schlozman et al. (2013, 138–139) note that race- and gender-based inequalities in turnout have their origins in socio-economic inequalities. As the outcomes of this study demonstrate, election reform laws can serve an important role in enhancing turnout among and bringing new poor voters into the active electorate.

6

Voting Rights, Election Administration, and Turnout for Racial Minorities

In the 2018 midterm election in Georgia, many individuals seeking to cast ballots for Stacy Abrams as the first black female major-party gubernatorial nominee in U.S. history were exposed to the dark side of how state governments administer elections. Abrams argues that using election administration to deny suffrage to certain groups has been perfected over the last two decades "in a way that lets us forget that it's real because it has so many pieces, and that's the architecture" (Rubin 2019).

Abrams contends that state election system architecture imposes costs on voters in three ways. First, there is registration access, as people cannot vote in the U.S. unless they are signed up to do so (excluding North Dakota, which doesn't have a voter registration law). Depending on the state, there are impediments put in place for registration. Some states, especially in the South, block or eliminate voters from the rolls (voter purging). The second is ballot access, where some of the most egregious practices occur, according to Abrams. These practices can range from strict voter ID laws in numerous states to practices requiring voters to pay a public notary to verify submission of an absentee ballot, as is the case for voters in Alabama and Mississippi.

This effectively translates into paying for the right to vote. Georgia closed 214 polling precincts from the state's total of 3,000, causing residents in some poorer areas to travel long distances to the nearest polling place. And finally, the secretary of state's office determines whether election ballots are actually counted, an issue that often receives far less attention than the first two. In Georgia in 2018 the state discarded absentee ballots because "people put the date in the wrong place because there were two lines that said 'Date.' One was birth date and the other was the date that you were submitting it, but it didn't say 'Birth Date' and 'Date of Submission,' it just said 'Date'" (Rubin 2019). Abrams' biggest challenge as a candidate was having absentee ballots counted that were rejected for this and other questionable reasons. Between

Accessible Elections. Michael Ritter and Caroline J. Tolbert, Oxford University Press (2021). © Oxford University Press. DOI: 10.1093/oso/9780197537251.001.0001.

registration access, ballot access, and having election ballots counted, election administration by state and local officials can play a large role in citizens' voting rights. Beyond Georgia, this chapter seeks to measure the effects of alternative voting laws and election administration on voter turnout for different racial and ethnic groups across the states.

Whether as a referendum on Donald Trump's first two years as president or because of high-profile subnational races, voter turnout in the 2018 midterm elections was historic, the highest turnout recorded for a midterm election in four decades. Overall, as a percentage of the citizen voting age population, turnout from 2014 to 2018 rose from 41.9% to 53.4%, more than 10 percentage points. Not only were young people significantly more likely to vote, but turnout rose by 13 percentage points (a 49% increase) among non-Hispanic Asians, 13 percentage points (50% increase) among Hispanics, and 11 percentage points among blacks (non-Hispanic) (Misra 2019; U.S. Census). Yet beyond 2018, turnout data shows that African American voting rates dipped significantly between 2012 and 2016, while Hispanic and Asian turnout rates remained flat. How do state laws regulating elections and implementation of the laws (election administration) affect voting rates for racial and ethnic minorities?

Recap Accessible Elections

While some states seek to restrict voting, as discussed previously, others have developed accessible election practices with many modes of convenience voting. By studying election practices—the laws plus the administration of these laws—this chapter tests if minority voters living in states with accessible elections have higher voter turnout over time. Using Catalist population data based on the voter rolls from all fifty states from 2008 to 2014, we explore whether racial and ethnic minorities living in states with (a) early voting, (b) home voting (no-excuse absentee or mail voting), (c) same day registration, and (d) quality election administration (proxied by Pew/MIT's Election Performance Index [EPI]) are more likely to become voters, even if they didn't vote in the previous midterm or presidential election. We compare these results to models using the new Cost of Voting Index (COVI) to measure ballot access (Li, Pomantell, and Schraufnagel 2018) which includes voter ID laws. The sample includes registered and unregistered individuals nationwide.

Because Catalist has vote histories (our 1% sample includes 2.4 million cases), we model change in individual turnout decisions over time (paralleling the models in Chapters 4 and 5). Are there differences when comparing voting decisions for white non-Hispanics to minority voters? Are there differences when comparing across whites, African Americans, Hispanics, and Asians? Results based on millions of voters from all fifty states suggest that state governments can improve turnout of racial and ethnic groups as well as non-Hispanic whites, but that different laws may benefit different groups living in different types of states. Rather than one-size-fits-all, this research suggests that different convenience voting laws benefit different demographic groups.

How Do Alternative Voting Laws Affect Minority Groups?

Measuring change over time is one of the most powerful research designs for understanding how state election laws impact political participation, because concerns about the endogeneity of the treatment are minimized. Studying state voter turnout rates over nearly a century (1920–2000), Springer (2014) compares the effects of recent alternative voting laws to Jim Crow voting laws decades earlier. Measuring the cumulative effects of various election laws and the longitudinal data allows measurement of change in voting rates over time. She finds that only same day registration stands out for significantly increasing turnout among the contemporary state election laws, and this beneficial effect pales in comparison to the negative effect of Jim Crow laws (literacy tests, poll taxes) used historically.

Some studies (Oliver 1996; Stein 1998) have found that minority voters are not more likely to use absentee/mail or in-person early voting methods than non-Hispanic whites. More recent research, however, has shown that African Americans and Hispanics *are* more likely than non-Hispanic whites to be in-person early voters (Herron and Smith 2012). This pattern for African Americans was found in Ohio in the 2008 and 2012 elections (Weaver 2015), in North Carolina in 2008 (Berman 2015), and in Florida in 2008 (Herron and Smith 2012). After these elections, a number of mostly Republican-controlled state governments began adopting restrictions on early voting and absentee/mail voting, restrictions that courts have tended to agree are partly designed to reduce turnout among Democratically aligned groups such as racial and ethnic minorities (*North Carolina State Conference of the NAACP v. McCrory* 2017). These restrictions included shortening early voting periods, reducing ways of transmitting completed absentee/mail ballots to election offices, and imposing stricter identification requirements in same day registration states (Brennan Center for Justice 2019). The results suggest that more restrictive early voting periods may have had a suppressive impact on minority turnout (Gronke and Stewart 2013; Herron and Smith 2012). Research reports that early voting laws do not appear to increase African American turnout rates in North Carolina (Walker, Herron, and Smith 2018). Whether or not early voting affects minority turnout is unclear.

What We Know About Race and State Election Laws

Stacy Abrams is not alone in arguing that race and ethnicity are still firmly connected to state voting laws. Academic research on this topic is extensive. A large part of the history of voting in the U.S. is connected to race (V.O. Key's *Southern Politics* [1949]). Before the Fifteenth Amendment was enacted in 1868, no federal guarantee of a right to vote existed for individuals regardless of race or ethnicity. Even so, with some brief advances in African American electoral success in the late 1860s and the 1870s during Reconstruction (Berman 2015; Keyssar 2009), the protected right to vote would not be established again until the Voting Rights Act (VRA) of 1965—and its extensions in 1970, 1975, 1982, 1992, and 2006. The eleven former Confederate states have been shown to have lower levels of political participation than the rest of the country (Key 1949; Kim, Petrocik, and Enokson 1975; Rosenstone and Hansen 2002).

Springer (2014) documents the long arc of political participation over the past century, showing that the legacies of slavery and Jim Crow laws (poll taxes and literacy tests) significantly reduced turnout in the Southern states. Keyssar (2009) notes that periods of expansion in voting rights have been followed by periods of restriction, as when the Jim Crow period followed Reconstruction. Some argue that a similar pattern has occurred today, particularly since the Supreme Court decided in *Crawford v. Marion County* (2008) that voter ID laws were constitutional even in the absence of voter fraud evidence; and in *Holder v. Shelby County* (2013), in which the Supreme Court decided that the VRA no longer mandated that states with histories of discriminatory voting systems get preclearance from the federal Department of Justice before changing their voting laws (Lopez 2014; Rhodes 2017).

Since these decisions, the number of states with restrictive identification laws has increased to thirty-five (National Conference of State Legislatures 2018), and a non-trivial number of states including North Carolina, Texas, and Wisconsin have made early voting, same day registration, and absentee voting more restrictive (Hasen 2014; Herron and Smith 2012).

Other restrictive state voting laws include racial gerrymanders, racially discriminatory voter purges, barriers to provisional voting, felon disenfranchisement, and other structural changes to a state's voting system that seems uniquely designed to disadvantage racial and ethnic minorities (Anderson 2018; Berman 2015; Curtist 2016; Weiser 2014). Even with the expansion of voting rights and the increase in the number of states with convenience voting laws since the 1980s (Larocca and Klemanski 2011), these more recent changes in state voting laws threaten the suffrage rights of racial and ethnic minorities. Other studies have focused on how felony disenfranchisement laws affect voter participation (Manza and Uggen 2006).

Voter ID Laws

Voter identification laws are another factor related to racial and ethnic minority group participation, but they are not a primary focus of this study. Such laws have existed in the U.S. since 1950, when South Carolina became the first state to adopt such a law; today, a total of thirty-five states have such laws (National Conference of State Legislature 2019). State voter ID laws vary in their stringency. Non–photo ID states either request or require individuals to present a form of non-photo documentation—such as a utility bill or a bank statement—at the polls to prove eligibility to vote. States with photo ID requirements stipulate that citizens show such a form of photo documentation—examples include driver's licenses or passports—to be able to cast a ballot. While the stated purpose of the adoption of these laws is to reduce fraud (Minnite 2011), patterns indicate that they are more likely to be adopted in states with large minority populations and Republican-controlled state legislatures (Rocha and Matsubayashi 2014). People less likely to have government-issued voter IDs include the elderly, the poor, and racial and ethnic minorities (Bentele and O'Brien 2013; Hicks et al. 2015; Vandewalker and Bentele 2015; Walker, Sanchez, Nuno, and Barreto 2018).

Research on the impact of voter identification laws on turnout, and particularly minority turnout, is inconclusive. Some research indicates that more stringent forms of these laws lower general turnout (Alvarez, Bailey, and Katz 2008; Dropp 2013; Vercelloti and Anderson 2007) and participation by racial and ethnic minorities relative to non-Hispanic whites (Hajnal, Lajevardi, and Nielson 2017). Possible explanations include the lack of necessary identification documents among certain segments of the population, including minorities (Walker, Sanchez, Nuno, and Barreto 2018), and the disproportionate likelihood that minorities compared to non-Hispanic whites will be asked to present identification at the polls (Atkeson, Kerevel, and Alvarez 2014; Atkeson, Bryant, et al. 2014; Stewart 2013). Other research finds that state voter ID laws do not depress voter turnout among racial and ethnic minorities differentially (Grimmer et al. 2017; Fraga 2018; Rocha and Matsubayashi 2014); turnout is lower overall, but not specifically lower for minorities. Numerous studies find that these laws have a minimal or null impact on overall voter turnout (Ansolabehere 2009; Alvarez et al. 2008; Berinsky 2005; Fraga 2018; Grimmer et al. 2017; Mycoff, Wagner, and Wilson 2007; Vercelloti and Anderson 2006). In this study, voter ID laws are measured as a component of the COVI.

Data and Methods

A challenge in empirically analyzing the effect of state election systems (the laws and implementation of the laws) on individual turnout decisions is whether other heterogeneous state factors are driving political behavior, not the election laws. Previous studies measuring change over time in voting rates have proven to be the most effective (Hanmer 2009; Springer 2014; Leighley and Nagler 2013). Measuring change in turnout rates minimizes concerns about endogenous treatments (election laws) that are really a function of other factors within states. Using data from the fifty states measuring state convenience voting laws and election administration merged with individual-level data on voting decisions using a national voter file (data described in Chapter 1), we measure the effects of state electoral practices on the change in rates of political participation. Multivariate logistic regression and lagged panel models are used to predict individual voting decisions and model whether individuals changed from not voting in a prior election to voting in a current election comparing 2008–2012 and 2010–2014.

The model setup is similar to that used in Chapters 4 and 5, where we predict whether a person voted in the 2012 or 2014 elections (outcome variables).

One of the explanatory/predictor variables is if they voted or not or 2010—along with what state they live in, so we can measure the presence/absence of alternative voting laws and quality election administration. The setup allows us to measure the change in the probability of an individual voting from the 2008 (presidential) or 2010 (midterm) elections to the following 2012 (presidential) or 2014 (midterm) elections. Explanatory variables—such as demographic factors and state election laws—will only have an impact on people who changed their voting behavior—non-voter in 2008 or 2010 to voting in 2012 or 2014, or vice versa. By using lagged panel models, we are focusing on predicting who changed their voting behavior.

Accessible Elections Model

We compare models predicting change in racial and ethnic group turnout using the COVI (discussed below) to the accessible elections model. Again, binary variables measure whether the state has adopted same day registration, early voting, or home voting (mail/no excuse absentee), coded 1 for the presence of the law and 0 for now law. These laws are updated biannually. The Pew Charitable Trusts/MIT Election Data and Science Lab's Election Performance Index (EPI) is made up of seventeen subcomponents and updated biannually, constructed from the same factors every two years, so its effects in one period can be compared to those of another. The accessible elections model places more weight on election administration, as we measure three primary voting laws and election administration in general. Despite the fact that state and local governments administer elections, election administration is rarely included in models predicting minority turnout. Since the outcome variable is voting in the election, logistic regression coefficients are reported with standard errors clustered by state.

As in previous chapters, at the individual level covariates are measured that have been associated with an individual's likelihood of voting, including a respondent's gender, education (propensity score of the likelihood of having a bachelor's degree), income (ordinal scale divided into twenty categories ranging from "$0 to $10,000" to "$141,000 or greater"), age (measured in years), news interest (as a proxy for political interest) and partisanship status (Republican or Democrat, compared to independents), home ownership, length of residence, and employment. The control variables and their coding are included in Appendix B.

Results

Non-Hispanic White and Ethnic/Racial Group Subsamples

Figure 6.1 displays the key logistic regression covariate results from four fully specified logistic regression models showing change in turnout for the midterm elections (2010 to 2014) and presidential elections (2008 to 2012) (models are listed in Appendix C), comparing a subsample of white non-Hispanics to minorities (African American, Hispanic, and Asians).[1] The bars around the dots represent the standard errors. Alternatively, we compare the change in the probability of voting for a subsample for racial

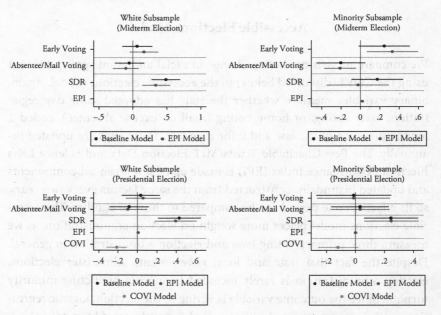

Figure 6.1. Effects of convenience voting laws on changing probability of voting from 2010 to 2014 (midterm) and from 2008 to 2012 (presidential) comparing white non-Hispanics to minorities, varying Election Performance Index.
Note: Logistic regression unstandardized coefficients with 95% confidence intervals. Only key coefficients presented here to conserve space, but see fully specified models found in Appendix Tables C1.5 and C1.6.

---

[1] Subsample models are estimated for white non-Hispanics compared to minority voters, and for African Americans, Hispanics, and Asians compared to white non-Hispanics. Catalist defines an individual's race/ethnicity from state voter file data, and from imputation using available well-corroborated commercial vendor sources.

and ethnic groups: non-Hispanic whites, African Americans, Hispanics, and Asians (Figures 6.5 and 6.7, discussed later in the chapter). The first set of models omits the control variable for the Election Performance Index, while the second set includes the control for election administration. Each model examines the effect of living in a state with the alternative voting laws on the probability of changing from being a non-voter to a voter.

The results show that white non-Hispanics are most likely to benefit from state laws allowing for same day voter registration in both midterm and presidential elections. While the media may frame same day registration laws as benefiting minority voters, white non-Hispanics may benefit the most. The size of the coefficient for same day registration laws (midterm elections) reduces modestly when controlling for election administration, suggesting that omitting a control for election administration can lead to biased results. White non-Hispanics are also significantly more likely to vote in states with improved overall election administrations in midterm elections.

The models on the right of Figure 6.1 show the results for minorities (black, Latino, or Asian) in the midterm election (top) and presidential election (bottom). Across the states in midterm elections, racial and ethnic groups benefit the most from early voting laws and improved election administration. Without controlling for election administration, the significance of early voting for minorities would be undetectable. For presidential elections, same day registration laws have a significant effect in increasing voting rates among minority groups. Since the outcome variable is measuring the change in the likelihood of voting for the same individuals (panel data), these results show that the beneficial effects of early voting and same day registration for minorities are considerable, consistent with previous research (Herron and Smith 2012, but see Walker et al. 2018).

Since logistic regression results can be difficult to substantively interpret, Figure 6.2 converts these results to predicted probabilities to better understand how same day registration shapes changes in the likelihood of voting in midterm and presidential elections for varying racial and ethnic groups. With all other factors held constant, white non-Hispanics are 10 percentage points more likely to vote in 2012 if they didn't vote in 2008 when living in same day registration states; they are also 5 percentage points more likely to vote in 2014 if they didn't vote in 2010 when living in same day registration states. Minorities also benefit from same day registration laws in presidential elections, with an average 6 percentage point increase in the probability

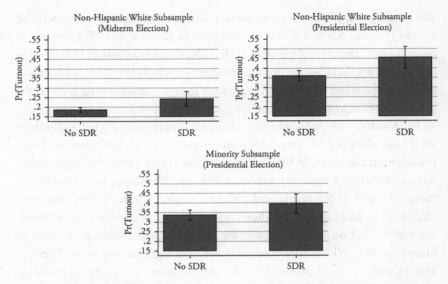

Figure 6.2. Impact of same day registration on change in probability of voting from 2010 to 2014 (midterm) or 2008 to 2012 (presidential), comparing white non-Hispanics and minorities.

Note: Predicted probabilities calculated from subsamples of non-voters in 2008 or 2010 among these subsamples from the corresponding EPI models in Figure 6.1, varying the presence versus non-presence of same day registration. All other variables held at mean values.

of becoming a voter if they were a non-voter in the previous presidential election.

This evidence shows that same day registration helps mobilize new voters across racial and ethnic groups, but whites benefit more than minorities. Since the outcome variable is measuring the change in the likelihood of voting, these are substantively large increases.

A 10% increased probability of voting for non-Hispanic whites who didn't vote in the previous election when living in a same day registration state, controlling for other laws, is really large. Some segment of non-voters is vulnerable to getting mobilized every election. Previous research on the effect sizes of same day registration are for the overall population, not non-voters. Our point is that previous research may have under-estimated the true effects of the laws by not using panel data.

Beyond the impact of convenience voting laws such as early voting or same day registration, election administration is also an important determinant of turnout among minorities. Figure 6.3 shows the effect of states' election

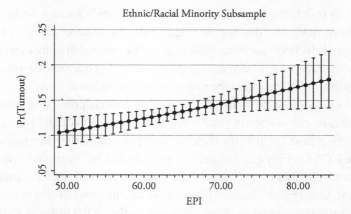

Figure 6.3. Impact of Election Performance Index on change in probability of voting in 2014 for minorities who didn't vote in 2010.

Note: Predicted probabilities with 95% confidence intervals calculated from subsample of non-voters in 2010 for subsample of ethnic/racial minority from Figure 6.1. EPI varied from minimum to maximum values. All other variables held at mean values.

administrations—proxied by the EPI—on the probability of voting in 2014 among ethnic/racial minorities who did not vote in 2010. Varying EPI from its minimum to maximum levels in the U.S. states, these simulations suggest that ethnic/racial minorities in states with the most accessible election administrations are nearly 8% more likely to vote than their counterparts in states with the least accessible election administrations.

Comparing Costs of Voting Index (COVI) to Convenience Voting

Instead of the three primary convenience voting laws and election administration, we also estimate models using the new COVI to measure how restrictive state election laws are in the aggregate (made up of more than a dozen factors) (Li, Pomante, and Schraufnagel 2018).[2] The index is focused

[2] The COVI includes: (1) registration deadlines; (2) voter registration restrictions (limitations on same day registration, felon disenfranchisement laws, mental competency required for registration); (3) registration drive restrictions; (4) preregistration laws; (5) voting inconvenience (existence of early voting, excuse/no-excuse voting, mail voting, or not); (6) strictness of voter ID laws; (7) poll hours.

heavily on restrictive laws (voter ID), while our study focuses on laws that promote turnout. The developers of this index rank American states every presidential election year from 1980 to 2016. The inclusion of this variable in our analyses serves a robustness check, showing that our models are robust to using this index instead of the convenience voting laws.

The COVI cannot be included in our main models predicting the effects of the laws on the change in voter turnout, since the COVI and the convenience voting laws include overlapping components. Other limitations are that the COVI is only constructed for presidential elections and cannot be used across election cycles because the index consists of different measures each year. Our analysis focuses on both presidential and midterm elections and over time comparisons. Thus, inclusion of the COVI index is a valuable robustness check, but not a substitute for measuring the state voting/registration laws directly.

The COVI logistic results in Figure 6.1 and corresponding predicted probabilities in Figure 6.4 show that states with restrictive electoral practices, including voter ID, disadvantage white non-Hispanics and minorities, and do not

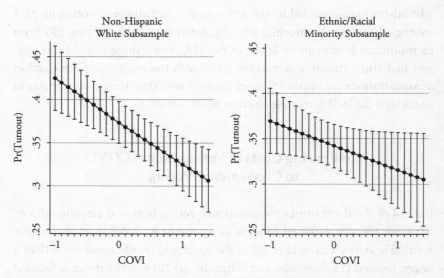

Figure 6.4. Impact of COVI on change in probability of voting from 2008 to 2012 among non-voters in 2008, comparing white non-Hispanic to racial/ethnic minorities.

Note: Predicted probabilities with 95% confidence intervals calculated from subsamples of non-voters in 2008 and for white non-Hispanics (left) and minorities (right) from Figure 6.1, varying COVI from minimum to maximum values. All other variables held at mean values.

uniquely disadvantage racial and ethnic groups (see Rocha and Matsubayashi 2014). The graph shows the probability of voting in the 2012 election for an individual who didn't vote in 2008, varying the COVI index between its lowest and highest values, with higher values indicating a more restrictive voting system. Residing in a state with more restrictive voting laws reduces white non-Hispanic voting rates (approximately 12%); minority voter turnout also drops steeply, but the confidence intervals for the slope of the line for whites and minorities overlap, meaning neither group is uniquely worse off.

Rather than one-size-fits-all, the analysis so far points to differences in the effects of state electoral practices—that is, the laws and implementation of the laws—on the probability of participating in politics for racial and ethnic groups. For non-Hispanic whites, same day registration is an important driver of turnout, while for ethnic/racial minorities early voting and same day registration laws are the most important. Living in a state with a more accessible election administration also positively shapes an individual's likelihood of voting. The overall accessibility of a state's election administration shape white and minority turnout in addition to the impacts of election reform laws such as early voting and same day registration.

Results for Ethnic/Racial Group Subsamples

Figure 6.5 uses the same lagged panel models as in the previous section, but instead unpacks the results for ethnic/racial minority subsamples—African Americans, Hispanics, and Asians—to detect unique effects of the alternative voting laws among different demographic groups. Non-Hispanic whites are the fourth category (results for non-Hispanic whites are identical to those in the previous section, and are included here as a reference group against which to compare the ethnic/racial minority results).

Figure 6.5 displays the logistic coefficient results for convenience voting laws and EPI on the likelihood of voting in 2014, controlling for voter history in 2010, for white non-Hispanics, African Americans, Hispanics, and Asians. To review, non-Hispanic whites are more likely to become voters if living in states with same day registration and improved election administration. In contrast, early voting is significantly likely to mobilize voters among African Americans and Hispanics. Hispanics turnout rates also increase when residing in states with higher quality election administration. For Asians, absentee and mail voting (home voting) has a positive and significant

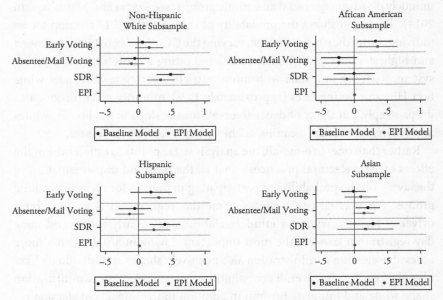

Figure 6.5. Effects of alternative voting laws on changing probability of voting from 2010 to 2014 (midterm) comparing across racial subgroups, varying Election Performance Index.

Note: Logistic regression points with 95% confidence intervals. Only key coefficients presented to conserve space, but these estimation points from fully specified models found in Appendix Table C1.7.

impact on turnout. Absentee and mail voting, however, are negatively and significantly related to turnout among African Americans. Together, these findings show that different alternative voting laws uniquely benefit individuals in different ethnic/racial group categories: Non-Hispanic whites (same day registration), African Americans (early voting), Hispanics (early voting and same day registration), and Asians (absentee/mail voting).

Since these are logistic regression coefficients, predicted probability measures aid in interpretation. Among subsamples of individuals who did not vote in 2010, early voting increased the probability of an African American individual voting by 4% in 2014, and a Hispanic individual by 2% by in the same election. Importantly, early voting's statistical significance for Hispanics is only apparent after controlling for EPI, again suggesting that omitting a control for election administration can lead to biased results. Figure 6.6 shows that Hispanics living in the most accessible election administration state are 6% more likely to vote than their counterparts in the least accessible election

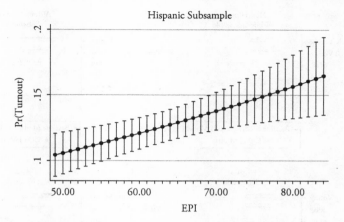

Figure 6.6. Impact of Election Performance Index on change in probability of Hispanic turnout from 2010 to 2014 among non-voters in 2010.

Note: Predicted probabilities with 95% confidence intervals calculated from subsample of Hispanic non-voters in 2010 from Figure 6.5, varying EPI from minimum to maximum values. All other variables held at mean values.

administration state. Both early voting (African Americans and Hispanics) and election administration (Hispanics) are important for turnout among these minority demographic groups.

Finally, Figure 6.7 displays logistic coefficients for alternative voting laws and election administration on the change in turnout among individuals in all four ethnic/racial groups for presidential elections (2008 to 2012). In presidential elections, we find that same day registration boosts the likelihood of voting across the board for African Americans, Hispanics, Asians, and non-Hispanic whites. A state with a more accessible election administration—as proxied by EPI—improves turnout among Asians. Conversely, more restrictive state voting systems—as indicated by the COVI index that includes voter ID laws—uniquely disadvantages whites, Hispanics, and Asians.

For the presidential elections, Figure 6.8 displays the degree to which same day registration changed the probability of voting in 2012 among African Americans, Hispanics, and Asians, provided they did not vote in 2008. Same day registration has the most pronounced substantive impact on Asian individuals, increasing their probability of voting by over 9%. This law also has a positive substantive impact on individuals within the other two categories—8% among Hispanics, and 5% among African Americans. These results demonstrate that same day registration does not only benefit non-Hispanic

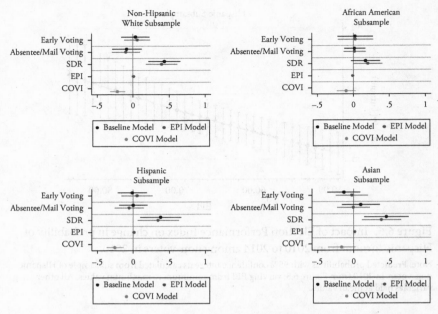

Figure 6.7. Effects of convenience voting laws on changing probability of voting from 2008 to 2012 (presidential) comparing across racial subgroups, varying Election Performance Index.

Note: Logistic regression points with 95% confidence intervals. Only key coefficients presented to conserve space, but these estimation points from fully specified models found in Appendix Tables C1.8 and C1.9.

whites in presidential elections, but—to varying extents—individuals in each of the other ethnic/racial groups as well.

The results in this section show that there are unique election laws effects linked to different ethnic/racial groups. Same day registration laws are beneficial for individuals in all four ethnic/racial groups in presidential elections, and for white non-Hispanics in midterm elections. Early voting is particularly beneficial for African Americans and Hispanics, and absentee/mail voting for Asians, in midterm elections. States that have more accessible election administrations (EPI), and less restrictive registration and voting regimes (COVI), also promote turnout to varying degrees across multiple ethnic/racial group categories. The general inference is that having overall more accessible state electoral practices—whether measured by convenience voting laws, EPI, or COVI—promotes turnout among individuals from a diverse array of ethnic/racial backgrounds.

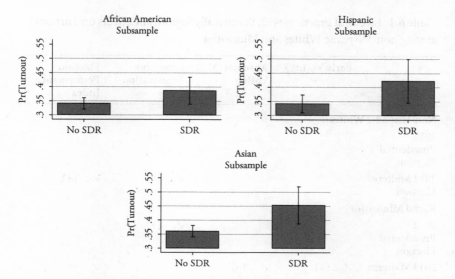

Figure 6.8. Impact of same day registration on the change in probability of voting (2008 to 2012) among non-voters in previous election, comparing white non-Hispanics and minorities.

Note: Predicted probabilities calculated from subsamples of racial and ethnic group non-voters in 2008 from the corresponding EPI models in Figure 6.7, varying the presence versus non-presence of same day registration. All other variables held at mean values.

Conclusion

Table 6.1 summarizes the key results from this chapter. One notable finding is that non-Hispanic Whites are significantly more likely to become voters in midterm and presidential elections when same day registration exists in their states, and are more likely to vote in states with higher EPI in midterm elections. Racial and ethnic minorities, considered both as a distinct category and as three distinct minority groups (African Americans, Hispanics, and Asians), benefit from all three alternative voting laws, and in states with higher EPI. Both non-Hispanic whites and racial minorities are significantly disadvantaged in states with higher barriers to registration and voting, as represented by the COVI results.

State governments play an important role in making voting accessible for all Americans. Electoral laws, rules and practices can be designed to increase voter turnout and create more equality across demographic groups. This

Table 6.1 Electoral Practices with Statistically Significant Effects on Turnout among non-Hispanic Whites and Minorities

	Early Voting	Absentee/Mail Voting	Same Day Registration	Election Performance Index
Non-Hispanic Whites				
2012 Presidential Election			✓ (+)	
2014 Midterm Election			✓ (+)	✓ (+)
Racial Minorities				
2012 Presidential Election			✓ (+)	
2014 Midterm Election	✓ (+)	✓ (−)		✓ (+)
African Americans				
2012 Presidential Election			✓ (+)	
2014 Midterm Election	✓ (+)	✓ (−)		
Hispanics				
2012 Presidential Election			✓ (+)	
2014 Midterm Election	✓ (+)		✓ (+)	✓ (+)
Asians				
2012 Presidential Election			✓ (+)	✓ (+)
2014 Midterm Election		✓ (+)		

study consistently found that states with improved election administration fostered higher voter turnout for white non-Hispanics and racial and ethnic minorities. But states can also impose barriers to political participation. The results shown here suggest that different convenience voting laws can benefit different demographic groups. Using panel survey data with vote histories and election data from state voter rolls, we test how state election laws and election administration shape voting rights in contemporary U.S. politics. We hope the results can contribute not only to academic science but also to practice and election law in the U.S. states to ensure that all Americans have a right to vote. Of the voting laws, same day registration has the greatest effect in increasing turnout in midterm and presidential elections for whites and minorities. But home voting (no-excuse absentee voting and mail voting) also helps convert Asian non-voters into voters, while early voting uniquely benefits African Americans and Hispanics.

7

Accessible Elections and Campaign Mobilization

In their often-cited work *Voice and Equality: Civic Voluntarism in American Politics*, Verba, Schlozman, and Brady (1995, 430) argue that people do not vote because "they can't; they don't want to; or because nobody asked." Based on the findings in Chapters 4 to 6, one can infer that individuals in states with more highly accessible electoral rules are exposed to fewer voting barriers, and are thus given more opportunities to vote. A key question, though, is whether more accessible electoral rules have a direct impact on individual voting decisions; or whether they also have an indirect effect on turnout, leading campaigns and parties to more actively mobilize citizens? A notable gap in the literature that needs to be filled pertains to how voting and registration reform laws shape these mobilization strategies. As noted in previous chapters, many scholars (Berinksy 2005; Donovan 2008; Karp and Banducci 2000, 2001; Neeley and Richardson 2001) emphasize that political interest, electoral competition, and mobilization are key factors conditioning the effects of these laws. Yet none of these studies directly measure how the laws influence campaign mobilization.

Previous research has long emphasized that competitive parties and campaigns are strategic and will do everything they can to win elections (Aldrich 1993). They tend to mobilize individuals who are already likely to vote in an election (Finkel 1993; Holbrook and McClurg 2005; Kramer 1973; Lazarsfeld, Berelson, and Gaudet 1944), such as partisans rather than independents, but some candidates also work to expand the size of the electorate by mobilizing new voters, as illustrated by Obama's successful 2008 and 2012 campaigns (Issenberg 2012).

High-socioeconomic-status individuals are common recruiting targets because they tend to be reliable voters from one election to the next (Rosenstone and Hansen 2002). What makes them likely voters and campaign targets is their abundance of politically relevant resources—time, money, and civic skills—that relate positively to participation. Individuals

Accessible Elections. Michael Ritter and Caroline J. Tolbert, Oxford University Press (2021). © Oxford University Press. DOI: 10.1093/oso/9780197537251.001.0001.

with more money can donate more to candidates, parties, and interest groups. Those with more time have more opportunities to volunteer for a campaign, or become better informed about an election. And those with more political interest are more likely to vote (Schlozman, Verba, and Brady 2013; Verba, Brady, and Schlozman 1995; also see Rosenstone and Hansen 2002, 7). Applying multivariate regression analyses to 1956–1988 campaign contact data available through the ANES, Rosenstone and Hansen (2002, 164–165, 287–290) evaluate which demographic groups are more likely to be mobilized by campaigns. Their findings confirm that high socioeconomic status citizens are more likely to be contacted by campaigns.

But rarely have the literatures on campaign mobilization and election reform crossed paths. The election reform literature generally assumes there is limited reason to believe that campaigns use these laws to bring new voters into the electorate (Berinsky 2005; Gronke et al. 2008a; and others). As discussed previously, many scholars find that these laws have a minimal effect on turnout, or generally advantage already likely voting groups if they do have an effect. This may explain the limited attention given to voter mobilization in the literature on state election reform.

However, over the past several decades, convenience voting reforms in the U.S. have become widespread, especially in swing states such as Florida. More recent research demonstrates the efficacy of certain modes of mobilization, especially early voting (Herron and Smith 2012, 2014), and leaves an opening for new research on election reform laws to identify their effects on campaign targeting of different demographic groups. In a unique contribution to the literature, Burden et al. (2014) argue that early voting, absentee voting, and same day registration impact voter mobilization. They find that states with combinations of these laws are related to higher turnout, while states with single laws (e.g., early voting by itself) depress turnout. This is because, according to the researchers, early voting and same day registration in combination lead to longer election periods in states, motivating political actors (e.g., parties, candidates, etc.) to campaign for longer stretches of time. In states with only early voting, however, the election period usually ends several days or weeks before election day, shortening the mobilization window for campaigns. While these inferences sound sensible, Burden et al. (2014) do not directly measure campaign contact, only theorizing that campaigns are more active in targeting voters because of these laws. This chapter attempts to fill in the missing gap from the literature.

Previous studies of election reform laws have several other limitations, some that have been discussed before. They also do not consistently examine both presidential and midterm elections, even though turnout and mobilization patterns vary significantly by the type of election. They rely primarily on U.S. Census data that cannot measure political interest and partisanship, although partisanship has been found to be the most important predictor of party contacting (Hersh 2015). They also do not account for potentially disparate effects of voting reform laws on mobilization of poor versus non-poor citizens. While previous research has made admirable contributions to the field, and has hypothesized that mobilization is a key factor behind election reform law use, none has empirically demonstrated this to be the case.

This chapter makes several contributions to the growing literature on election reform. First, it directly models the relationship between state election reform laws, election administration, and campaign contact, using a 2010, 2012, and 2014 Cooperative Congressional Election Study (CCES) question asking if citizens were contacted face-to-face, by phone call, via electronic message, or through the mail by a political candidate or campaign.[1] Specifically, respondents were queried, "Did a candidate or political campaign organization contact you during the [insert election year] election?" The CCES collects representative state and congressional district samples, and measures political interest and partisanship of respondents, thereby facilitating a robust analysis of how the laws affect mobilization in all fifty states. The Catalist data used in the previous chapters does not include a question on campaign contact. Building on the research design from Schlozman et al. (2013), a secondary analysis is conducted using subsamples of those contacted compared to those not contacted by political campaigns to predict voter turnout. This strategy helps identify how variation in campaign contact shapes voter turnout associated with election reform laws.

This study has focused on how the state election reform laws affect the most disadvantaged members of society. Continuing in this exploration, this chapter compares how state voting laws and election administration structure mobilization of an unlikely voting group (the poor) compared to a more likely voting group (the non-poor). The subsample strategy is used to understand if the laws equalize voter recruitment between these demographic groups.

---

[1] Previous research has shown these mobilization methods to be positively related to turnout (Green and Gerber 2008).

Finally, variations in mobilization are examined in midterm and presidential elections, accounting for increased campaign mobilization in presidential elections (Hersh 2015).

Direct Voter Mobilization

Recent literature on campaign contact and turnout demonstrates that the impact of mobilization depends on the type of recruitment. Impersonal campaign mobilization techniques, such as robocalls, have been found to have no effect on turnout (Green and Gerber 2015); likewise, television and radio advertisements, as well as blanket modes of campaigning across large geographic areas, have minimal effects (Parry et al. 2008). Conversely, direct campaign contact—in the form of in-person, phone call, mail, or electronic message voter recruitment—has been found to increase turnout through information and social pressure mechanisms (Green and Gerber 2015; Mossberger, Tolbert, and McNeal 2008, Chapter 4; Parry et al. 2008; Sinclair 2012). Individuals who are contacted directly by campaigns become more informed when these agents tell them about policies, candidates, and elections. Campaigns may also inform potential voters of state registration requirements, or prompt them to mail in absentee ballots, for example. This helps citizens unfamiliar with the process of registering and voting to more easily navigate a state's election administration and cast a ballot (Mossberger et al. 2008).

Beyond direct mobilization, individuals can be psychologically coerced into voting by targeted campaign messages revealing that their vote history is state public record, implying that a non-vote will be a blemish on their vote history records (Green and Gerber 2008). Campaigns can also send mail with information on the turnout of a potential voter's neighbors, providing social pressure if they choose not to participate. Targeted messages communicate that casting a ballot is a civic duty, with the implication being that non-voters are nonideal citizens (Green and Gerber 2008; Hershey 2015; Sinclair 2012). These social pressure mechanisms have been shown to be effective in increasing voter turnout.

A long history of research demonstrates the efficacy of campaign contact and voter recruitment, just a sampling of which is discussed here. In a landmark study, Gosnell (1927) uses field experiments to show that campaign letters (the treatment effect) increased turnout by 1% in the

1924 presidential election and 9% in a 1925 municipal election among Chicagoans.[2] Also using a campaign experiment, Eldersveld (1956) reports that personalized campaign messages increased turnout in Ann Arbor, Michigan, and the sizes of these effects were non-trivial. Cutright and Ross (1958), examining campaign effects in a medium-sized Midwestern city, and testing their hypotheses using multivariate regression find that turnout for the Democratic Party increased by almost 2% when party activists contacted potential voters, while this effect was nearly 7% for Republican turnout. These patterns hold in the modern era as well. Drawing on the 1952–1996 ANES data coupled with regression analysis, Weilhouwer (2000) finds a statistically significant and positive relationship between campaigns and parties who contact prospective voters via phone or in-person and political participation. Niven (2000, 2004), in another illustration, uses panel data to show that face-to-face party recruitment is significantly related to turnout in Florida municipal and state elections. A positive relationship between party contact and mobilization is also reported in Ohio state elections (Calderia, Clausen, and Patterson 1990).

Other research using randomized field experiments corroborates these earlier findings. Green and Gerber (2008) and Sinclair (2012) use mail or door-to-door canvassing field experiments, along with local-, state-, and national-level datasets coupled with multivariate regression, to show that individuals are encouraged to vote at higher rates when the recruiter is also a local resident, or if the campaign message reminds citizens of the voting habits of their fellow neighbors or community (see also Gerber, Green, and Larimer 2008). Sinclair (2012) argues that social pressure leads people to internalize a social norm of voting, which has a positive effect on turnout. Mossberger et al. (2008) use ANES data and multivariate analyses to show that campaigns use the internet and email to mobilize political activity. Online campaigns provide relevant election information via such messages, spurring greater participation (Bimber 2003; Bimber and Davis 2003).

These modes of direct mobilization are not insignificant tools in the modern campaign's toolbox. Much the opposite is the case. With discoveries (e.g., Gosnell 1927) and re-discoveries (e.g., Green and Gerber 2008; Sinclair 2012) regarding the efficacy of direct voter recruitment, campaigns and parties have recently invested more time and resources into targeted voter mobilization (Darr and Levendusky 2009; Masket 2009; also see 2012

---

[2] The control group was non-recipients of campaign letters.

Obama Campaign Legacy Report). The 2008 and 2012 Obama campaign compiled a dataset consisting of the whole country's voting age population to construct voter-targeting plans (this later became the Catalist data used in previous chapters) (Issenberg 2012). Population datasets include information on individual voter histories, demographic characteristics (either based on public record, or imputed), and other factors associated with turnout (e.g., the imputed likelihood of subscribing to a news publication as a proxy for political interest) (Hersh 2015). By tailoring their direct mobilization strategies using this wealth of information, the Democratic Party could efficiently target individuals who might be persuaded to vote for Obama. Today, both the Democratic and Republican Parties have national voter databases they use to fuel these direct campaigning efforts (Hersh 2015, 67–68).

Widening Participation Gaps

But do these direct mobilization techniques help recruit individuals from groups less likely to participate in elections? Some scholars say yes. Parry et al. (2008) examine how in-person, mail, phone, and television and radio advertisement mobilization relates to turnout in the 2002 Senate elections in Missouri and Arkansas. Using voter history data (panel), they split their sample of 1,001 respondents into consistent, intermittent, and seldom voter groups. Consistent voters cast ballots in most elections, intermittent every four years, and the seldom group rarely if at all. The first group is mostly populated by high-SES citizens, while the third is dominated by individuals from the lower classes. Interestingly, they find that direct campaign contact (in-person, mail, or phone) significantly increases turnout among the seldom voter group, while this variable is only marginally significant among intermittent voters, and has no effect on consistent voters. The researchers conclude that consistent and intermittent voters are more likely to cast ballots, even if not contacted by campaigns. However, seldom voters are those most in need of campaign cues to vote, which is why the effect is most pronounced among them. Similar findings are also present in Niven's (2004) work. Mobilization appears to make a large difference in converting habitual nonvoters into voters, all else held constant. This suggests that election reform laws may have their largest voter mobilization effect on the poor.

Green and Gerber (2015) also test hypotheses on whether direct and personal campaign contact methods—such as door-to-door canvassing—increase an individual's likelihood of becoming a registered voter or casting a ballot. Using experimental treatment and control group designs across a number of American cities, Green and Gerber consistently demonstrate that direct and personalized campaign canvassing is most effective in motivating individuals to register to vote.

Social Networks

In a ground-breaking new study, Rolfe (2012) studies voter mobilization occurring within social networks. In this research, voting is defined as a social act. Using survey and precinct-level data along with quantitative methods, she demonstrates that individual-level correlates of voting (e.g., income and education) are imperfect predictors of turnout, with turnout also being strongly explained by social networks. The results show that an individual is more likely to vote when associates in their network also participate. This chapter explores whether state electoral rules—election reform laws and administration—create institutional networks that foster campaign contact strategies, an important factor leading to turnout. Instead of individual social networks, the focus is on state electoral practices.

Party Campaign Strategy

Sasha Issenberg's (2012) landmark book *The Victory Lab* details the landscape of modern electoral campaigns, and how they use big data sources to identify candidate and party supporters in the electorate. In a series of small case studies about twenty-first-century U.S. political campaigns—with the Obama campaign in 2008 being a leading example—Issenberg examines how parties use information about American citizens (voting histories, available demographic information, and an array of details on individual product consumption, home ownership, and media usage preferences, among other measures) to construct mobilization strategies and micro-target voters in a way not possible a decade earlier. The micro-targeting mobilization strategies using big data have been game changers, helping to pave the way to victory for Obama in two elections (see Hersh 2015).

Whereas Issenberg (2012) argues that big data has allowed campaigns to make precise and well-calibrated mobilization strategies, Hersh (2015) shows that big data does not always give campaigns perfect knowledge of voters, and is in fact contingent on the quality of the data state governments provide. Using population data (Catalist) built from state voter rolls discussed earlier, he is interested in how state data collection laws structure campaign mobilization strategies and voter recruitment; states have varying laws about how much information can be collected on individuals, and this affects the precision of mobilization campaigns. He contends that states with more permissive data collection laws allow campaigns to more precisely identify likely supporters in the electorate. Hersh's (2015) results show that campaign knowledge of potential voters is imperfect and strongly contingent on the leniency of state laws allowing data collection on individuals.

The literature discussed so far in this chapter was made possible in part by extensive use of experimental data with randomized treatment and control groups, as well as large sample survey and population data. But the existing literature has not explored how state election reform laws and the administration of elections shape campaign mobilization. To address this gap in the literatures on campaigning and election reform laws, this chapter uses a unique large sample two-step mobilization-turnout modeling technique to try to better understand whether state election reform laws and administration are systematically related to the likelihood that campaigns will contact and recruit voters. These are possible relationships that have not been widely studied by scholars working in these areas of research. Recent research by Hershey provides an exception.

Election Reform Laws and Campaign Strategy

Early voting, no-excuse absentee and mail voting, and same day registration are tools that parties now use to mobilize voters. Campaigns have redrawn their mobilization strategies to take advantage of them. According to Hershey (2015, 162):

> The traditional plan of building a campaign toward a big finish on Election Day doesn't work very well if large numbers of voters cast their ballots in October. To take advantage of early and no-excuse absentee voting, party organizations must be prepared to explain these options to their likely supporters and to mobilize early voters. The traditional GOTV [Get Out the Vote] drive, which used to take place during the weekend before Election

Day, has now become at least six weeks long. On the other hand, candidates then have the benefit of access to "running lists" telling who has requested absentee ballots and who has submitted them or voted early—though not, of course, how each individual voted.

To maximize their electoral success, political parties utilize early voting and no-excuse absentee or mail voting to mobilize supporters or persuadable voters over a longer period time. Same day registration likely keeps parties engaged in mobilization efforts until election day or the end of an early voting period.[3] Longer periods of mobilization likely equate to higher levels of turnout attributable to campaign activities. Additional research (Ashok et al. 2016) has shown that likely voters (e.g., more partisan, older, and higher SES) are more likely to cast ballots near the beginning of an early voting period, while less likely voters (e.g., less partisan, younger, and lower SES) are more likely to wait until the end of this period to do so. Therefore, in states with extensive mobilization periods, parties are likely to mobilize both likely and unlikely voting groups. These election laws structure mobilization, and there is a reasonable expectation that the poor are an attractive mobilization target, especially later in an election period.

Other recent work points to the need to account for mobilization when measuring the impact of convenience voting laws. In one of these studies, using a sample of active voters from Maryland voter file data for the 2010 general election, Herrnson, Hanmer, and Koh (2018) find that individuals are more likely to be absentee and early voters if they are exposed to certain informational messages regarding the existence of the laws in the state. In another, employing national survey data and voter registration files from three states (Florida, Georgia, and North Carolina) for the 2004 and 2008 elections, Miller and Chaturvedi (2018) find that party contact is significantly related to election day voting and early voting. An additional study, that of Galicki (2018), reinforces the findings of these other studies and emphasizes how indirect changes in voting laws—such as when states adopt new convenience voting laws, or impose new voter constraints—shapes voter mobilization patterns. While these studies show the importance of mobilization in structuring the impact of convenience voting laws, our study builds on them to

---

[3] Burden et al. (2014) differentiate between modes of same day registration that allow registration and voting on election day as well as during the early voting period preceding an election, and registration and voting only on the day of the election (with the latter referred to as Election Day Registration).

test whether these impacts are generalizable across all fifty American states and in both midterm and presidential elections.

The expansion of election reform laws in the American states over the past three decades is an attempt to widen the American electorate to include a broader segment of the population. State electoral practices are important determinants of which demographic groups are targets of party mobilization efforts, with political parties doing the heavy lifting.

Research Hypotheses

This study considers whether the accessibility of a state's electoral rules structures the targeting strategies employed by candidates and campaigns to recruit voters and, if so, how this subsequently impacts turnout among citizens. Several testable hypotheses are derived from the accessible elections framework when applied to the subject of mobilization:

H1: Individuals residing in states with election reform laws (early voting, no-excuse absentee or mail voting, and same day registration) and better election administration are more likely to be contacted by parties and candidate campaigns.

H2: Individuals contacted by campaigns are more likely to vote, compared to individuals who are not contacted.

H3: Poor individuals living in states with early voting, no-excuse absentee voting, or same day registration and improved election administration are more likely to be contacted.

H4: The effects of election reform laws on contacting will be more pronounced in higher salience presidential elections than midterm elections. These effects should be consistent for poor and non-poor citizens.

Data and Methods

Pooled cross-sectional time-series data from the 2010, 2012, and 2014 Cooperative Congressional Election Study (CCES) is used for the empirical analysis in this chapter, building on research by Burden et al. (2014).

The CCES is an online survey that uses statistical matching based on the American Community Survey to build a representative sample of Americans. Individuals are thus the unit of analysis. Although the results hold when using multilevel modeling for state factors combined with individual-level factors, more logistic regression models are presented here for simplicity. The total survey sample includes 165,602 respondents spread over the three election years. The 2008 CCES is excluded because it does not include a variable measuring campaign contact. Two separate datasets are created; one for the midterm election years with a sample of 111,176, and one for the presidential election with a sample of 54,426. Subsamples of poor respondents with household incomes at or below the federal poverty line are created for the two midterm election (n = 22,781) and one presidential election (n = 12,262) years.

The first dependent variable is whether a respondent was contacted by a campaign in these elections. Individuals reporting being contacted are coded 1, and they are coded 0 if not. Because of the binary form of the outcome variable, logistic regression is used for the statistical modeling. The second dependent variable, whether a respondent voted, is also dichotomously coded 1 for voting, and 0 for non-voting, as discussed and used in the previous chapters.

Following the Schlozman et al. (2013) design, campaign contacting and turnout models are divided into two stages: the first is mobilization and second is voting. The first stage consists of the full sample and examines which factors influence an individual's likelihood of being contacted by a campaign (candidate or party). The second stage subsamples respondents into contacted or not contacted categories and utilizes the same factors from the previous model to determine if campaign mobilization, election reform laws, and a state's election administration increases the propensity of individuals to vote in elections. The CCES survey data is merged with state aggregate variables measuring the presence of election reform laws and election administration performance. While Schlozman et al. (2013) were interested primarily in the demographic attributes of voters, this study is primarily interested in characteristics of the respondent's state. Because respondents reside in states with more or less competitive elections and different state voting laws and administration, standard errors are clustered by state in the statistical models.

A similar modeling strategy used in Chapters 4 to 5 is followed here, with a similar set of explanatory variables. Election reform laws and state election administration are also interacted with each other to see if a difference in the average quality of a state election administration moderates the propensity of campaigns to use these election reform provisions to contact potential voters. To measure electoral competition across the states and different years, this study includes a variable representing the margin of victory in the 2012 presidential election, and the closest senatorial, gubernatorial, or average of House races at the state level in 2010 and 2014. Other control variables include income, male/female, age, education, African American, Hispanic, Asian, other race, non-Hispanic white (reference group), strong partisan, political interest, length of residence, employment, and home ownership. Finally, a year dummy variable is included to control for potential temporal heterogeneity.

Discussion and Results

Presidential Election Campaign Contact

Table 7.1 reports logistic models to predict campaign contact based on demographic factors and state contextual variables in the 2012 presidential election. In the baseline model (column 1), same day registration is shown to have a positive and significant effect on campaign contact in presidential elections, consistent with the law's beneficial effects on turnout in the previous chapters. This effect remains after election administration is included as a control variable in the second model. In fact, election administration—across the last four models—has a consistently positive and significant impact on voter mobilization. In states with improved election administration, parties and candidate campaigns are significantly more likely to reach out to voters (see Hersh 2015). Additionally, in the fourth model, the significantly positive no-excuse absentee/mail voting variable coefficient and the significantly negative no-excuse absentee and EPI interaction variable coefficient indicates that individuals are more likely to be contacted to vote in no-excuse absentee/mail voting states, but this effect becomes less pronounced when absentee/mail voting states have more accessible election administrations.

This is an important addition to the literature on state election reform laws. Same day registration, no-excuse absentee/mail voting, and the overall

Table 7.1 Individual Likelihood of Being Contacted by a Campaign in 2012 Presidential Election, Varying Convenience Voting Laws and Election Performance Index

	Baseline	Convenience Voting Laws + EPI	Early Voting × EPI	Absentee/ Mail Voting × EPI	SDR × EPI
Early Voting	−0.106	−0.080	0.342	−0.096	−0.080
	(0.131)	(0.132)	(0.815)	(0.121)	(0.132)
Absentee/Mail Voting	0.096	0.078	0.081	1.406*	0.077
	(0.140)	(0.140)	(0.142)	(0.733)	(0.140)
SDR	0.276**	0.226**	0.230**	0.237*	0.070
	(0.107)	(0.109)	(0.114)	(0.121)	(1.227)
EPI		0.014*	0.017**	0.023**	0.013*
		(0.007)	(0.008)	(0.008)	(0.007)
Early Voting × EPI			−0.006		
			(0.012)		
Absentee/Mail Voting × EPI				−0.019*	
				(0.010)	
SDR × EPI					0.002
					(0.017)
Pseudo R^2	0.161	0.162	0.162	0.163	0.162
N	54426	54426	54426	54426	54426

Note: Based on CCES data measuring voting behavior of eligible voters in 2012 election. To conserve space, only the primary covariates are reported here. Full regression models are reported in Appendix Table C1.10. The estimates are unstandardized logistic regression coefficients. Robust standard errors in parentheses are clustered by state. Multilevel models reveal similar results. P-values are based on two-tailed tests.

* $p < 0.10$, ** $p < 0.05$, *** $p < 0.001$.

quality of a state's election administration are all significant predictors of campaign mobilization in presidential elections.

To make these results more interpretable, Figure 7.1 displays the substantive effects of same day registration on the probability of an individual being contacted by a campaign, holding other variables at their mean values. Relative to residing in a non–same day registration state, being in a same day registration state increases an individual's likelihood of being contacted by 6.5%, from 55.5% to 62%. Same day registration substantially enhances the likelihood that a person will be mobilized to vote.

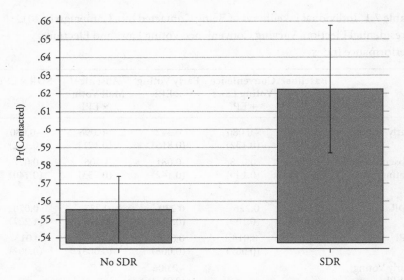

Figure 7.1. Probability of being contacted by a campaign in 2012 presidential election, varying same day registration.

Note: Line reports probability of being contacted in states with and without same day registration in 2012 from Model 1 in Table 7.1. All other variables held at mean values. Ninety percent confidence intervals included too.

Campaign Contact and Voting

The previous section found that the quality of election administration can push campaigns to recruit new voters in presidential elections. Did the election laws' mobilization impacts make a meaningful difference in an individual's decision to cast a ballot? This question is assessed in the four logistic regression models listed in Table 7.2. The first two models predict turnout in the presidential election among those who were not contacted; and the second two models examine this outcome among those who were contacted. Columns 2 and 4 report the fully specified models controlling for election administration.

What emerges from the empirical results is that early voting, quality state election administration, and campaign contact appear to go together to increase voter turnout. Among those who were not contacted, same day registration is related to a lower likelihood of voting. However, this result is no longer significant after state election administration is included in the second model (the fully specified model). Conversely, among individuals

Table 7.2 Campaign Contact Effect on Voting in 2012 Presidential Election, Varying Convenience Voting Laws and Election Performance Index

	No Contact	No Contact + EPI	Contact	Contact + EPI
Early Voting	−0.077	−0.086	0.176**	0.188**
	(0.082)	(0.085)	(0.075)	(0.073)
Absentee/Mail Voting	−0.031	−0.022	−0.050	−0.057
	(0.091)	(0.094)	(0.091)	(0.088)
SDR	−0.210**	−0.190**	−0.056	−0.073
	(0.084)	(0.088)	(0.101)	(0.102)
EPI		−0.005		0.005
		(0.005)		(0.004)
Pseudo R^2	0.072	0.072	0.054	0.054
N	22770	22770	31656	31656

Note: Based on CCES data measuring voting behavior of eligible voters in the 2012 election. To conserve space, only the primary covariates are reported here. Full regression models are reported in Appendix Table C1.11. The estimates are unstandardized logistic regression coefficients. Robust standard errors in parentheses are clustered by state. Multilevel models reveal similar results. P-values are based on two-tailed tests.

* $p < 0.10$, ** $p < 0.05$, *** $p < 0.001$.

who were contacted, in-person early voting has a positive and significant impact on voting in presidential elections. Together, these findings suggest that early voting—by itself—does not translate into higher turnout in presidential elections. When joined together with campaign recruitment strategies, this law can enhance turnout.

To understand the substantive size of the factors shaping voting probabilities, Figures 7.2 translates the in-person early voting logistic results into predicted probabilities. All other covariates for these simulations are held at their mean values. According to the early voting results, provided that an individual has been contacted by a campaign, the law increases their propensity of voting by approximately 3%. During presidential elections, mobilization and early voting increase a person's probability of voting.

Midterm Election Campaign Contact

Table 7.3 reports the results of the models predicting campaign or party contact for the overall population in midterm elections. The first model estimates

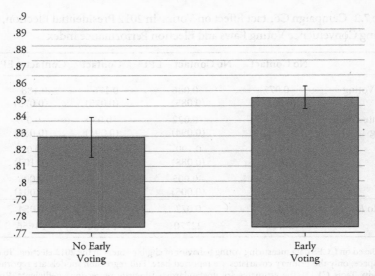

Figure 7.2. Probability of voting in 2012 presidential election in states with and without in-person early voting (contacted by a campaign).

Note: Bars report probability of voting in states with and without in-person early voting in 2012 for Model 4 in Table 7.2. All other variables held at mean values. Ninety percent confidence intervals included.

baseline effects by only including the state election laws; the second model incorporates election administration; and the third, fourth, and fifth models include interactions between each of the election laws and election administration to determine if the on average quality of a state's election administration moderates the likelihood that campaigns will use these reform measures to contact prospective voters. As for key results, the baseline model shows that same day registration has a positive and significant effect on the probability that campaigns will contact voters. In fact, after controlling for EPI, the impact of same day registration on mobilization increases, indicating that a state's election administration works in tandem with same day registration to incentivize campaigns to contact prospective voters.

But are these findings substantively significant? To answer this, Figure 7.3 converts same day registration logistic results from Models 1 and 2 into predicted probabilities. The results reveal that same day registration improves an individual's prospects of being contacted by approximately 5%. The statistical significance of this substantive effect is only discernible after controlling for a state's election administration (EPI measure), demonstrating the

Table 7.3 Individual Likelihood of Being Contacted by a Campaign in 2010 and 2014 Midterm Elections, Varying Convenience Voting Laws and Election Performance Index

	Baseline	Election Reform Laws + EPI	Early Voting × EPI	Absentee/ Mail Voting × EPI	SDR × EPI
Early Voting	−0.066	−0.068	−0.567	−0.064	−0.069
	(0.101)	(0.100)	(0.346)	(0.100)	(0.099)
Absentee/Mail Voting	0.075	0.072	0.072	−0.161	0.075
	(0.099)	(0.099)	(0.095)	(0.312)	(0.099)
SDR	0.191**	0.202**	0.190**	0.197**	−0.215
	(0.081)	(0.086)	(0.082)	(0.084)	(0.350)
EPI		−0.002	−0.006	−0.004	−0.003
		(0.003)	(0.004)	(0.004)	(0.003)
Early Voting × EPI			0.007		
			(0.005)		
Absentee/Mail Voting × EPI				0.003	
				(0.004)	
SDR × EPI					0.006
					(0.005)
Pseudo R^2	0.173	0.173	0.174	0.173	0.173
N	111176	111176	111176	111176	111176

Note: Based on CCES data measuring voting behavior of eligible voters in the 2010 and 2014 elections. To conserve space, only the primary covariates are reported here. Full regression models are reported in Appendix Table C1.12. The estimates are unstandardized logistic regression coefficients. Robust standard errors in parentheses are clustered by state. Multilevel models reveal similar results. P-values are based on two-tailed tests.

$^*p < 0.10,\ ^{**}p < 0.05,\ ^{***}p < 0.001$.

importance of controlling for this factor when seeking to understand the impact of alternative voting laws.

Campaign Contact and Voting

After establishing that an alternative voting law (same day registration) shapes campaign targeting strategies directed at individuals among the general population in midterm elections, the next question is whether this translates into higher propensities of voting among those who were contacted. Table 7.4 reports the results from four logistic regression models: the first two examine how alternative voting laws and election administration impact turnout

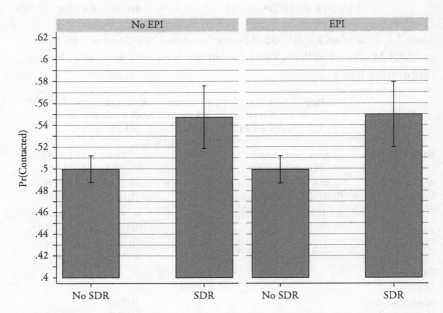

Figure 7.3. Probability of being contacted by a campaign in 2010 or 2014 midterm elections in states with and without same day registration, varying Election Performance Index.

Note: Bars on left report the probability of being contacted in 2010 or 2014 for Model 1 in Table 7.3 that does not include the EPI covariate. The bars on the right report the same relationship, but based on Model 2 that includes this covariate. All other variables held at mean values. Ninety percent confidence intervals included.

Table 7.4 Campaign Contact Effect on Voting in 2010 and 2014 Midterm Elections, Varying Convenience Voting Laws and Election Performance Index

	No Contact	No Contact + EPI	Contact	Contact + EPI
Early Voting	−0.036	−0.047	0.001	−0.001
	(0.108)	(0.104)	(0.104)	(0.105)
Absentee/Mail Voting	0.124	0.123	0.176**	0.163*
	(0.112)	(0.112)	(0.087)	(0.093)
SDR	0.083	0.111	0.091	0.127**
	(0.074)	(0.075)	(0.060)	(0.063)
EPI		−0.004		−0.006
		(0.003)		(0.004)
Pseudo R^2	0.144	0.144	0.110	0.110
N	51220	51220	59956	59956

Note: Based on CCES data measuring voting behavior of eligible voters in the 2010 and 2014 elections. To conserve space, only the primary covariates are reported here. Full regression models are reported in Appendix Table C1.13. The estimates are unstandardized logistic regression coefficients. Robust standard errors in parentheses are clustered by state. Multilevel models reveal similar results. *P*-values are based on two-tailed tests. Year fixed effects are also included.

* $p < 0.10$, ** $p < 0.05$, *** $p < 0.001$.

decisions among those who were not contacted, and the second two for those who were contacted. The first and third models are estimated without the control for election administration, while the second and fourth include this factor.

Among those who were not contacted (the first two models), neither alternative voting laws nor election administration significantly shapes an individual's likelihood of voting. In contrast, among those who were contacted (second two models), both no-excuse absentee/mail voting and same day registration have positive and significant impacts on voter turnout. The same day registration result, in fact, is only detectable after controlling for EPI in the fourth model, again showing the importance of controlling for a state's election administration to better understand the impact of these laws.

Do Accessible Elections Help Mobilization the Poor?

Presidential Election

Do alternative voting laws and election administration shape a campaign's likelihood of contacting poor people, a harder group to identify and mobilize? Individuals with a family income between $20,000 and $29,999 are defined as poor, consistent with the poverty threshold set by the U.S. Department of Health and Human Services. In Table 7.5, five logistic regression models are presented, following the same modeling strategy as in Chapter 4 (one baseline model, then a model with the election administration variable, followed by three models with interaction variables between each voting law and election administration). Of the election reform laws, only same day registration has a positive and significant effect on campaign contact of poor individuals. But this only persists without a control for election administration. After accounting for the overall performance of a state's election administration—which has a significant effect on increasing campaign contact—same day registration no longer has an independent effect on this outcome.

A state's election administration is a consistently positive predictor of campaign contact in these models. Additionally, in the latter three models, a state's election administration has a moderating influence on no-excuse absentee/mail's impact relating to mobilization of the poor. The significantly negative interaction effect in this case indicates that poor individuals are less

Table 7.5 Poor Person Likelihood of Being Contacted by a Campaign in 2012 Presidential Election, Varying Convenience Voting Laws and Election Performance Index (Subsample of the Poor)

	Baseline	Convenience Voting Laws + EPI	Early Voting × EPI	Absentee/ Mail Voting × EPI	SDR × EPI
Early Voting	0.118	0.146	0.754	0.135	0.145
	(0.108)	(0.108)	(0.742)	(0.100)	(0.108)
Absentee/Mail Voting	-0.072	-0.089	-0.086	1.069	-0.091
	(0.117)	(0.119)	(0.121)	(0.710)	(0.120)
SDR	0.251**	0.181	0.191	0.198	-0.353
	(0.120)	(0.125)	(0.128)	(0.129)	(1.233)
EPI		0.018**	0.023**	0.026***	0.018**
		(0.006)	(0.007)	(0.007)	(0.007)
Early Voting × EPI			-0.009		
			(0.011)		
Absentee/Mail Voting × EPI				-0.017*	
				(0.010)	
SDR × EPI					0.007
					(0.016)
Pseudo R^2	0.134	0.135	0.135	0.136	0.135
N	12262	12262	12262	12262	12262

Note: Based on CCES data measuring voting behavior of eligible voters in 2012 election. To conserve space, only the primary covariates are reported here. Full regression models are reported in Appendix Table C1.14. The estimates are unstandardized logistic regression coefficients. Robust standard errors in parentheses are clustered by state. Multilevel models reveal similar results. P-values are based on two-tailed tests.
* $p < 0.10$, ** $p < 0.05$, *** $p < 0.001$.

likely to be contacted in no-excuse absentee/mail voting states during presidential elections.

Together, these findings indicate that campaigns are more likely to make an effort to bring impoverished individuals into the active electorate when states have on average higher quality election administration, and same day registration, a law that is more likely to be used to cast a ballot by individuals—such as the poor—who tend to decide to vote later in an election period.

To make these results more understandable, Figure 7.4 converts the same day registration logistic regression results from Model 1 into predicted probabilities. Significantly, residing in a same day registration state substantively increases a poor person's probability of being mobilized by a campaign to vote by 6%.

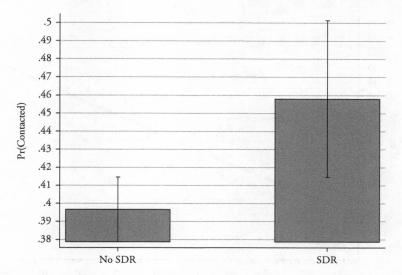

Figure 7.4. Probability of a poor person being contacted by a campaign in 2012 presidential election, varying same day registration.

Note: Line represents poor person's probability of being contacted in states with and without same day registration in 2012 for Model 1 in Table 7.5. All other variables held at mean values. Ninety percent confidence intervals included

Figure 7.5 translates the EPI logistic regression results from Model 2 to predicted probabilities to show how a state's election administration shapes a poor person's likelihood of being contacted by a campaign. Varying EPI from minimum to maximum values, poor individuals are 20% more likely to be targeted to vote in states with the most accessible election administrations, compared to their counterparts in states with the least accessible election administrations. For the poor, residing in a state with a more accessible election administration makes a meaningful difference in incentivizing campaigns to mobilize them to vote.

Midterm Elections

Following the same modeling technique used in Table 7.5, Table 7.6 uses logistic analyses applied to a subsample of the poor in the 2010 and 2014 midterm elections. Of the reform laws, the baseline model shows that only same day registration is significantly related to campaign contact directed at the

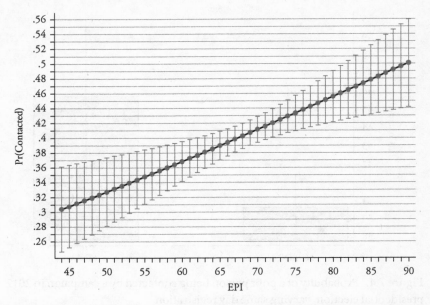

Figure 7.5. Probability of a poor person being contacted by a campaign in 2012 presidential election, varying Election Performance Index.

Note: Line represents poor person's probability of being contacted based on a state's EPI in 2012 for Model 2 in Table 7.5. All other variables held at mean values. Ninety percent confidence intervals included.

poor, and positively so. This effect holds after controlling for election administration quality in a state. In fact, the fifth model shows a significant and positive interaction effect between EPI and same day registration, illustrating that the poor are more likely to be contacted in same day registration states that have the most accessible election administrations.

Figure 7.6 converts the same day registration and EPI effects from model five into predicted probabilities. The intention is to show how same day registration's impact on mobilization is shaped by the overall quality of election administration throughout a state. Although at lower EPI values there is no discernible difference between non–same day registration and same day registration states in terms of campaign contact, when EPI reaches the value of 74 residing in a same day registration makes a poor individual significantly more likely to be contacted. Same day registration states with an EPI value at or above 74 in 2014 include Colorado, Connecticut, Maine, Maryland, Minnesota, Montana, North Dakota, and Wisconsin, while same day registration states with an EPI value below 74 include Idaho, Iowa, New

Table 7.6 Poor Person Likelihood of Being Contacted by a Campaign in 2010 and 2014 Midterm Elections, Varying Convenience Voting Laws and Election Performance Index (Subsample of the Poor)

	Baseline	Convenience Voting Laws + EPI	Early Voting × EPI	Absentee/ Mail Voting × EPI	SDR × EPI
Early Voting	−0.077	−0.081	−0.436	−0.083	−0.083
	(0.110)	(0.108)	(0.467)	(0.108)	(0.107)
Absentee/Mail Voting	0.085	0.081	0.081	0.185	0.088
	(0.114)	(0.114)	(0.112)	(0.390)	(0.114)
SDR	0.165*	0.185*	0.179**	0.186**	−0.720
	(0.093)	(0.094)	(0.091)	(0.095)	(0.456)
EPI		−0.003	−0.006	−0.003	−0.005
		(0.004)	(0.005)	(0.005)	(0.004)
Early Voting × EPI			0.005		
			(0.007)		
Absentee/Mail Voting × EPI				−0.002	
				(0.006)	
SDR × EPI					0.013**
					(0.006)
Pseudo R^2	0.155	0.155	0.155	0.155	0.156
N	22781	22781	22781	22781	22781

Note: Based on CCES data measuring voting behavior of eligible voters in the 2010 and 2014 elections. To conserve space, only the primary covariates are reported here. Full regression models are reported in Appendix Table C1.15. The estimates are logistic regression coefficients. The estimates are unstandardized logistic regression coefficients. Robust standard errors in parentheses are clustered by state. Multilevel models reveal similar results. P-values are based on two-tailed tests.

* $p < 0.10$, ** $p < 0.05$, *** $p < 0.001$.

Hampshire, and Wyoming. At the EPI values of 74 to 91, the difference in a poor person's likelihood of being contacted by a campaign in a same day registration relative to a non–same day registration state increases from 5% to 10%. Coupling a state's same day registration law with a highly accessible election administration maximizes the likelihood that a poor individual will be recruited by a campaign to vote in the 2010 or 2014 midterm elections.

Conclusion

The evidence shown in this chapter suggests that accessible elections—election reform laws and election administration—influence campaign

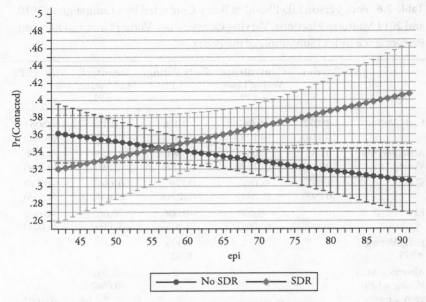

Figure 7.6. Probability of a poor person being contacted by a campaign in 2010 and 2014 midterm elections in states with and without same day registration, varying Election Performance Index.

Note: Lines report probabilities of being contacted in states with and without same day registration in 2010 or 2014 from Model 5 in Table 7.6. EPI varied from minimum to maximum values. All other variables held at mean values. Ninety percent confidence intervals included.

decisions to recruit more citizens to become voters. This is especially the case in presidential elections, when the impact of these factors on mobilization is coupled with high-stimulus election campaigns. Among alternative voting laws, no-excuse absentee/mail voting and same day registration structure campaign contact. Election administration is also a significant predictor of campaign contact in presidential elections. After controlling for campaign contact, in-person early voting (in presidential elections) and same day registration (in midterm elections) are related to a higher likelihood of voting, showing that the interaction of mobilization and liberalized voting laws produces higher turnout. States with same day registration (in presidential and midterm elections) and higher election administration performance (in presidential and midterm elections), also, are more likely to have campaigns that recruit poor persons to vote.

Tables 7.7 and 7.8 provide a summary of election reform laws with statistically significant effects on mobilization. This evidence is a response to

Table 7.7   Electoral Practices with Statistically Significant Effects on Mobilization

	Early Voting	Absentee/Mail Voting	Same Day Registration	Election Performance Index
2012 Presidential Election	✓ (+)	✓ (+)	✓ (+)	
2010/2014 Midterm Elections			✓ (+)	✓ (+)

Table 7.8   Electoral Practices with Statistically Significant Effects on Mobilization among the Poor

	Early Voting	Absentee/Mail Voting	Same Day Registration	Election Performance Index
2012 Presidential Election			✓ (+)	✓ (+)
2010/2014 Midterm Elections			✓ (+)	✓ (+)

prior election reform law research holding that these laws must be paired with mobilization strategies to have an effect on turnout (see Berinsky 2005; Gronke et al. 2008; Karp and Banducci 2001). Having an accessible election administration also promotes mobilization of eligible voters in presidential and midterm elections, and the poor in midterms. In sum, states with more accessible electoral rules motivate campaigns to recruit potential voters, and, in some cases, increase their likelihood of voting.

Hershey (2015) and Aldrich (2011) emphasize that campaigns and parties are endogenous to their political environments. This means that parties shape, and are shaped by, election laws. Schattschneider (1942), for example, writes that the "whole history of suffrage [expansion . . . is] intimately associated with parties." Parties promote suffrage expansions when doing so advantages them and disadvantages their opponents. In the late 1700s, the Jeffersonian Republicans removed the property requirements associated with voting to appeal to less affluent citizens, giving them a new constituency and a strategic asset relative to the Federalist Party. A century later, Republicans hoped to win the African American vote with the passage of the

Fifteenth Amendment. The Democratic Party, during the Lyndon Johnson administration, tried to do the same with the 1965 Voting Rights Act, facilitating the demise of literacy tests and poll taxes that barred racial minorities and impoverished citizens from access to the ballot (Springer 2014). The National Voter Registration Act (NVRA) in 1993, passed during the Bill Clinton administration, and blocked by his predecessor, George H. W. Bush, can be considered a law adopted to advantage population groups tending to support the Democratic Party (the same expected to be advantaged by the NVRA) (Keyssar 2009). With the proliferation of election reform laws over the past several decades, one can consider the expansion of election reform laws to be an attempt by political parties to widen their mobilization strategies and bring more citizens to the polls. Since the poor undervote, and parties can gain a strategic advantage by winning them to their side, a natural expectation is that these reform laws are used to mobilize this demographic.

This chapter's results have several implications. One, when considering the full impact of these laws, it is necessary to determine how these laws shape the mobilization strategies of political campaigns. These laws do not only have a direct impact on turnout but also have an indirect effect on turnout through the mechanism of campaign mobilization. Future research on election reform laws needs to control for the electoral context of a state to precisely estimate the impacts of these laws on mobilization and turnout. Distinguishing the influence of these laws in midterm and presidential elections is important since campaigns, parties, and other voter recruitment organizations invest more resources in mobilization during higher-salience presidential elections. Most importantly, the quality of how state governments administer elections often moderates the effects of the election reform laws on voter mobilization. Alternative voting laws and election administration are key factors in how frequently campaigns contact voters among the general population and even the poorest members of society.

8

Conclusion

How the States Can Help Americans Vote

While the scholarly research has generally downplayed the positive benefits of state election reform efforts in the realm of alternative voting laws—at least in their potential to significantly increase turnout or reduce the demographic biases in who votes—party activists and election reformers have continued to advocate for significant reforms of the U.S. election system. Do election reformers and campaigns know something the academics do not? Reforming state election systems not only protects state voter roll systems from hackers and election inference, a topic of growing salience, but may expand participation in elections. In the lead-up to the contested 2018 midterm elections, the first national elections since Donald Trump took office, more than 16 million registered voters were removed from state voter rolls (Robinson 2018). Now more than ever is a time to critically re-evaluate the components on state election systems—what works and what does not.

In the introduction we argued that state governments should make elections accessible, and thus it makes sense that political elites may seek to mobilize voters using these new laws. There is no reason to expect that ordinary citizens would be aware of changes to state election laws, so if we see behavior changing, other factors are likely the cause. This mechanism is analyzed in Chapter 7, finding that candidates, parties, and campaigns are more likely to mobilize and contact people in states with convenience voter laws. This is evidence that elites are playing a key role in making individuals aware of new voting laws and how they can participate. Change in political elite behavior after adoption of new voting laws can result in the mobilization of new voters. While convenience voting laws may make voting easier and less costly, we believe elite political mobilization is more important than simply reducing the costs of voting alone.

Election reformers in the states have had a number of important victories, as well as disappointing losses. Victories include the passage of automatic voter registration (AVR) in Oregon, California, and seventeen other states

Accessible Elections. Michael Ritter and Caroline J. Tolbert, Oxford University Press (2021). © Oxford University Press.
DOI: 10.1093/oso/9780197537251.001.0001.

as of 2020, while setbacks encompass voting restrictions—including voter ID laws and shortened early voting days and hours—passed in twenty-three states since 2010 (Brennan Center for Justice 2018; Weister and Feldman 2018). Despite the ups and downs of the legal battles over election reform adoption, this study sought to critically re-evaluate the effects of convenience voting laws on voter turnout, turnout among disadvantaged Americans, and voter mobilization. It did so by making some significant improvements in framing, data quality, and research design.

Because of data limitations, many previous studies lacked large enough samples of the population from each of the fifty states, and certainly large enough samples of citizens living at or below the federal poverty level for scientific study, as well as racial and ethnic minority groups.

Leveraging election data based on the voter rolls from all fifty states combined with government and commercial data, this study was able to hone in on the voting decisions of millions of Americans in both midterm and presidential elections. As the decision to vote (or not vote) is habitual (Plutzer 2002), studying vote histories over time sought to predict what factors were associated with citizens changing their decision of whether to vote in elections. Panel data with repeated observations for the same individuals provides a higher bar with which to make causal inferences than cross-sectional surveys that do not vary over time. While much of the previous research has focused on higher turnout presidential elections, the influence of accessible state election systems may be most important in lower turnout midterm elections. Both midterm and presidential elections are analyzed.

The research sought to measure the complex, dynamic nature of state election rules and practices in a more holistic fashion using the framework of accessible elections. Accessible elections are defined by state governments with high quality election administration (see Gerken 2009), as well as a core set of convenience voting laws that open balloting to the largest percent of the eligible voting population as possible. This includes scoring above average in election administration (including ballot design, sufficient polling places, polling hours, well-trained poll workers, counting ballots, and managing voter records). Citizens demand from their state governments the same type of service quality customers would expect from any solid business. This includes passing laws such as no- excuse absentee or all-mail voting, in-person early voting, and same day registration making registering to vote and casting a ballot easier. It is the combination of these laws and quality of election administration that may matter for voter turnout. The problem is that previous research has not measured election administration and state voting laws at the same time. We argue that election administration performance is a critical omitted factor in a long history of studying voter turnout in the U.S.

Using a myriad of empirical analyses, our results reveal that the quality of how well state governments administer elections is an important factor in predicting voter turnout in both presidential and midterm elections. This is a novel finding. The quality of overall election administration by state governments improves voter turnout of the general population and even the poorest, most disadvantaged citizens in lower turnout off-year elections. And while state voting and registration laws independently improve participation rates, uniquely the quality of election administration can also boost voter mobilization and the contacting of citizens by parties and campaigns. In nearly half of the empirical tests in this project, election administration performance was a statistically significant predictor of participation in recent U.S. elections. The use of panel data with repeated observations for the same individuals indicated that non-voters are more likely to become voters in states with improved administration of elections.

In combination with election administration, same day registration was found to be the single most important law in increasing participation rates of citizens. Same day registration laws were a statistically significant predictor of higher overall voter turnout rates in both presidential and midterm elections; more importantly, such laws reduce demographic biases in the electorate by significantly increasing the probability that poor people and racial and ethnic minorities will vote in elections. In both midterm and presidential elections, same day registration laws provide an incentive to parties and campaigns to contact voters and mobilize them to participate, including not only individuals in the general populace but poor individuals as well. Same day registration laws were a significant predictor of voter turnout in more than 60% of the empirical tests presented in this study. We conclude that all fifty states would benefit from improved election administration and the adoption of same day registration. The use of panel models shows that non-voters are more likely to convert to voters in states with same day registration laws.

Much of the scholarly literature has dismissed the other election reforms analyzed in this study as having only a modest effect on turnout, or in benefiting demographic groups already likely to vote (older, affluent, and educated people). But again, our study provides some different answers, especially when we control for state election administration. Early voting is one of those surprising findings. After controlling for election administration, early voting is found to be associated with higher voter turnout for the general population in midterm elections (Herron and Smith 2014; Herron and Smith 2012) and for African Americans and Hispanics in particular in midterm elections (see Chapters 4 and 6). Because so much of the existing research has focused on presidential elections exclusively, this finding may have been obscured.

Additionally, individuals are significantly more likely to cast ballots in early voting states after they have been contacted by a campaign or party, attesting to the importance of pairing this voting law with voter recruitment strategies to boost turnout. Because panel models are used throughout the study, the results show that non-voters are more likely to become voters in states with early voting laws. In midterm elections, early voting also is associated with more voter mobilization by campaigns. In almost 20% of the empirical tests, early voting was found to have a beneficial effect on voter turnout. This is a non-trivial effect.

Mail voting (no-excuse absentee voting/mail voting) also has beneficial effects, even if it is a less consistent predictor of increased political participation. In midterm elections, absentee/mail voting was found to increase turnout by individuals in the general populace.

Additionally, in presidential elections, absentee/mail voting was found to boost voting by poor people, as well as the probability that a poor person would convert from a non-voter to a voter. In midterm elections, the same laws had a significantly positive impact on voter turnout among Asian Americans. Regarding mobilization, in presidential elections, these laws are also significantly related to a higher probability of a citizen being contacted by a campaign or party to vote. While the beneficial effects were more limited, in nearly 20% of the empirical tests, absentee/mail voting was found to be a significant independent predictor of higher voter turnout.

In sum, no-excuse absentee/mail voting, early voting, same day registration, and a well-performing election administration can improve turnout and stimulate campaigns to recruit individuals to vote. The findings are robust to many alternative specifications and tests. For social scientists, the study highlights how the effects of state election reform laws can be better identified by controlling for election administration. While the poor and racial and ethnic minorities were a focus for this study, this framework can be expanded to focus on turnout of different demographic groups.

Simultaneously controlling for election administration and voting reform laws shows that election reform laws not only positively shape turnout, but also help turn non-voters into voters (Chapter 4). Chapter 5 illustrated that these positive effects are not limited to individuals in high-propensity voting groups, as suggested by past (Berinsky 2005; Gronke et al. 2008) and even more recent literature (Burden et al. 2014, 2017); rather, these laws can increase turnout among the poor, and even help them change from inactive to active voters, thereby fostering greater turnout parity in state voter turnout. This is also an update of Piven and Cloward's (1977) research findings; whereas these authors conclude that the poor engage in protests, strikes, and sit-ins in times of large-scale economic disruption, this research shows that mundane election reform laws can increase turnout among this demographic.

Chapter 6 found that a one-size-fits-all package of election reforms doesn't work; rather, different alternative voting laws tend to benefit different racial and ethnic groups, with home voting have the strongest effect for Asian Americans and early voting for African Americans and Hispanics, while all groups tend to benefit from same day registration. Accessible elections may help ameliorate the legacy of two-tiered pluralism (e.g., non-Hispanic white versus racial minority) present in American politics (Hero 1992).

Chapter 7 demonstrated, uniquely in the literature on voting reform laws, how these laws encourage campaigns, candidates, and parties to target voters (both low and higher socioeconomic status [SES]) and mobilize them to vote. These results held under alternative specifications of election administration performance. Building on recent research on convenience voting and election reform laws, this study recognizes that individual decisions to vote and the strategy of campaigns and parties are structured by state government laws as well as the administration of these laws.

In election reform research, Alvarez, Atkeson, and Hall (2013, 19–38) consider a state's "electoral ecosystem" or election administration to be an important structuring influence behind individual voting behavior. Election administration is found to be one of the most important factors in this study. States with more accessible electoral rules—represented by election reform laws and a highly performing election administration—have citizens who are more likely to vote and make use of these laws. The opposite likely occurs in states with less accessible electoral rules. Future research should evaluate how the accessibility of a state's voting system affects the working poor, a demographic group of interest in the realm of public policy.

Whereas the definition of "poor" in this study encompasses individuals at or below the federal poverty threshold, broadening the focus to include the working poor would raise the income threshold to 150% or 200% of the federal poverty line. A key expectation of the accessible elections framework is that states with more accessible electoral rules want their citizens to vote, including but not limited to the rich and poor, white and minority, and young and old.

While states with accessible electoral practices have poor citizens and racial and ethnic minorities who are more likely to partake in elections in part because the act of voting is encouraged by their government, future studies could examine how other disadvantaged demographic groups (the young, low educated, veterans, immigrants, and others) are impacted by the overall accessibility of a state's voting system. Testing the effects of accessible electoral rules on these other demographic groups would be valuable.

Other election reform laws can be examined within the accessible electoral systems framework. Waldman (2016, 200), chair of the Brennan Center for Justice, notes that as of 2016 "nineteen states had passed twenty-five bills making it harder to vote," including shortened early voting window laws in a few states, restraints imposed on same day registration in North Carolina, and adoption of strict photo ID laws in many others (also see Brennan Center for Justice 2016). While the effects of photo ID laws are mixed (see Hicks, McKee, and Smith 2016, 413), the other two policy changes have depressed turnout among some groups such as African Americans (see Herron and Smith 2014). A 7.1% decline in African American turnout from 66.7% in 2012 to 59.6% in 2016, as reported by the Brookings Institution, suggests that these restrictive voting laws have had an impact (Frey 2017). Building on this recent research, upcoming work could examine how these restrictive voting laws impact the overall accessibility of a state's electoral practices, and how this impacts turnout among disadvantaged voting groups.

A new frontier for election reform is the impact of automatic voter registration (AVR) laws in the U.S. What began in Oregon as AVR in 2016 has spread across the states, expanding motor voter laws (1993) that allowed people to register to vote when getting a driver's license. Prior research has found young people and low-educated people are more likely to vote because of same day registration laws, and this study finds that poor people and minorities benefit from same-day registration. AVR is an extension of same day registration. According to the National Conference of State Legislatures (2020), eighteen states and the District of Columbia have this new election reform measure, making voter registration "opt-out" instead of "opt-in." This law involves the government registering or updating the registration information of eligible citizens to vote based upon pre-existing citizen identification data from government agencies, such as the state Department of Motor Vehicles, rather than citizens registering themselves, and provided citizens do not decline this option. This electoral arrangement is more typical of European democracies, which also tend to have higher turnout. Accessible voting laws continue to change the composition of state electorates by increasing voting rates of disadvantage groups—racial and ethnic minorities, young, and poor—and we anticipate AVR possibly having a similar effect on political participation.

For policy activists and political actors interested in increasing turnout and access to the ballot, this study shows when and how state voting laws can work. The summary tables at the end of each chapter show that a myriad of factors are associated with more accessible state election systems. We hope the results reported here offer hope in the ability of state governments to expand participation in democratic elections more equally. Election administration in combination with state voting reform laws, especially same day registration and early voting, defines accessible election practices for citizens. If they choose to, state governments can help Americans vote.

APPENDIX A

Summary Statistics

Table A1.1 Convenience Voting Laws and Election Performance Index in the American States

State	Year	Election Performance Index	No-Excuse Absentee/ Mail Voting	Early Voting	Same Day Registration
Alabama	2006	0.41	0	0	0
	2008	0.41	0	0	0
	2010	0.47	0	0	0
	2012	0.57	0	0	0
	2014	0.49	0	0	0
	2016	0.66	0	0	0
	2018	0.66	0	0	0
Alaska	2006	0.71	1	1	0
	2008	0.71	1	1	1
	2010	0.64	1	1	0
	2012	0.72	1	1	1
	2014	0.66	1	1	0
	2016	0.78	1	1	1
	2018	0.78	1	1	0
Arizona	2006	0.62	1	0	0
	2008	0.62	1	0	1
	2010	0.60	1	0	0
	2012	0.66	1	0	1
	2014	0.64	1	0	0
	2016	0.71	1	0	1
	2018	0.71	1	0	0
Arkansas	2006	0.56	0	1	0
	2008	0.56	0	1	0
	2010	0.63	0	1	0
	2012	0.63	0	1	0

Continued

Table A1.1 *Continued*

State	Year	Election Performance Index	No-Excuse Absentee/ Mail Voting	Early Voting	Same Day Registration
	2014	0.59	0	1	0
	2016	0.65	0	1	0
	2018	0.65	0	1	0
California	2006	0.52	1	1	0
	2008	0.52	1	1	0
	2010	0.43	1	1	0
	2012	0.55	1	1	0
	2014	0.54	1	1	0
	2016	0.62	1	1	0
	2018	0.62	1	1	1
Colorado	2006	0.69	1	1	0
	2008	0.69	1	1	0
	2010	0.75	1	1	0
	2012	0.79	1	1	0
	2014	0.80	1	1	1
	2016	0.76	1	1	1
	2018	0.76	1	1	1
Connecticut	2006	0.67	0	0	1
	2008	0.67	0	0	1
	2010	0.74	0	0	1
	2012	0.76	0	0	1
	2014	0.81	0	0	1
	2016	0.80	0	0	1
	2018	0.80	0	0	1
Delaware	2006	0.72	0	0	0
	2008	0.72	0	0	0
	2010	0.75	0	0	0
	2012	0.75	0	0	0
	2014	0.80	0	0	0
	2016	0.84	0	0	0
	2018	0.84	0	0	0
Florida	2006	0.68	1	1	0

Table A1.1 *Continued*

State	Year	Election Performance Index	No-Excuse Absentee/ Mail Voting	Early Voting	Same Day Registration
	2008	0.68	1	1	0
	2010	0.66	1	1	0
	2012	0.70	1	1	0
	2014	0.67	1	1	0
	2016	0.73	1	1	0
	2018	0.73	1	1	0
Georgia	2006	0.75	0	1	0
	2008	0.75	1	1	0
	2010	0.65	1	1	0
	2012	0.68	1	1	0
	2014	0.67	1	1	0
	2016	0.72	1	1	0
	2018	0.72	1	1	0
Hawaii	2006	0.69	1	1	0
	2008	0.69	1	1	0
	2010	0.60	1	1	0
	2012	0.66	1	1	0
	2014	0.59	1	1	0
	2016	0.69	1	1	0
	2018	0.69	1	1	0
Idaho	2006	0.58	1	1	1
	2008	0.58	1	1	1
	2010	0.50	1	1	1
	2012	0.60	1	1	1
	2014	0.57	1	1	1
	2016	0.58	1	1	1
	2018	0.58	1	1	1
Illinois	2006	0.62	0	1	0
	2008	0.62	0	1	0
	2010	0.59	0	1	0
	2012	0.72	1	1	0

Continued

Table A1.1 *Continued*

State	Year	Election Performance Index	No-Excuse Absentee/ Mail Voting	Early Voting	Same Day Registration
	2014	0.73	1	1	0
	2016	0.81	1	1	1
	2018	0.81	1	1	1
Indiana	2006	0.55	0	1	0
	2008	0.55	0	1	0
	2010	0.62	0	1	0
	2012	0.69	0	1	0
	2014	0.66	0	1	0
	2016	0.75	0	1	0
	2018	0.75	0	1	0
Iowa	2006	0.73	1	1	0
	2008	0.73	1	1	1
	2010	0.68	1	1	1
	2012	0.72	1	1	1
	2014	0.71	1	1	1
	2016	0.79	1	1	1
	2018	0.79	1	1	1
Kansas	2006	0.58	1	1	0
	2008	0.58	1	1	0
	2010	0.63	1	1	0
	2012	0.62	1	1	0
	2014	0.63	1	1	0
	2016	0.64	1	1	0
	2018	0.64	1	1	0
Kentucky	2006	0.63	0	0	0
	2008	0.63	0	0	0
	2010	0.64	0	0	0
	2012	0.65	0	0	0
	2014	0.60	0	0	0
	2016	0.67	0	0	0
	2018	0.67	0	0	0
Louisiana	2006	0.66	0	1	0
	2008	0.66	0	1	0

Table A1.1 *Continued*

State	Year	Election Performance Index	No-Excuse Absentee/ Mail Voting	Early Voting	Same Day Registration
	2010	0.67	0	1	0
	2012	0.72	0	1	0
	2014	0.65	0	1	0
	2016	0.76	0	1	0
	2018	0.76	0	1	0
Maine	2006	0.66	1	1	1
	2008	0.66	1	1	1
	2010	0.72	1	1	1
	2012	0.69	1	1	1
	2014	0.75	1	1	1
	2016	0.71	1	1	1
	2018	0.71	1	1	1
Maryland	2006	0.69	0	0	0
	2008	0.69	0	0	0
	2010	0.67	0	1	0
	2012	0.77	0	1	0
	2014	0.77	0	1	1
	2016	0.77	0	1	1
	2018	0.77	0	1	1
Massachusetts	2006	0.61	0	0	0
	2008	0.61	0	0	0
	2010	0.62	0	0	0
	2012	0.71	0	0	0
	2014	0.69	0	0	0
	2016	0.81	0	0	0
	2018	0.81	0	0	0
Michigan	2006	0.72	1	1	0
	2008	0.72	1	1	0
	2010	0.72	1	1	0
	2012	0.77	1	1	0
	2014	0.76	1	1	0

Continued

Table A1.1 *Continued*

State	Year	Election Performance Index	No-Excuse Absentee/ Mail Voting	Early Voting	Same Day Registration
	2016	0.76	1	1	0
	2018	0.76	1	1	0
Minnesota	2006	0.75	1	1	1
	2008	0.75	1	1	1
	2010	0.77	1	1	1
	2012	0.79	1	1	1
	2014	0.83	1	1	1
	2016	0.84	1	1	1
	2018	0.84	1	1	1
Mississippi	2006	0.39	0	0	0
	2008	0.39	0	0	0
	2010	0.42	0	0	0
	2012	0.44	0	0	0
	2014	0.59	0	0	0
	2016	0.67	0	0	0
	2018	0.67	0	0	0
Missouri	2006	0.73	0	0	0
	2008	0.73	0	0	0
	2010	0.68	0	0	0
	2012	0.74	0	0	0
	2014	0.78	0	0	0
	2016	0.79	0	0	0
	2018	0.79	0	0	0
Montana	2006	0.63	1	1	1
	2008	0.63	1	1	1
	2010	0.71	1	1	1
	2012	0.74	1	1	1
	2014	0.75	1	1	1
	2016	0.75	1	1	1
	2018	0.75	1	1	1
Nebraska	2006	0.70	1	1	0
	2008	0.70	1	1	0
	2010	0.59	1	1	0

Table A1.1 *Continued*

State	Year	Election Performance Index	No-Excuse Absentee/ Mail Voting	Early Voting	Same Day Registration
	2012	0.74	1	1	0
	2014	0.73	1	1	0
	2016	0.80	1	1	0
	2018	0.80	1	1	0
Nevada	2006	0.68	1	1	0
	2008	0.68	1	1	0
	2010	0.69	1	1	0
	2012	0.80	1	1	0
	2014	0.74	1	1	0
	2016	0.82	1	1	0
	2018	0.82	1	1	0
New Hampshire	2006	0.59	0	0	1
	2008	0.59	0	0	1
	2010	0.61	0	0	1
	2012	0.69	0	0	1
	2014	0.66	0	0	1
	2016	0.72	0	0	1
	2018	0.72	0	0	1
New Jersey	2006	0.64	1	1	0
	2008	0.64	1	1	0
	2010	0.60	1	1	0
	2012	0.64	1	1	0
	2014	0.62	1	1	0
	2016	0.69	1	1	0
	2018	0.69	1	1	0
New Mexico	2006	0.70	1	1	0
	2008	0.70	1	1	0
	2010	0.69	1	1	0
	2012	0.74	1	1	0
	2014	0.63	1	1	0
	2016	0.74	1	1	0

Continued

Table A1.1 *Continued*

State	Year	Election Performance Index	No-Excuse Absentee/ Mail Voting	Early Voting	Same Day Registration
	2018	0.74	1	1	0
New York	2006	0.58	0	0	0
	2008	0.58	0	0	0
	2010	0.46	0	0	0
	2012	0.60	0	0	0
	2014	0.61	0	0	0
	2016	0.68	0	0	0
	2018	0.68	0	0	0
North Carolina	2006	0.67	1	1	0
	2008	0.67	1	1	1
	2010	0.67	1	1	1
	2012	0.77	1	1	1
	2014	0.69	1	1	1
	2016	0.74	1	1	1
	2018	0.74	1	1	1
North Dakota	2006	0.87	1	1	1
	2008	0.87	1	1	1
	2010	0.91	1	1	1
	2012	0.90	1	1	1
	2014	0.84	1	1	1
	2016	0.83	1	1	1
	2018	0.83	1	1	1
Ohio	2006	0.59	1	1	0
	2008	0.59	1	1	0
	2010	0.63	1	1	1
	2012	0.70	1	1	1
	2014	0.71	1	1	0
	2016	0.77	1	1	0
	2018	0.77	1	1	0
Oklahoma	2006	0.57	1	1	0
	2008	0.57	1	1	0
	2010	0.51	1	1	0

Table A1.1 *Continued*

State	Year	Election Performance Index	No-Excuse Absentee/ Mail Voting	Early Voting	Same Day Registration
	2012	0.56	1	1	0
	2014	0.57	1	1	0
	2016	0.60	1	1	0
	2018	0.60	1	1	0
Oregon	2006	0.58	1	1	0
	2008	0.58	1	1	0
	2010	0.71	1	1	0
	2012	0.71	1	1	0
	2014	0.77	1	1	0
	2016	0.72	1	1	0
	2018	0.72	1	1	0
Pennsylvania	2006	0.67	0	0	0
	2008	0.67	0	0	0
	2010	0.65	0	0	0
	2012	0.74	0	0	0
	2014	0.70	0	0	0
	2016	0.80	0	0	0
	2018	0.80	0	0	0
Rhode Island	2006	0.65	0	0	0
	2008	0.65	0	0	1
	2010	0.65	0	0	0
	2012	0.67	0	0	1
	2014	0.65	0	0	0
	2016	0.74	0	0	1
	2018	0.74	0	0	0
South Carolina	2006	0.57	0	0	0
	2008	0.57	0	0	0
	2010	0.57	0	0	0
	2012	0.67	0	0	0
	2014	0.74	0	0	0
	2016	0.79	0	0	0

Continued

Table A1.1 *Continued*

State	Year	Election Performance Index	No-Excuse Absentee/ Mail Voting	Early Voting	Same Day Registration
	2018	0.79	0	0	0
South Dakota	2006	0.68	1	1	0
	2008	0.68	1	1	0
	2010	0.70	1	1	0
	2012	0.70	1	1	0
	2014	0.71	1	1	0
	2016	0.67	1	1	0
	2018	0.67	1	1	0
Tennessee	2006	0.65	0	1	0
	2008	0.65	0	1	0
	2010	0.69	0	1	0
	2012	0.70	0	1	0
	2014	0.64	0	1	0
	2016	0.68	0	1	0
	2018	0.68	0	1	0
Texas	2006	0.66	0	1	0
	2008	0.66	0	1	0
	2010	0.68	0	1	0
	2012	0.65	0	1	0
	2014	0.60	0	1	0
	2016	0.69	0	1	0
	2018	0.69	0	1	0
Utah	2006	0.59	1	1	0
	2008	0.59	1	1	0
	2010	0.70	1	1	0
	2012	0.72	1	1	0
	2014	0.64	1	1	0
	2016	0.70	1	1	0
	2018	0.70	1	1	0
Vermont	2006	0.68	1	1	0
	2008	0.68	1	1	0
	2010	0.61	1	1	0
	2012	0.64	1	1	0

Table A1.1 *Continued*

State	Year	Election Performance Index	No-Excuse Absentee/ Mail Voting	Early Voting	Same Day Registration
	2014	0.74	1	1	0
	2016	0.86	1	1	0
	2018	0.86	1	1	1
Virginia	2006	0.65	0	0	0
	2008	0.65	0	0	0
	2010	0.71	0	0	0
	2012	0.71	0	0	0
	2014	0.82	0	0	0
	2016	0.79	0	0	0
	2018	0.79	0	0	0
Washington	2006	0.72	1	0	0
	2008	0.72	1	0	0
	2010	0.69	1	0	0
	2012	0.73	1	0	0
	2014	0.71	1	0	0
	2016	0.77	1	0	0
	2018	0.77	1	0	0
West Virginia	2006	0.55	0	1	0
	2008	0.55	0	1	0
	2010	0.57	0	1	0
	2012	0.65	0	1	0
	2014	0.68	0	1	0
	2016	0.77	0	1	0
	2018	0.77	0	1	0
Wisconsin	2006	0.80	1	1	1
	2008	0.80	1	1	1
	2010	0.74	1	1	1
	2012	0.79	1	1	1
	2014	0.82	1	1	1
	2016	0.84	1	1	1
	2018	0.84	1	1	1

Continued

Table A1.1 *Continued*

State	Year	Election Performance Index	No-Excuse Absentee/ Mail Voting	Early Voting	Same Day Registration
Wyoming	2006	0.62	1	1	1
	2008	0.62	1	1	1
	2010	0.62	1	1	1
	2012	0.68	1	1	1
	2014	0.61	1	1	1
	2016	0.73	1	1	1
	2018	0.73	1	1	0

Source: State election reform laws data from National Conference of State Legislatures (2018a, 2018b) and Larocca and Klemanski (2011). EPI data available from MIT Election Data and Science Lab (2016) and Pew Charitable Trusts (2016) from 2008 to 2016; EPI for year 2018 duplication of EPI of year 2016.

Note: Only states that implemented laws as of 2018 are included in this table. Alaska and Rhode Island have same day registration in presidential but not midterm elections.

Control Variable Coding

<u>Catalist</u>: Vote margin (candidate's margin of victory over nearest competitor in a presidential election; or closest senatorial, gubernatorial, or average of House of Representative's contests in a state in a midterm election); Number of Ballot Initiatives (count measure in election year); Male (male = 1; female = 0); Age (continuous variable ranging from 17–99); Length of Residence (continuous variable measuring number of years individual has resided at a home); Education (propensity score measure of an individual's likelihood of having a college degree); non-Hispanic White (non-Hispanic White = 1; other = 0); African American (African American = 1; other = 0); Hispanic (Hispanic = 1; other = 0); Asian (Asian = 1; other = 0); Other Race (Other Race = 1; other = 0); Partisan (Republican or Democrat = 1; other = 0); News Interest (propensity score measure of an individual's likelihood of having a subscription to a news publication); Home Ownership (propensity score measure of an individual's likelihood of owning a home); Employed (employed = 1; other = 0. Based on a series of propensity score measures examining an individual's likelihood of being employed in one of several professions—manual labor, professional work, executive work, and home-based work. Individuals with over 50% probability of being employed are listed as such).

<u>CCES</u>: Vote margin (candidate's margin of victory over nearest competitor in a presidential election; or closest senatorial, gubernatorial, or average of House of Representative's contests in a state in a midterm election); Number of Ballot Initiatives (count measure in election year); Male (male = 1; female = 0); Age (continuous variable); Length of Residence (less than month = 0; two to six months = 1; seven to eleven months = 2; one to two years = 3; three to four years = 4; five or more years = 5); Education (no high school degree = 0; high school degree = 1; some college = 2; two-year college degree = 3; four-year college degree = 4; post-graduate education = 5); non-Hispanic White (non-Hispanic White = 1; other = 0); African American (African American = 1; other = 0); Hispanic (Hispanic = 1; other = 0); Asian (Asian = 1; other = 0); Other Race (Other Race = 1; other = 0); Strong Partisan (Strong Republican or Democrat = 1; other = 0); Political Interest (no interest = 0; sporadic interest = 1; more steady interest = 2; interest most of time = 3); Home Ownership (own home = 1; other = 0); Employed (employed full or part time = 1; other = 0).

APPENDIX C

Full Data Tables

Chapter 4

Midterm Elections

Table C1.1 Effects of Convenience Voting Laws on Changing Probability of Voting from 2010 to 2014, Varying Election Performance Index (Lagged Panel Models)

	Election Reform Laws	Election Reform Laws + EPI	In-Person Early Voting × EPI	No-Excuse Absentee/ Mail Voting × EPI	Same Day Registration × EPI
Vote 2010	2.05***	2.05***	2.05***	2.05***	2.05***
	(0.072)	(0.070)	(0.069)	(0.068)	(0.069)
In-Person Early Voting	0.10	0.19*	−0.60	0.15	0.20*
	(0.112)	(0.106)	(0.616)	(0.096)	(0.108)
Absentee/Mail Voting	−0.07	−0.11	−0.12	−1.51**	−0.12
	(0.108)	(0.093)	(0.093)	(0.477)	(0.091)
SDR	0.43***	0.28**	0.23*	0.20*	1.38*
	(0.119)	(0.122)	(0.122)	(0.119)	(0.716)
EPI		0.01**	0.01	0.03×10^{-1}	0.02**
		(0.005)	(0.007)	(0.006)	(0.005)
Early Voting × EPI			0.01		
			(0.009)		
Absentee/Mail Voting × EPI				0.02**	
				(0.007)	
SDR × EPI					−0.01
					(0.010)
State Vote Margin	0.01***	0.01***	0.01***	0.01***	0.01***
	(0.003)	(0.002)	(0.002)	(0.002)	(0.002)
Number of Ballot Initiatives	0.03*	0.04***	0.04***	0.05***	0.04***
	(0.017)	(0.012)	(0.011)	(0.010)	(0.012)
Household Income	0.00	0.00	0.00	0.00	0.00
	(0.004)	(0.004)	(0.004)	(0.004)	(0.004)
Missing Income	−0.31***	−0.31***	−0.31***	−0.31***	−0.31***
	(0.071)	(0.069)	(0.068)	(0.066)	(0.070)

Continued

Table C1.1 *Continued*

	Election Reform Laws	Election Reform Laws + EPI	In-Person Early Voting × EPI	No-Excuse Absentee/ Mail Voting × EPI	Same Day Registration × EPI
Male	0.01[*]	0.01[*]	0.01	0.01	0.01
	(0.008)	(0.008)	(0.008)	(0.008)	(0.008)
Age	0.01[***]	0.01[***]	0.01[***]	0.01[***]	0.01[***]
	(0.002)	(0.002)	(0.002)	(0.002)	(0.002)
Education	1.54[***]	1.57[***]	1.58[***]	1.59[***]	1.58[***]
	(0.080)	(0.085)	(0.088)	(0.086)	(0.087)
Black	−0.01	−0.01	−0.02	−0.02	−0.01
	(0.050)	(0.052)	(0.051)	(0.052)	(0.052)
Hispanic	−0.36[***]	−0.31[***]	−0.29[***]	−0.29[***]	−0.31[***]
	(0.035)	(0.031)	(0.031)	(0.027)	(0.031)
Asian	−0.46[***]	−0.42[***]	−0.40[***]	−0.39[***]	−0.41[***]
	(0.070)	(0.077)	(0.080)	(0.076)	(0.077)
Other Race	−0.41[***]	−0.39[***]	−0.39[***]	−0.38[***]	−0.39[***]
	(0.087)	(0.085)	(0.084)	(0.084)	(0.085)
Partisan	0.18[**]	0.24[***]	0.24[***]	0.26[***]	0.24[***]
	(0.065)	(0.064)	(0.063)	(0.062)	(0.064)
News Interest	0.15[***]	0.15[***]	0.15[***]	0.15[***]	0.15[***]
	(0.016)	(0.016)	(0.016)	(0.016)	(0.016)
Length of Residence	0.01[***]	0.01[***]	0.01[***]	0.01[***]	0.01[***]
	(0.002)	(0.001)	(0.001)	(0.002)	(0.001)
Employed	−0.17[***]	−0.17[***]	−0.17[***]	−0.17[***]	−0.17[***]
	(0.011)	(0.011)	(0.011)	(0.011)	(0.012)
Home Ownership	0.34[***]	0.33[***]	0.33[***]	0.33[***]	0.32[***]
	(0.034)	(0.033)	(0.035)	(0.037)	(0.033)
Constant	−4.43[***]	−5.23[***]	−4.78[***]	−4.46[***]	−5.34[***]
	(0.258)	(0.397)	(0.523)	(0.484)	(0.433)
Pseudo R^2	0.267	0.268	0.268	0.269	0.268
N	2,321,466	2,321,466	2,321,466	2,321,466	2,321,466

Note: Based on Catalist data (2016) measuring voting behavior of same eligible voters in the 2010 and 2014 elections. The Vote 2010 variable is included to control for turnout in past election. The estimates are unstandardized logistic regression coefficients. Robust standard errors in parentheses are clustered by state. Multilevel models reveal similar results. *P*-values are based on two-tailed tests.

[*] $p < 0.10$, [**] $p < 0.05$, [***] $p < 0.001$.

Presidential Election

Table C1.2 Effects of Convenience Voting Laws on Changing Probability of Voting from 2008 to 2014, Varying Election Performance Index (EPI) (Lagged Panel Models)

	Election Reform Laws	Election Reform Laws + EPI	In-Person Early Voting × EPI	No-Excuse Absentee/Mail Voting × EPI	Same Day Registration × EPI
Vote 2008	1.88***	1.88***	1.88***	1.88***	1.88***
	(0.071)	(0.071)	(0.070)	(0.071)	(0.071)
Early Voting	0.02	0.04	0.43	0.03	0.04
	(0.096)	(0.090)	(0.653)	(0.090)	(0.091)
Absentee/ Mail Voting	−0.05	−0.06	−0.06	0.47	−0.06
	(0.093)	(0.093)	(0.095)	(0.694)	(0.092)
SDR	0.41***	0.38***	0.39***	0.39***	−0.98
	(0.113)	(0.112)	(0.107)	(0.105)	(1.183)
EPI		0.00	0.01	0.01	0.04×10^{-1}
		(0.006)	(0.009)	(0.009)	(0.006)
Early Voting × EPI			−0.01		
			(0.010)		
Absentee/ Mail Voting × EPI				−0.01	
				(0.010)	
SDR × EPI					0.02
					(0.016)
State Vote Margin	0.00	0.00	0.00	0.00	0.00
	(0.004)	(0.004)	(0.004)	(0.004)	(0.004)
Number of Ballot Initiatives	0.02*	0.02*	0.02	0.01	0.02*
	(0.009)	(0.011)	(0.010)	(0.010)	(0.010)
Household Income	0.01**	0.01**	0.01**	0.01**	0.01**
	(0.004)	(0.004)	(0.004)	(0.004)	(0.004)
Missing Income	−0.76***	−0.76***	−0.76***	−0.76***	−0.76***
	(0.096)	(0.095)	(0.096)	(0.095)	(0.095)
Male	−0.08***	−0.08***	−0.08***	−0.08***	−0.08***
	(0.011)	(0.011)	(0.011)	(0.011)	(0.011)
Age	0.01***	0.01***	0.01***	0.01***	0.01***
	(0.001)	(0.001)	(0.001)	(0.001)	(0.001)
Education	1.63***	1.63***	1.63***	1.62***	1.62***
	(0.084)	(0.085)	(0.086)	(0.084)	(0.085)
Black	0.21***	0.21***	0.22***	0.22***	0.21***
	(0.039)	(0.039)	(0.043)	(0.041)	(0.040)
Hispanic	−0.02	−0.01	−0.02	−0.02	−0.02
	(0.048)	(0.045)	(0.045)	(0.043)	(0.045)

Continued

Table C1.2 *Continued*

	Election Reform Laws	Election Reform Laws + EPI	In-Person Early Voting × EPI	No-Excuse Absentee/Mail Voting × EPI	Same Day Registration × EPI
Asian	−0.35***	−0.34***	−0.34***	−0.35***	−0.34***
	(0.039)	(0.041)	(0.041)	(0.040)	(0.041)
Other Race	−0.09	−0.10	−0.10	−0.10	−0.10
	(0.143)	(0.142)	(0.141)	(0.141)	(0.142)
Partisan	0.24***	0.25***	0.25***	0.24***	0.25***
	(0.058)	(0.057)	(0.052)	(0.058)	(0.057)
News Interest	0.19***	0.19***	0.19***	0.19***	0.19***
	(0.015)	(0.015)	(0.015)	(0.016)	(0.015)
Length of Residence	−0.00	−0.00	−0.00	−0.00	−0.00
	(0.002)	(0.002)	(0.002)	(0.002)	(0.002)
Employed	−0.18***	−0.18***	−0.18***	−0.18***	−0.18***
	(0.024)	(0.024)	(0.024)	(0.024)	(0.024)
Home Ownership	0.28***	0.28***	0.28***	0.28***	0.28***
	(0.018)	(0.018)	(0.018)	(0.018)	(0.018)
Constant	−1.94***	−2.09***	−2.34***	−2.35***	−2.02***
	(0.325)	(0.393)	(0.565)	(0.530)	(0.405)
Pseudo R^2	0.248	0.248	0.248	0.248	0.248
N	2,218,389	2,218,389	2,218,389	2,218,389	2,218,389

Note: Based on Catalist data (2016) measuring voting behavior of same eligible voters in the 2008 and 2012 elections. Vote 2008 variable is included to control for turnout in past election. The estimates are unstandardized logistic regression coefficients. Robust standard errors in parentheses are clustered by state. Multilevel models reveal similar results. *P*-values are based on two-tailed tests.

* $p < 0.10$, ** $p < 0.05$, *** $p < 0.001$.

Chapter 5

Midterm Elections

Table C1.3 Effects of Convenience Voting Laws and Election Performance Index on Change in Probability of Voting among the Poor from 2010 to 2014, Varying Election Performance Index (EPI) (Lagged Panel Models)

	Baseline	EPI
Vote 2010	1.98***	1.99***
	(0.069)	(0.068)
Early Voting	0.08	0.11
	(0.085)	(0.089)
Absentee/Mail Voting	0.02	0.01
	(0.074)	(0.072)

Table C1.3 *Continued*

	Baseline	EPI
SDR	0.30**	0.25*
	(0.140)	(0.141)
EPI		0.05×10^{-1}
		(0.004)
Household Income		
State Vote Margin	0.01***	0.01***
	(0.002)	(0.002)
Number of Ballot Initiatives	0.03**	0.04***
	(0.011)	(0.010)
Male	−0.06***	−0.06***
	(0.019)	(0.019)
Age	0.01***	0.01***
	(0.002)	(0.002)
Education	2.95***	2.96***
	(0.131)	(0.133)
Black	0.18***	0.18***
	(0.045)	(0.046)
Hispanic	−0.20***	−0.18***
	(0.037)	(0.037)
Asian	−0.16	−0.14
	(0.129)	(0.134)
Other Race	−0.12*	−0.12*
	(0.070)	(0.070)
Partisan	0.24**	0.26***
	(0.077)	(0.074)
News Interest	0.14***	0.15***
	(0.022)	(0.022)
Length of Residence	0.01**	0.01***
	(0.002)	(0.002)
Employed	−0.21***	−0.21***
	(0.016)	(0.016)
Home Ownership	0.28***	0.28***
	(0.031)	(0.030)
Constant	−4.72***	−4.96***
	(0.221)	(0.379)
Pseudo R^2	0.231	0.231
N	312,232	312,232

Note: Based on Catalist data (2016) measuring voting behavior of same eligible voters in the 2010 and 2014 elections. The Vote 2010 variable is included to control for turnout in past election. The estimates are unstandardized logistic regression coefficients. Robust standard errors in parentheses are clustered by state. Multilevel models reveal similar results. *P*-values are based on two-tailed tests.

* $p < 0.10$, ** $p < 0.05$, *** $p < 0.001$.

Table C1.4 Effects of Election Reform Laws on Changing Probability of Voting among the Poor from 2008 to 2012, Varying Election Administration Performance (Lagged Panel Model; Catalist)

	Baseline	EPI
Vote 2008	1.63***	1.63***
	(0.055)	(0.055)
Early Voting	−0.09	−0.11
	(0.078)	(0.068)
Absentee/Mail Voting	0.20**	0.21***
	(0.069)	(0.061)
SDR	0.37***	0.42***
	(0.085)	(0.092)
EPI		−0.01*
		(0.006)
State Vote Margin	−0.00	0.00
	(0.004)	(0.003)
Number of Ballot Initiatives	0.01	0.01
	(0.010)	(0.009)
Missing Income		
Male	−0.15***	−0.15***
	(0.017)	(0.017)
Age	0.01***	0.01***
	(0.001)	(0.001)
Education	2.54***	2.55***
	(0.095)	(0.092)
Black	0.41***	0.40***
	(0.034)	(0.034)
Hispanic	0.11**	0.09
	(0.052)	(0.055)
Asian	−0.11**	−0.14**
	(0.055)	(0.057)
Other Race	−0.00	−0.00
	(0.058)	(0.059)
Partisan	0.27***	0.27***
	(0.059)	(0.054)
News Interest	0.19***	0.19***
	(0.020)	(0.020)
Length of Residence	−0.00	−0.00
	(0.001)	(0.002)
Employed	−0.15***	−0.16***
	(0.023)	(0.022)
Home Ownership	0.29***	0.29***
	(0.030)	(0.030)

Table C1.4 *Continued*

	Baseline	EPI
Constant	−2.02***	−1.74***
	(0.287)	(0.353)
Pseudo R^2	0.163	0.163
N	296,178	296,178

Note: Based on Catalist data (2016) measuring voting behavior of same eligible voters in the 2008 and 2012 elections. The Vote 2008 variable is included to control for turnout in past election. The estimates are unstandardized logistic regression coefficients. Robust standard errors in parentheses are clustered by state. Multilevel models reveal similar results. *P*-values are based on two-tailed tests.
* $p < 0.10$, ** $p < 0.05$, *** $p < 0.001$.

Chapter 6

Table C1.5 Effects of Convenience Voting Laws on Changing Probability of Voting from 2010 to 2014, Varying Election Administration Performance (Catalist)

	Non-Hispanic White Subsample Model		Ethnic/Racial Minority Subsample Model	
Vote 2010	2.08***	2.08***	1.98***	1.98***
	(0.063)	(0.060)	(0.105)	(0.104)
Early Voting	0.06	0.16	0.24*	0.33**
	(0.112)	(0.107)	(0.135)	(0.135)
Absentee/Mail Voting	−0.05	−0.10	−0.20	−0.21**
	(0.109)	(0.097)	(0.128)	(0.084)
SDR	0.48***	0.34**	0.17	−0.03
	(0.107)	(0.106)	(0.136)	(0.164)
EPI		0.01***		0.02**
		(0.004)		(0.007)
State Vote Margin	0.01***	0.01***	0.02***	0.02***
	(0.003)	(0.002)	(0.005)	(0.003)
Number of Ballot Initiatives	0.03*	0.04***	0.03	0.04**
	(0.017)	(0.012)	(0.021)	(0.014)
Household Income	0.01	0.01*	−0.02***	−0.02***
	(0.004)	(0.003)	(0.004)	(0.004)
Missing Income	−0.30***	−0.30***	−0.39***	−0.39***
	(0.082)	(0.079)	(0.052)	(0.053)
Male	0.05***	0.05***	−0.12***	−0.12***
	(0.008)	(0.008)	(0.025)	(0.026)
Age	0.01***	0.01***	0.01***	0.01***
	(0.002)	(0.002)	(0.002)	(0.002)
Education	1.39***	1.42***	2.03***	2.04***
	(0.082)	(0.084)	(0.099)	(0.102)

Continued

Table C1.5 *Continued*

	Non-Hispanic White Subsample Model		Ethnic/Racial Minority Subsample Model	
Partisan	0.20**	0.26***	0.16**	0.22**
	(0.067)	(0.065)	(0.074)	(0.081)
News Interest	0.15***	0.15***	0.14***	0.14***
	(0.016)	(0.015)	(0.024)	(0.024)
Length of Residence	0.00***	0.00***	0.01**	0.01***
	(0.001)	(0.001)	(0.002)	(0.002)
Employed	−0.18***	−0.18***	−0.19***	−0.18***
	(0.014)	(0.014)	(0.018)	(0.017)
Home Ownership	0.34***	0.33***	0.35***	0.33***
	(0.032)	(0.032)	(0.047)	(0.046)
Constant	−4.25***	−5.11***	−5.47***	−6.15***
	(0.239)	(0.380)	(0.454)	(0.585)
Pseudo R^2	0.266	0.267	0.234	0.235
N	1,706,970	1,706,970	614,496	614,496

Note: The estimates are unstandardized logistic regression coefficients. Robust standard errors in parentheses are clustered by state. Multilevel models reveal similar results. *P*-values are based on two-tailed tests.

* $p < 0.10$, ** $p < 0.05$, *** $p < 0.001$.

Table C1.6 Effects of Convenience Voting Laws on Changing Probability of Voting from 2008 to 2012, Varying Election Administration Performance (Catalist)

	Non-Hispanic White Subsample Models			Ethnic/Racial Minority Subsample Models		
Vote 2008	1.95***	1.95***	1.96***	1.72***	1.72***	1.72***
	(0.060)	(0.060)	(0.061)	(0.089)	(0.089)	(0.089)
Early Voting	0.03	0.06		−0.01	−0.01	
	(0.101)	(0.091)		(0.132)	(0.128)	
Absentee/ Mail Voting	−0.09	−0.10		0.03	0.03	
	(0.104)	(0.099)		(0.102)	(0.104)	
SDR	0.43***	0.39***		0.24**	0.25**	
	(0.113)	(0.110)		(0.096)	(0.096)	
EPI		0.01			−0.00	
		(0.006)			(0.007)	
COVI			−0.21***			−0.12*
			(0.053)			(0.070)
State Vote Margin	0.00	−0.00	0.01**	0.00	0.00	0.01**
	(0.004)	(0.004)	(0.004)	(0.004)	(0.005)	(0.004)
Number of Ballot Initiatives	0.02*	0.02*	−0.00	0.01	0.01	−0.00
	(0.010)	(0.011)	(0.008)	(0.010)	(0.012)	(0.008)

Table C1.6 *Continued*

	Non-Hispanic White Subsample Models			Ethnic/Racial Minority Subsample Models		
Household Income	0.02***	0.02***	0.02***	−0.01*	−0.01*	−0.01*
	(0.004)	(0.004)	(0.004)	(0.004)	(0.004)	(0.004)
Missing Income	−0.73***	−0.74***	−0.75***	−0.85***	−0.85***	−0.85***
	(0.109)	(0.106)	(0.107)	(0.095)	(0.095)	(0.095)
Male	−0.02	−0.02	−0.02	−0.24***	−0.24***	−0.24***
	(0.011)	(0.011)	(0.011)	(0.023)	(0.023)	(0.023)
Age	0.01***	0.01***	0.01***	0.00	0.00	0.00
	(0.001)	(0.001)	(0.001)	(0.001)	(0.001)	(0.001)
Education	1.60***	1.60***	1.54***	1.53***	1.53***	1.52***
	(0.087)	(0.088)	(0.086)	(0.096)	(0.098)	(0.096)
Partisan	0.23***	0.24***	0.20***	0.30***	0.30***	0.29***
	(0.062)	(0.060)	(0.057)	(0.065)	(0.065)	(0.055)
News Interest	0.20***	0.20***	0.20***	0.13***	0.13***	0.13***
	(0.015)	(0.015)	(0.017)	(0.019)	(0.019)	(0.020)
Length of Residence	−0.00	−0.00	−0.00	−0.00	−0.00	−0.00
	(0.002)	(0.002)	(0.002)	(0.003)	(0.003)	(0.003)
Employed	−0.21***	−0.21***	−0.20***	−0.13***	−0.13***	−0.13***
	(0.027)	(0.027)	(0.026)	(0.023)	(0.022)	(0.023)
Home Ownership	0.28***	0.28***	0.30***	0.31***	0.31***	0.31***
	(0.020)	(0.019)	(0.021)	(0.027)	(0.027)	(0.030)
Constant	−2.09***	−2.36***	−2.37***	−1.57***	−1.56***	−1.86***
	(0.364)	(0.426)	(0.314)	(0.278)	(0.333)	(0.299)
Pseudo R^2	0.261	0.261	0.261	0.201	0.201	0.201
N	1,642,177	1,642,177	1,642,177	576,212	576,212	576,212

Note: The estimates are unstandardized logistic regression coefficients. Robust standard errors in parentheses are clustered by state. Multilevel models reveal similar results. P-values are based on two-tailed tests.

* $p < 0.10$, ** $p < 0.05$, *** $p < 0.001$.

Table C1.7 Effects of Convenience Voting Laws on Changing Probability of Voting from 2010 to 2014, Varying Election Administration Performance (Catalist)

	Non-Hispanic White Subsample Models		African American Subsample Models		Hispanic Subsample Models		Asian Subsample Models	
Vote 2008	2.08*** (0.063)	2.08*** (0.060)	2.07*** (0.045)	2.07*** (0.045)	1.77*** (0.126)	1.77*** (0.126)	1.93*** (0.101)	1.93*** (0.102)
Early Voting	0.06 (0.112)	0.16 (0.107)	0.32* (0.135)	0.35* (0.151)	0.19 (0.157)	0.30* (0.135)	-0.01 (0.093)	0.10 (0.126)
Absentee/ Mail Voting	-0.05 (0.109)	-0.10 (0.097)	-0.23 (0.138)	-0.23* (0.123)	-0.06 (0.124)	-0.13 (0.110)	0.20* (0.091)	0.15* (0.079)
SDR	0.48*** (0.107)	0.34** (0.106)	0.00 (0.158)	-0.10 (0.185)	0.39*** (0.117)	0.23* (0.122)	0.28 (0.203)	0.17 (0.215)
EPI		0.01** (0.004)		0.01 (0.009)		0.02** (0.005)		0.01 (0.007)
State Vote Margin	0.01*** (0.003)	0.01*** (0.002)	0.02*** (0.005)	0.02*** (0.004)	0.02*** (0.004)	0.01*** (0.003)	0.02*** (0.004)	0.01** (0.004)
Number of Ballot Initiatives	0.03* (0.017)	0.04*** (0.012)	0.04** (0.017)	0.04** (0.013)	0.02* (0.013)	0.05** (0.015)	0.04** (0.014)	0.06** (0.019)
Household Income	0.01 (0.004)	0.01* (0.003)	-0.01* (0.004)	-0.01** (0.004)	-0.01* (0.004)	-0.01* (0.005)	-0.02** (0.008)	-0.02* (0.009)
Missing Income	-0.30*** (0.082)	-0.30*** (0.079)	-0.41*** (0.068)	-0.41*** (0.069)	-0.25*** (0.059)	-0.26*** (0.057)	-0.41*** (0.080)	-0.42*** (0.079)
Male	0.05*** (0.008)	0.05*** (0.008)	-0.21*** (0.018)	-0.21*** (0.018)	-0.02 (0.018)	-0.02 (0.018)	-0.03* (0.016)	-0.03* (0.015)
Age	0.01*** (0.002)	0.01*** (0.002)	0.01*** (0.001)	0.01*** (0.001)	0.02*** (0.002)	0.02*** (0.002)	0.02*** (0.002)	0.02*** (0.002)

Education	1.39***	1.42***	2.33***	2.34***	2.31***	2.30***	1.77***	1.76***
	(0.082)	(0.084)	(0.149)	(0.151)	(0.088)	(0.087)	(0.184)	(0.187)
Partisan	0.20**	0.26***	0.15	0.19*	0.16**	0.20***	0.12*	0.15**
	(0.067)	(0.065)	(0.101)	(0.109)	(0.055)	(0.060)	(0.065)	(0.066)
News Interest	0.15***	0.15***	0.16***	0.16***	0.11***	0.11***	0.07*	0.07*
	(0.016)	(0.015)	(0.021)	(0.022)	(0.018)	(0.018)	(0.039)	(0.038)
Length of Residence	0.00***	0.00***	0.01**	0.01**	0.01***	0.01***	0.00**	0.01**
	(0.001)	(0.001)	(0.002)	(0.002)	(0.002)	(0.002)	(0.002)	(0.002)
Employed	-0.18***	-0.18***	-0.16***	-0.16***	-0.17***	-0.17***	-0.19***	-0.18***
	(0.014)	(0.014)	(0.027)	(0.025)	(0.012)	(0.012)	(0.040)	(0.039)
Home Ownership	0.34***	0.33***	0.42***	0.41***	0.25***	0.24***	0.22***	0.21***
	(0.032)	(0.032)	(0.036)	(0.040)	(0.037)	(0.029)	(0.043)	(0.039)
Constant	-4.25***	-5.11***	-5.53***	-5.93***	-5.50***	-6.12***	-4.93***	-5.44***
	(0.239)	(0.380)	(0.468)	(0.726)	(0.375)	(0.417)	(0.419)	(0.660)
Pseudo R^2	0.266	0.267	0.266	0.267	0.208	0.208	0.212	0.212
N	1,706,970	1,706,970	302,701	302,701	228,336	228,336	65,201	65,201

Note: The estimates are unstandardized logistic regression coefficients. Robust standard errors in parentheses are clustered by state. Multilevel models reveal similar results. *P*-values are based on two-tailed tests.

* $p < 0.10$, ** $p < 0.05$, *** $p < 0.001$.

Table C1.8 Effects of Convenience Voting Laws on Changing Probability of Voting from 2008 to 2012, Varying Election Administration Performance and COVI (Catalist)

	Non–Hispanic White Subsample Models			African American Subsample Models		
Vote 2008	1.95*** (0.060)	1.95*** (0.060)	1.96*** (0.061)	1.82*** (0.054)	1.82*** (0.054)	1.82*** (0.054)
Early Voting	0.03 (0.101)	0.06 (0.091)		0.02 (0.125)	0.03 (0.125)	
Absentee/Mail Voting	−0.09 (0.104)	−0.10 (0.099)		0.02 (0.074)	0.02 (0.079)	
SDR	0.43*** (0.113)	0.39*** (0.110)		0.17* (0.102)	0.20** (0.102)	
EPI		0.01 (0.006)			−0.01 (0.008)	
COVI			−0.21*** (0.053)			−0.10 (0.067)
State Vote Margin	0.00 (0.004)	−0.00 (0.004)	0.01** (0.004)	0.00 (0.005)	0.00 (0.005)	0.01 (0.004)
Number of Ballot Initiatives	0.02* (0.010)	0.02* (0.011)	−0.00 (0.008)	−0.00 (0.012)	−0.00 (0.012)	−0.00 (0.010)
Household Income	0.02*** (0.004)	0.02*** (0.004)	0.02*** (0.004)	0.00 (0.005)	0.00 (0.005)	0.00 (0.005)
Missing Income	−0.73*** (0.109)	−0.74*** (0.106)	−0.75*** (0.107)	−0.89*** (0.100)	−0.89*** (0.101)	−0.90*** (0.102)
Male	−0.02 (0.011)	−0.02 (0.011)	−0.02 (0.011)	−0.31*** (0.022)	−0.31*** (0.022)	−0.31*** (0.022)

	(1)	(2)	(3)	(4)	(5)	(6)
Age	0.01***	0.01***	0.01***	-0.00	-0.00	-0.00
	(0.001)	(0.001)	(0.001)	(0.001)	(0.001)	(0.001)
Education	1.60***	1.60***	1.54***	1.71***	1.71***	1.71***
	(0.087)	(0.088)	(0.086)	(0.128)	(0.130)	(0.144)
Partisan	0.23***	0.24***	0.20***	0.29***	0.29***	0.28***
	(0.062)	(0.060)	(0.057)	(0.090)	(0.089)	(0.078)
News Interest	0.20***	0.20***	0.20***	0.14***	0.14***	0.14***
	(0.015)	(0.015)	(0.017)	(0.026)	(0.025)	(0.027)
Length of Residence	-0.00	-0.00	-0.00	-0.00	-0.00*	-0.00
	(0.002)	(0.002)	(0.002)	(0.002)	(0.002)	(0.002)
Employed	-0.21***	-0.21***	-0.20***	-0.15***	-0.15***	-0.14***
	(0.027)	(0.027)	(0.026)	(0.025)	(0.024)	(0.025)
Home Ownership	0.28***	0.28***	0.30***	0.37***	0.37***	0.38***
	(0.020)	(0.019)	(0.021)	(0.036)	(0.036)	(0.036)
Constant	-2.09***	-2.36***	-2.37***	-1.25***	-1.04*	-1.46***
	(0.364)	(0.426)	(0.314)	(0.340)	(0.434)	(0.306)
Pseudo R^2	0.261	0.261	0.261	0.226	0.226	0.226
N	1,642,177	1,642,177	1,642,177	287,459	287,459	287,459

Note: The estimates are unstandardized logistic regression coefficients. Robust standard errors in parentheses are clustered by state. Multilevel models reveal similar results. *P*-values are based on two-tailed tests.

* $p < 0.10$, ** $p < 0.05$, *** $p < 0.001$.

Table C1.9 Effects of Convenience Voting Laws on Changing Probability of Voting from 2008 to 2012, Varying Election Performance Index and COVI (Catalist)

	Hispanic Subsample Models			Asian Subsample Models		
Vote 2008	1.55*** (0.114)	1.55*** (0.114)	1.54*** (0.113)	1.54*** (0.061)	1.55*** (0.062)	1.55*** (0.064)
Early Voting Law	−0.02 (0.103)	0.05 (0.110)		−0.14 (0.115)	−0.02 (0.114)	
Absentee/Mail Voting Law	−0.00 (0.099)	−0.06 (0.104)		0.10 (0.134)	−0.00 (0.115)	
SDR Law	0.38** (0.145)	0.35** (0.145)		0.45** (0.158)	0.39** (0.138)	
EPI		0.01 (0.007)			0.02** (0.009)	
COVI			−0.26*** (0.060)			−0.17* (0.098)
State Vote Margin	−0.00 (0.004)	−0.01 (0.005)	0.01** (0.003)	0.00 (0.007)	−0.01 (0.009)	0.01 (0.008)
Number of Ballot Initiatives	0.03*** (0.007)	0.03*** (0.009)	0.01* (0.005)	0.02** (0.012)	0.04*** (0.012)	0.01 (0.010)
Household Income	−0.00 (0.004)	−0.00 (0.005)	−0.00 (0.004)	−0.01 (0.009)	−0.01 (0.009)	−0.01 (0.009)
Missing Income	−0.68*** (0.119)	−0.68*** (0.116)	−0.70*** (0.116)	−0.75*** (0.090)	−0.76*** (0.090)	−0.76*** (0.087)
Male	−0.18*** (0.010)	−0.19*** (0.010)	−0.18*** (0.010)	−0.11*** (0.026)	−0.10*** (0.026)	−0.10*** (0.025)
Age	0.00*** (0.001)	0.00*** (0.001)	0.01*** (0.001)	0.01*** (0.001)	0.01*** (0.001)	0.01*** (0.001)
Education	1.98*** (0.111)	1.96*** (0.115)	1.99*** (0.111)	1.63*** (0.150)	1.61*** (0.162)	1.60*** (0.159)
Partisan	0.31*** (0.056)	0.31*** (0.056)	0.29*** (0.043)	0.22*** (0.059)	0.24*** (0.049)	0.21*** (0.062)
News Interest	0.09*** (0.025)	0.09*** (0.025)	0.09** (0.026)	0.10*** (0.024)	0.10*** (0.024)	0.10*** (0.024)
Length of Residence	0.00 (0.003)	0.00 (0.003)	0.00 (0.003)	0.00 (0.003)	0.00 (0.003)	0.00 (0.003)
Employed	−0.06*** (0.018)	−0.07*** (0.019)	−0.07*** (0.020)	−0.14*** (0.025)	−0.13*** (0.025)	−0.15*** (0.026)
Home Ownership	0.27*** (0.022)	0.26*** (0.023)	0.27*** (0.023)	0.24*** (0.030)	0.24*** (0.033)	0.24*** (0.031)
Constant	−1.75*** (0.285)	−1.90*** (0.326)	−2.35*** (0.238)	−2.00*** (0.597)	−2.51*** (0.464)	−2.35** (0.716)

Table C1.9 *Continued*

	Hispanic Subsample Models			Asian Subsample Models		
Pseudo R^2	0.188	0.188	0.189	0.171	0.172	0.170
N	210,760	210,760	210,760	60,700	60,700	60,700

Note: The estimates are unstandardized logistic regression coefficients. Robust standard errors in parentheses are clustered by state. Multilevel models reveal similar results. *P*-values are based on two-tailed tests.

$^*p < 0.10,$ $^{**}p < 0.05,$ $^{***}p < 0.001.$

Chapter 7

Table C1.10 Individual Likelihood of Being Contacted by a Campaign in 2012 Presidential Election, Varying Convenience Voting Laws and Election Performance Index (EPI) (CCES)

	Baseline	Convenience Voting Laws + EPI	Early Voting × EPI	Absentee/ Mail Voting × EPI	SDR × EPI
Early Voting	−0.106	−0.080	0.342	−0.096	−0.080
	(0.131)	(0.132)	(0.815)	(0.121)	(0.132)
Absentee/Mail Voting	0.096	0.078	0.081	1.406*	0.077
	(0.140)	(0.140)	(0.142)	(0.733)	(0.140)
SDR	0.276**	0.226**	0.230**	0.237*	0.070
	(0.107)	(0.109)	(0.114)	(0.121)	(1.227)
EPI		0.014*	0.017**	0.023**	0.013*
		(0.007)	(0.008)	(0.008)	(0.007)
Early Voting × EPI			−0.006		
			(0.012)		
Absentee/Mail Voting × EPI				−0.019*	
				(0.010)	
SDR × EPI					0.002
					(0.017)
Vote Margin	0.018***	0.013**	0.013**	0.013***	0.013**
	(0.004)	(0.004)	(0.004)	(0.004)	(0.004)
Number of Ballot Initiatives	0.012	0.018	0.016	0.011	0.018
	(0.011)	(0.012)	(0.012)	(0.012)	(0.013)
Household Income	0.067***	0.068***	0.067***	0.067***	0.068***
	(0.007)	(0.007)	(0.007)	(0.007)	(0.007)
Missing Income	0.490***	0.492***	0.491***	0.486***	0.492***
	(0.059)	(0.058)	(0.059)	(0.059)	(0.057)
Male	−0.098**	−0.098**	−0.098**	−0.098**	−0.098**
	(0.031)	(0.031)	(0.031)	(0.031)	(0.031)

Continued

Table C1.10 *Continued*

	Baseline	Convenience Voting Laws + EPI	Early Voting × EPI	Absentee/ Mail Voting × EPI	SDR × EPI
Age	0.028***	0.028***	0.028***	0.028***	0.028***
	(0.001)	(0.001)	(0.001)	(0.001)	(0.001)
Education	0.188***	0.188***	0.188***	0.188***	0.188***
	(0.012)	(0.012)	(0.012)	(0.012)	(0.012)
Black	−0.883***	−0.874***	−0.870***	−0.861***	−0.874***
	(0.065)	(0.063)	(0.068)	(0.067)	(0.063)
Hispanic	−0.711***	−0.686***	−0.688***	−0.686***	−0.686***
	(0.069)	(0.068)	(0.066)	(0.066)	(0.068)
Asian	−0.693***	−0.671***	−0.676***	−0.687***	−0.672***
	(0.145)	(0.149)	(0.143)	(0.142)	(0.148)
Other Race	−0.031	−0.029	−0.030	−0.035	−0.029
	(0.087)	(0.084)	(0.084)	(0.084)	(0.084)
Strong Partisan	0.207***	0.211***	0.212***	0.214***	0.211***
	(0.038)	(0.039)	(0.039)	(0.039)	(0.039)
Political Interest	0.384***	0.384***	0.384***	0.384***	0.384***
	(0.022)	(0.022)	(0.022)	(0.022)	(0.022)
Length of Residence	0.119***	0.121***	0.121***	0.120***	0.121***
	(0.012)	(0.012)	(0.012)	(0.012)	(0.012)
Employed	−0.075**	−0.079**	−0.079**	−0.079**	−0.079**
	(0.037)	(0.036)	(0.037)	(0.037)	(0.036)
Home Ownership	0.129**	0.123**	0.124**	0.128**	0.123**
	(0.044)	(0.043)	(0.043)	(0.042)	(0.043)
Constant	−4.655***	−5.206***	−5.458***	−5.882***	−5.192***
	(0.336)	(0.506)	(0.620)	(0.635)	(0.542)
Pseudo R^2	0.161	0.162	0.162	0.163	0.162
N	54,426	54,426	54,426	54,426	54,426

Note: Based on CCES data measuring voting behavior of eligible voters in 2012 election. The estimates are unstandardized logistic regression coefficients. Robust standard errors in parentheses are clustered by state. Multilevel models reveal similar results. *P*-values are based on two-tailed tests.
* $p < 0.10$, ** $p < 0.05$, *** $p < 0.001$.

Table C1.11 Campaign Contact Effect on Voting in 2012 Presidential Election, Varying Convenience Voting Laws and Election Performance Index (EPI) (CCES)

	No Contact	No Contact + EPI	Contact	Contact + EPI
Early Voting	−0.077	−0.086	0.176**	0.188**
	(0.082)	(0.085)	(0.075)	(0.073)
Absentee/Mail Voting	−0.031	−0.022	−0.050	−0.057
	(0.091)	(0.094)	(0.091)	(0.088)
SDR	−0.210**	−0.190**	−0.056	−0.073
	(0.084)	(0.088)	(0.101)	(0.102)

Table C1.11 *Continued*

	No Contact	No Contact + EPI	Contact	Contact + EPI
EPI		-0.005		0.005
		(0.005)		(0.004)
Vote Margin	-0.002	0.000	0.004	0.002
	(0.003)	(0.003)	(0.003)	(0.003)
Number of Ballot Initiatives	0.007	0.005	-0.002	0.001
	(0.006)	(0.007)	(0.007)	(0.008)
Household Income	0.000	0.000	0.007	0.008
	(0.010)	(0.010)	(0.008)	(0.008)
Missing Income	-0.262**	-0.262**	-0.273**	-0.272**
	(0.104)	(0.103)	(0.083)	(0.083)
Male	-0.155***	-0.155***	-0.052	-0.051
	(0.045)	(0.045)	(0.043)	(0.043)
Age	0.013***	0.013***	0.012***	0.012***
	(0.002)	(0.002)	(0.002)	(0.002)
Education	0.159***	0.159***	0.189***	0.189***
	(0.018)	(0.018)	(0.021)	(0.021)
Black	-0.957***	-0.959***	-0.047	-0.041
	(0.080)	(0.080)	(0.096)	(0.096)
Hispanic	-0.839***	-0.850***	-0.213*	-0.205*
	(0.064)	(0.064)	(0.109)	(0.110)
Asian	-0.468***	-0.477***	-0.526**	-0.517**
	(0.142)	(0.142)	(0.171)	(0.174)
Other Race	-0.421**	-0.424**	-0.148	-0.148
	(0.176)	(0.176)	(0.103)	(0.102)
Strong Partisan	0.276***	0.274***	0.401***	0.401***
	(0.048)	(0.047)	(0.036)	(0.036)
Political Interest	0.174***	0.174***	0.294***	0.295***
	(0.027)	(0.027)	(0.026)	(0.026)
Length of Residence	0.086***	0.085***	0.049**	0.049**
	(0.016)	(0.016)	(0.020)	(0.020)
Employed	0.086	0.086	-0.063	-0.066
	(0.056)	(0.056)	(0.061)	(0.062)
Home Ownership	0.068	0.070	0.169**	0.168**
	(0.058)	(0.058)	(0.054)	(0.054)
Constant	-1.324***	-1.110***	-1.020***	-1.221***
	(0.256)	(0.312)	(0.215)	(0.250)
Pseudo R^2	0.072	0.072	0.054	0.054
N	22,770	22,770	31,656	31,656

Note: Based on CCES data measuring voting behavior of eligible voters in the 2012 election. The estimates are unstandardized logistic regression coefficients. Robust standard errors in parentheses are clustered by state. Multilevel models reveal similar results. P-values are based on two-tailed tests.
* $p < 0.10$, ** $p < 0.05$, *** $p < 0.001$.

Table C1.12 Individual Likelihood of Being Contacted by a Campaign in 2010 and 2014 Midterm Elections, Varying Convenience Voting Laws and Election Performance Index (EPI) (CCES)

	Baseline	Election Reform Laws + EPI	Early Voting × EPI	Absentee/ Mail Voting × EPI	SDR × EPI
Early Voting	−0.066 (0.101)	−0.068 (0.100)	−0.567 (0.346)	−0.064 (0.100)	−0.069 (0.099)
Absentee/Mail Voting	0.075 (0.099)	0.072 (0.099)	0.072 (0.095)	−0.161 (0.312)	0.075 (0.099)
SDR	0.191** (0.081)	0.202** (0.086)	0.190** (0.082)	0.197** (0.084)	−0.215 (0.350)
EPI		−0.002 (0.003)	−0.006 (0.004)	−0.004 (0.004)	−0.003 (0.003)
Early Voting × EPI			0.007 (0.005)		
Absentee/Mail Voting × EPI				0.003 (0.004)	
SDR × EPI					0.006 (0.005)
Vote Margin	0.007** (0.003)	0.008** (0.003)	0.008** (0.003)	0.008** (0.003)	0.008** (0.003)
Number of Ballot Initiatives	0.015 (0.009)	0.014 (0.010)	0.017* (0.010)	0.015 (0.010)	0.013 (0.010)
Household Income	0.066*** (0.005)	0.066*** (0.005)	0.066*** (0.005)	0.066*** (0.005)	0.065*** (0.005)
Missing Income	0.486*** (0.043)	0.484*** (0.043)	0.485*** (0.043)	0.485*** (0.043)	0.482*** (0.044)
Male	−0.055** (0.023)	−0.055** (0.023)	−0.055** (0.022)	−0.055** (0.023)	−0.055** (0.023)
Age	0.026*** (0.001)	0.026*** (0.001)	0.026*** (0.001)	0.026*** (0.001)	0.026*** (0.001)
Education	0.176*** (0.008)	0.176*** (0.008)	0.175*** (0.008)	0.176*** (0.008)	0.175*** (0.008)
Black	−0.260*** (0.043)	−0.261*** (0.043)	−0.262*** (0.044)	−0.261*** (0.043)	−0.261*** (0.043)
Hispanic	−0.465*** (0.032)	−0.471*** (0.033)	−0.464*** (0.034)	−0.468*** (0.033)	−0.473*** (0.033)
Asian	−0.478*** (0.065)	−0.485*** (0.066)	−0.477*** (0.065)	−0.480*** (0.065)	−0.488*** (0.067)
Other Race	0.038 (0.046)	0.036 (0.045)	0.040 (0.045)	0.038 (0.045)	0.036 (0.045)
Strong Partisan	0.295*** (0.030)	0.295*** (0.030)	0.295*** (0.030)	0.295*** (0.030)	0.295*** (0.030)

Table C1.12 *Continued*

	Baseline	Election Reform Laws + EPI	Early Voting × EPI	Absentee/ Mail Voting × EPI	SDR × EPI
Political Interest	0.465***	0.464***	0.465***	0.465***	0.465***
	(0.012)	(0.011)	(0.012)	(0.011)	(0.011)
Length of Residence	0.140***	0.140***	0.140***	0.140***	0.140***
	(0.009)	(0.009)	(0.009)	(0.009)	(0.009)
Employed	−0.113***	−0.113***	−0.113***	−0.113***	−0.113***
	(0.026)	(0.026)	(0.026)	(0.026)	(0.026)
Home Ownership	0.298***	0.300***	0.298***	0.299***	0.301***
	(0.031)	(0.031)	(0.031)	(0.031)	(0.031)
Constant	−4.202***	−4.106***	−3.885***	−4.011***	−4.057***
	(0.254)	(0.286)	(0.275)	(0.305)	(0.282)
Pseudo R^2	0.173	0.173	0.174	0.173	0.173
N	111,176	111,176	111,176	111,176	111,176

Note: Based on CCES data measuring voting behavior of eligible voters in the 2010 and 2014 elections. The estimates are unstandardized logistic regression coefficients. Robust standard errors in parentheses are clustered by state. Multilevel models reveal similar results. *P*-values are based on two-tailed tests.

* $p < 0.10$, ** $p < 0.05$, *** $p < 0.001$.

Table C1.13 Campaign Contact Effect on Voting in 2010 and 2014 Midterm Elections, Varying Convenience Voting Laws and Election Performance Index (CCES)

	No Contact	No Contact + EPI	Contact	Contact + EPI
Early Voting	−0.036	−0.047	0.001	−0.001
	(0.108)	(0.104)	(0.104)	(0.105)
Absentee/Mail Voting	0.124	0.123	0.176**	0.163*
	(0.112)	(0.112)	(0.087)	(0.093)
SDR	0.083	0.111	0.091	0.127**
	(0.074)	(0.075)	(0.060)	(0.063)
EPI		−0.004		−0.006
		(0.003)		(0.004)
Vote Margin	0.006**	0.007**	0.010**	0.011**
	(0.003)	(0.003)	(0.004)	(0.004)
Number of Ballot Initiatives	0.024**	0.021*	0.008	0.006
	(0.012)	(0.012)	(0.010)	(0.010)
Household Income	−0.007	−0.008	0.030***	0.029**
	(0.007)	(0.007)	(0.009)	(0.009)
Missing Income	−0.210***	−0.213***	0.016	0.011
	(0.057)	(0.056)	(0.081)	(0.081)

Continued

Table C1.13 *Continued*

	No Contact	No Contact + EPI	Contact	Contact + EPI
Male	0.066**	0.066**	0.177***	0.177***
	(0.031)	(0.031)	(0.027)	(0.027)
Age	0.022***	0.022***	0.022***	0.022***
	(0.001)	(0.001)	(0.001)	(0.001)
Education	0.163***	0.163***	0.110***	0.110***
	(0.012)	(0.012)	(0.014)	(0.014)
Black	−0.478***	−0.480***	−0.433***	−0.436***
	(0.070)	(0.070)	(0.057)	(0.058)
Hispanic	−0.503***	−0.518***	−0.308***	−0.328***
	(0.077)	(0.077)	(0.088)	(0.086)
Asian	−0.852***	−0.867***	−0.438***	−0.464***
	(0.103)	(0.102)	(0.101)	(0.105)
Other Race	−0.124	−0.128	−0.222***	−0.228***
	(0.097)	(0.098)	(0.056)	(0.056)
Strong Partisan	0.355***	0.355***	0.303***	0.301***
	(0.036)	(0.036)	(0.030)	(0.029)
Political Interest	0.451***	0.450***	0.518***	0.518***
	(0.015)	(0.015)	(0.020)	(0.020)
Length of Residence	0.122***	0.121***	0.164***	0.162***
	(0.017)	(0.016)	(0.016)	(0.016)
Employed	0.210***	0.210***	0.064**	0.066**
	(0.049)	(0.049)	(0.030)	(0.029)
Home Ownership	0.113**	0.117**	0.076**	0.084**
	(0.050)	(0.049)	(0.038)	(0.035)
Constant	−4.808***	−4.572***	−4.107***	−3.805***
	(0.279)	(0.281)	(0.347)	(0.299)
Pseudo R^2	0.144	0.144	0.110	0.110
N	51,220	51,220	59,956	59,956

Note: Based on CCES data measuring voting behavior of eligible voters in the 2010 and 2014 elections. The estimates are unstandardized logistic regression coefficients. Robust standard errors in parentheses are clustered by state. Multilevel models reveal similar results. *P*-values are based on two-tailed tests. Year fixed effects are also included.

* $p < 0.10$, ** $p < 0.05$, *** $p < 0.001$.

Table C1.14 Poor Person Likelihood of Being Contacted by a Campaign in 2012 Presidential Election, Varying Convenience Voting Laws and Election Performance Index (EPI) (Subsample of the Poor)

	Baseline	Convenience Voting Laws + EPI	Early Voting × EPI	Absentee/ Mail Voting × EPI	SDR × EPI
Early Voting	0.118	0.146	0.754	0.135	0.145
	(0.108)	(0.108)	(0.742)	(0.100)	(0.108)
Absentee/Mail Voting	−0.072	−0.089	−0.086	1.069	−0.091
	(0.117)	(0.119)	(0.121)	(0.710)	(0.120)
SDR	0.251**	0.181	0.191	0.198	−0.353
	(0.120)	(0.125)	(0.128)	(0.129)	(1.233)
EPI		0.018**	0.023**	0.026***	0.018**
		(0.006)	(0.007)	(0.007)	(0.007)
Early Voting × EPI			−0.009		
			(0.011)		
Absentee/Mail Voting × EPI				−0.017*	
				(0.010)	
SDR × EPI					0.007
					(0.016)
Vote Margin	0.020***	0.014**	0.014**	0.014**	0.013**
	(0.004)	(0.004)	(0.004)	(0.004)	(0.004)
Number of Ballot Initiatives	0.004	0.011	0.009	0.006	0.011
	(0.010)	(0.011)	(0.011)	(0.011)	(0.012)
Age	0.024***	0.024***	0.024***	0.024***	0.024***
	(0.002)	(0.002)	(0.002)	(0.002)	(0.002)
Education	0.276***	0.276***	0.276***	0.276***	0.276***
	(0.027)	(0.027)	(0.027)	(0.027)	(0.027)
Black	−0.805***	−0.787***	−0.781***	−0.777***	−0.789***
	(0.080)	(0.086)	(0.089)	(0.089)	(0.086)
Hispanic	−0.602***	−0.568***	−0.572***	−0.570***	−0.569***
	(0.132)	(0.132)	(0.130)	(0.129)	(0.132)
Asian	−0.927**	−0.875**	−0.879**	−0.886**	−0.877**
	(0.390)	(0.388)	(0.386)	(0.382)	(0.386)
Other Race	0.148	0.147	0.145	0.143	0.149
	(0.186)	(0.184)	(0.184)	(0.183)	(0.184)
Strong Partisan	0.173**	0.175**	0.176**	0.177**	0.175**
	(0.063)	(0.062)	(0.063)	(0.063)	(0.063)
Political Interest	0.332***	0.332***	0.332***	0.331***	0.332***
	(0.034)	(0.034)	(0.034)	(0.034)	(0.034)
Length of Residence	0.123***	0.125***	0.125***	0.124***	0.125***
	(0.027)	(0.027)	(0.027)	(0.027)	(0.028)

Continued

Table C1.14 *Continued*

	Baseline	Convenience Voting Laws + EPI	Early Voting × EPI	Absentee/ Mail Voting × EPI	SDR × EPI
Employed	−0.081	−0.090	−0.089	−0.090	−0.090
	(0.063)	(0.063)	(0.063)	(0.063)	(0.063)
Home Ownership	0.142**	0.142**	0.143**	0.145**	0.142**
	(0.064)	(0.065)	(0.066)	(0.065)	(0.065)
Constant	−4.701***	−5.385***	−5.743***	−5.967***	−5.333***
	(0.417)	(0.492)	(0.604)	(0.592)	(0.509)
Pseudo R^2	0.134	0.135	0.135	0.136	0.135
N	12,262	12,262	12,262	12,262	12,262

Note: Based on CCES data measuring voting behavior of eligible voters in 2012 election. The estimates are unstandardized logistic regression coefficients. Robust standard errors in parentheses are clustered by state. Multilevel models reveal similar results. *P*-values are based on two-tailed tests.
$^*p < 0.10$, $^{**}p < 0.05$, $^{***}p < 0.001$.

Table C1.15 Poor Person Likelihood of Being Contacted by a Campaign in 2010 and 2014 Midterm Elections, Varying Convenience Voting Laws and Election Performance Index (EPI) (Subsample of the Poor)

	Baseline	Convenience Voting Laws + EPI	Early Voting × EPI	Absentee/ Mail Voting × EPI	SDR × EPI
Early Voting	−0.077	−0.081	−0.436	−0.083	−0.083
	(0.110)	(0.108)	(0.467)	(0.108)	(0.107)
Absentee/Mail Voting	0.085	0.081	0.081	0.185	0.088
	(0.114)	(0.114)	(0.112)	(0.390)	(0.114)
SDR	0.165*	0.185*	0.179**	0.186**	−0.720
	(0.093)	(0.094)	(0.091)	(0.095)	(0.456)
EPI		−0.003	−0.006	−0.003	−0.005
		(0.004)	(0.005)	(0.005)	(0.004)
Early Voting × EPI			0.005		
			(0.007)		
Absentee/Mail Voting × EPI				−0.002	
				(0.006)	
SDR × EPI					0.013**
					(0.006)
Vote Margin	0.010**	0.010**	0.011**	0.010**	0.010**
	(0.003)	(0.003)	(0.003)	(0.003)	(0.003)
Number of Ballot Initiatives	0.033**	0.032**	0.034**	0.031**	0.030**
	(0.012)	(0.013)	(0.014)	(0.014)	(0.013)

Table C1.15 *Continued*

	Baseline	Convenience Voting Laws + EPI	Early Voting × EPI	Absentee/ Mail Voting × EPI	SDR × EPI
Male	0.026	0.026	0.027	0.026	0.027
	(0.051)	(0.051)	(0.051)	(0.051)	(0.051)
Age	0.027***	0.027***	0.027***	0.027***	0.027***
	(0.002)	(0.002)	(0.002)	(0.002)	(0.002)
Education	0.229***	0.229***	0.229***	0.229***	0.228***
	(0.025)	(0.025)	(0.025)	(0.025)	(0.025)
Black	−0.206**	−0.208**	−0.210**	−0.208**	−0.208**
	(0.081)	(0.080)	(0.080)	(0.080)	(0.080)
Hispanic	−0.436***	−0.450***	−0.446***	−0.451***	−0.456***
	(0.102)	(0.106)	(0.106)	(0.107)	(0.107)
Asian	−0.610**	−0.621**	−0.616**	−0.623**	−0.627**
	(0.219)	(0.215)	(0.212)	(0.213)	(0.218)
Other Race	−0.056	−0.060	−0.057	−0.061	−0.064
	(0.123)	(0.124)	(0.123)	(0.123)	(0.125)
Strong Partisan	0.339***	0.338***	0.338***	0.338***	0.338***
	(0.050)	(0.050)	(0.050)	(0.050)	(0.050)
Political Interest	0.436***	0.436***	0.436***	0.436***	0.437***
	(0.025)	(0.025)	(0.025)	(0.025)	(0.025)
Length of Residence	0.123***	0.122***	0.122***	0.122***	0.121***
	(0.020)	(0.021)	(0.021)	(0.021)	(0.021)
Employed	−0.081	−0.080	−0.081	−0.080	−0.082
	(0.066)	(0.066)	(0.066)	(0.066)	(0.066)
Home Ownership	0.361***	0.363***	0.362***	0.363***	0.366***
	(0.062)	(0.061)	(0.061)	(0.060)	(0.061)
Constant	−4.440***	−4.258***	−4.096***	−4.303***	−4.138***
	(0.342)	(0.427)	(0.457)	(0.444)	(0.443)
Pseudo R^2	0.155	0.155	0.155	0.155	0.156
N	22,781	22,781	22,781	22,781	22,781

Note: Based on CCES data measuring voting behavior of eligible voters in the 2010 and 2014 elections. The estimates are unstandardized logistic regression coefficients. Robust standard errors in parentheses are clustered by state. Multilevel models reveal similar results. *P*-values are based on two-tailed tests. Year fixed effects are also included.

* $p < 0.10$, ** $p < 0.05$, *** $p < 0.001$.

References

2012 Campaign Legacy Report. 2013. Technical report Obama for America, 639–645.

Aldrich, John H. 1993. "Turnout and Rational Choice." *American Journal of Political Science* 37:246–278.

Aldrich, John H. 2011. *Why Parties? A Second Look*. Chicago, IL: University of Chicago Press.

Alvarez, R. Michael, Lonna Rae Atkeson, and Thad E. Hall. 2013. *Evaluating Elections: A Handbook of Methods and Standards*. New York, NY: Cambridge University Press.

Alvarez, R. Michael, Delia Bailey, and Jonathan N. Katz. 2008. "The Effect of Voter Identification Laws on Turnout." Social Science Working Paper 1267R, California Institute of Technology.

Alvarez, R. Michael, and Bernard Grofman, eds. 2014. *Election Administration in the United States: The State of Reform after Bush v. Gore*. New York, NY: Cambridge University Press.

Alvarez, R. Michael, and Thad E. Hall. 2014. "Resolving Voter Registration Problems: Making Registration Easier, Less Costly, and More Accurate." In *Election Administration in the United States: The State of Reform after Bush v. Gore*, eds. R. Michael Alvarez and Bernard Grofman, 186–198. New York, NY: Cambridge University Press.

Alvarez, Michael R., Ines Levin, and J. Andrew Sinclair. 2012. "Making Voting Easier: Convenience Voting in the 2008 Presidential Election." *Political Research Quarterly* 65: 248–262.

Anderson, Carol. 2018. *One Person, No Vote: How Voter Suppression Is Destroying Our Democracy*. New York, NY: Bloomsbury Publishing.

Angrist, Joshua D., and Jorn-Steffen Pischke. 2008. *Mostly Harmless Econometrics: An Empiricist's Companion*. Princeton, NJ: Princeton University Press.

Ansolabehere, Stephen. 2009. "Effects of Identification Requirements on Voting: Evidence from the Experiences of Voters on Election Day." *PS: Political Science & Politics* 42 (1): 127–130.

Ansolabehere, Stephen, and Eitan Hersh. 2014. "Voter Registration: The Process and Quality of Lists." In *The Measure of American Elections*, eds. Barry C. Burden and Charles Stewart III. New York, NY: Cambridge University Press.

Ansolabehere, Stephen, and Charles Stewart III. 2005. "Residual Vote Attributable to Technology." *Journal of Politics* 67 (2): 365–389.

Arceneaux, Kevin, Thad Kousser, and Megan Mullin. 2012. "Get Out the Vote-by-Mail? A Randomized Field Experiment Testing the Effect of Mobilization in Traditional and Vote-by-Mail Precincts." *Political Research Quarterly* 65 (4): 882–894.

Ashok, Vivekinan, Daniel Feder, Mary McGrath, and Eitan Hersh. 2016. "The Dynamic Election: Patterns of Early Voting Across Time, State, Party, and Age." *Election Law Journal* 15 (2): 115–128.

Atkeson, Lonna Rae, R. Michael Alvarez, Thad E. Hall, and J. Andrew Sinclair. 2014. "Balancing Fraud Prevention and Electoral Participation: Attitudes toward Voter Identification." *Social Science Quarterly* 95 (5): 1381–1398.

Atkeson, Lonna Rae, Yann P. Kerevel, R. Michael Alvarez, and Thad E. Hall. 2014. "Who Asks for Voter Identification? Explaining Poll-Worker Discretion." *Journal of Politics* 76 (4): 944–957.

Atkeson, Lonna Rae, and Kyle L. Saunders. 2008. "Election Administration and Voter Confidence." In *Democracy in the States: Experimentation in Election Reform.* Washington, DC: Brookings Institution Press, 21–34.

Bardach, Eugene. 1977. *The Implementation Game: What Happens After a Bill Becomes a Law.* Boston, MA: MIT Press.

Barreto, Matt, Stephen A. Nuno, and Gabriel R. Sanchez. 2009. "The Disproportionate Impact of Voter-ID Requirements on the Electorate—New Evidence from Indiana." *PS: Political Science and Politics* 42 (1): 111–116.

Barreto, Matt A., Matthew J. Streb, and Mara Marks Fernando Guerra. 2006. "Do Absentee Voters Differ from Polling Place Voters? New Evidence from California." *Public Opinion Quarterly* 70 (Summer): 224–234.

Bartels, Larry M. 2008. *Unequal Democracy: The Political Economy of the New Gilded Age.* Princeton, NJ: Princeton University Press.

Bentele, Keith G., and Erin E. O'Brien. 2013. "Jim Crow 2.0? Why States Consider and Adopt Restrictive Voter Access Policies." *Perspectives on Politics* 11 (4): 1088–1116.

Berinsky, Adam J. 2005. "The Perverse Consequences of Electoral Reform in the United States." *American Politics Research* 33:471–490.

Berinsky, Adam J., Nancy Burns, and Michael W. Traugott. 2001. "Who Votes by Mail? A Dynamic Model of the Individual-Level Consequences of Voting-by-Mail Systems." *Public Opinion Quarterly* 65:178–197.

Berman, Ali. 2015. *Give Us the Ballot: The Modern Struggle for Voting Rights in America.* Picador.

Bimber, Bruce. 2003. *Information and American Democracy: Technology in the Evolution of Political Power.* Cambridge University Press.

Bimber, Bruce, and Richard Davis. 2003. *Campaigning Online: The Internet in U.S. Elections.* Oxford University Press.

Blais, Andre. 2000. *To Vote or Not to Vote: The Merits and Limits of Rational Choice Theory.* Pittsburg, PA: University of Pittsburg Press.

Bowler, Shaun, and Todd Donovan. 2008. "Mobilizing Political Engagement and Participation in Diverse Societies: The Impact of Institutional Arrangements." In *Designing Democratic Government: Making Institutions Work,* eds. Margaret Levi, James Johnson, Jack Knight, and Susan Stokes, 40–61. New York, NY: Russell Sage Foundation.

Brady, Henry E., Sidney Verba, and Kay Lehman Schlozman. 1995. "Beyond SES: A Resource Model of Political Participation." *The American Political Science Review* 89, no. 2 (June): 271–294.

Brennan Center for Justice. 2016. "Voting Laws Roundup 2016." https://www.brennancenter.org/analysis/voting-laws-roundup-2016 (accessed November 16, 2016).

Brennan Center for Justice. 2018. "Automatic Voter Registration." https://www.brennancenter.org/analysis/automatic-voter-registration (accessed August 1, 2018).

Brennan Center for Justice. 2019. "New Voting Restrictions in America." https://www.brennancenter.org/new-voting-restrictions-america (accessed May 24, 2019).

Brians, Craig Leonard, and Bernard Grofman. 2001. "Election Day Registration's Effect on U.S. Voter Turnout." *Social Science Quarterly* 82 (March): 170–183.

Brown, Robert D., Robert A. Jackson, and Gerald C. Wright. 1999. "Registration, Turnout, and State Party Systems." *Political Research Quarterly* 52 (3): 463–479.

Burden, Barry C. 2014. "Registration and Voting: A View from the Top." In *The Measure of American Elections*, eds. Barry C. Burden and Charles Stewart III. New York, NY: Cambridge University Press.

Burden, Barry C., David T. Canon, Kenneth R. Mayer, and Donald P. Moynihan. 2014. "Electoral Laws, Mobilization, and Turnout: The Unanticipated Consequences of Election Reform." *American Journal of Political Science* 58, (1) (January): 95–109.

Burden, Barry C., David T. Canon, Kenneth R. Mayer, and Donald P. Moynihan. 2017. "The Complicated Partisan Effects of State Election Laws." *Political Research Quarterly* 70 (3): 1–13.

Burden, Barry C., and Charles Stewart III. 2014. *The Measure of American Elections*. New York, NY: Cambridge University Press.

Caldeira, Gregory A., Aage R. Clausen, and Samuel C. Patterson. 1990. "Partisan Mobilization and Electoral Participation." *Electoral Studies* 9 (3): 191–204.

Campbell, Angus, Philip E. Converse, Warren E. Miller, and Donald E. Stokes. 1960. *The American Voter*. New York: John Wiley and Sons, Inc.

Cantoni, Enrico, and Vincent Pons. 2019. "Strict ID Laws Don't Stop Voters: Evidence from a U.S. National Panel, 2008–2016." Working Paper 25522, National Bureau of Economic Research, Cambridge, MA.

Carter, Elisabeth, and David M. Farrell. 2010. "Electoral Systems and Election Management." In *Comparing Democracies: Elections and Voting in the 21st Century*, eds. Lawrence LeDuc, Richard G. Niemi, and Pippa Norris, 3rd edition, 25–44. Thousand Oaks, CA: Sage Publications.

Catalist. 2016. "Catalist Data." http://www.catalist.us/data/ (accessed October 1, 2016).

Cooperative Congressional Election Study. 2008–2014. "CCES Dataverse." http://projects.iq.harvard.edu/cces/data (accessed October 1, 2016).

Cox, Gary W., and Michael C. Munger 1989. "Closeness, Expenditures, and Turnout in the 1982 U.S. House Elections." *American Political Science Review* 83 (1): 217–231.

Crawford v. Marion County Election Board. 2008. 553 U.S. 181.

Current Population Survey. 2000–2016. "Voting and Registration Supplement." *United States Census Bureau*. http://www.census.gov/topics/public-sector/voting.html (accessed July 1, 2018).

Curtist, Michael Kent. 2016. "Using the Voting Rights Act to Discriminate: North Carolina's Use of Racial Gerrymanders, Two Racial Quotas, Safe Harbors, Shields, and Inoculations to Undermine Multiracial Coalitions and Black Political Power." *Wake Forest Law Review* 51: 421–492.

Cutright, Phillips, and Peter H. Rossi. 1958. "Grass Roots Politicians and the Vote." *American Sociological Review* 23 (2): 171–179.

Darr, Joshua P., and Matthew S. Levendusky. 2009. "Relying on the Ground Game: The Placement and Effect of Campaign Field Offices." *American Politics Research* 42 (3): 529–548.

Desilver, Drew. 2016. "U.S. Turnout Trails Most Developed Countries." *Pew Research Center*. http://www.pewresearch.org/fact-tank/2016/08/02/u-s-voter-turnout-trails-most-developed-countries/ (accessed September 15, 2016).

Donovan, Todd. 2008. "A Goal for Reform." In *Democracy in the States*, eds. Bruce E. Cain, Todd Donovan, and Caroline J. Tolbert, 186–198. Washington, DC: Brookings Institution Pres.

Downs, Anthony. 1957. *An Economic Theory of Democracy*. New York, NY: Harper and Row.

Dropp, Kyle A. 2013. "Voter ID Laws and Voter Turnout." Working paper, draft as of September 21.

Dyck, Joshua J., and James G. Gimpel. 2005. "Distance, Turnout, and the Convenience of Voting." *Social Science Quarterly* 86 (5): 531–546.

Elazar, David J. 1972. *American Federalism: A View from the States*. New York, NY: Thomas Y. Cromwell.

Elazar, Daniel J. 1994. *The American Mosaic: The Impact of Space, Time, and Culture on American Politics*. Boulder, CO: Westview Press.

Eldersveld, Samuel J. 1956. "Experimental Propaganda Techniques and Voting Behavior." *American Political Science Review* 50:154–165.

Erikson, Robert S. 2015. "Income Inequality and Policy Responsiveness." *Annual Review of Political Science* 18 (May): 11–29.

Epstein, Jennifer. 2013. "Obama Signs Order Creating Election Reform Commission." *Politico.* https://www.politico.com/blogs/politico44/2013/03/obama-signs-order-creating-election-reform-commission-160422 (accessed June 1, 2013).

Ewald, Alec C. 2009. *The Way We Vote: The Local Dimension of American Suffrage*. Nashville, TN: Vanderbilt University Press.

Fenster, Mark J. 1994. "The Impact of Allowing Day of Registration Voting on Turnout in U.S. Elections from 1960 to 1992." *American Politics Research* 22 (1): 74–87.

Finkel, Steven. 1993. "Reexamining the 'Minimal Effects' Model in Recent Presidential Elections." *Journal of Politics* 55:1–21.

Fitzgerald, Mary. 2005. "Greater Convenience but Not Greater Turnout: The Impact of Alternative Voting Methods on Electoral Participation in the United States." *American Politics Research* 33 (October): 842–867.

Florida Department of State. 2016a. "County Reporting Status." *Florida Election Watch.* http://enight.elections.myflorida.com/CountyReportingStatus/ (accessed November 16, 2016).

Florida Department of State. 2016b. "Vote-by-Mail Request and Early Voting Statistics." *Division of Elections.* https://countyballotfiles.elections.myflorida.com/FVRSCountyBallotReports/AbsenteeEarlyVotingReports/PublicStats (accessed November 16, 2016).

Fortier, John C. 2006. *Absentee and Early Voting: Trends, Promises, and Perils*. Washington, DC: American Enterprise Institute Press.

Fraga, Bernard L. 2018. *The Turnout Gap: Race, Ethnicity, and Political Inequality in a Diversifying America*. Cambridge: Cambridge University Press.

Franko, William W., Nathan J. Kelly, and Christopher Witko. 2016. "Class Bias in Voter Turnout, Representation, and Income Inequality." *Perspectives on Politics* 14 (2): 351–368.

Franko, William W., and Christopher Witko. 2017. *The New Economic Populism: How States Respond to Economic Inequality*. New York City, NY: Oxford University Press.

Frey, William H. 2017. "Census Shows Pervasive Decline in 2016 Minority Voter Turnout." *Brookings Institution.* https://www.brookings.edu/blog/the-avenue/2017/05/18/census-shows-pervasive-decline-in-2016-minority-voter-turnout/ (accessed May 28, 2017).

Fullmer, Elliot B. 2015a. "Early Voting: Do More Sites Lead to Higher Turnout?" *Election Law Journal* 14 (2): 81–96.

Fullmer, Elliot B. 2015b. "The Site Gap: Racial Inequalities in Early Voting Access." *American Politics Research* 43 (2): 283–303.

Gaventa, John. 1980. *Power and Powerlessness: Quiescence and Rebellion in an Appalachian Valley*. Champaign, IL: University of Illinois Press.

Galicki, Celestyna. 2018. "Convenience Voting and Voter Mobilization: Applying a Continuum Model." *Representation: Journal of Representative Democracy* 247–261.

Garnett, Holly Ann. 2019. "Early Voting: Comparing Canada, Finland, Germany, and Switzerland." *Election Law Journal* 18 (2): 116–131.

Gaventa, John. 1980. *Power and Powerlessness: Quiescence and Rebellion in an Appalachian Valley*. Champaign, IL: University of Illinois Press.

Gerber, Alan S., Donald P. Green, and Christopher W. Larimer. 2008. "Social Pressure and Voter Turnout: Evidence from a Large-Scale Field Experiment." *American Political Science Review* 102 (1): 33–48.

Gerken, Heather. 2009. *The Democracy Index*. Princeton, NJ: Princeton University Press.

Giammo, Joseph D., and Brian J. Brox. 2010. "Reducing the Costs of Participation: Are States Getting a Return on Early Voting?" *Political Research Quarterly* 63:295–303.

Gilens, Martin. 2012. *Affluence and Influence: Economic Inequality and Political Power in America*. Princeton, NJ: Princeton University Press.

Gimpel, James G., Joshua J. Dyck, and Daron R. Shaw. 2006. "Location, Knowledge, and Time Pressures in the Spatial Structure of Convenience Voting." *Electoral Studies* 25:35–58.

Gosnell, Harold F. 1927. *Getting Out the Vote: An Experiment in the Stimulation of Voting*. Chicago, IL: University of Chicago Press.

Green, Donald P., and Alan S. Gerber. 2015. *Get Out the Vote: How to Increase Voter Turnout*. 3rd ed. Washington, DC: Brookings Institution Press.

Griffin, John D., and Brian Newman. 2008. *Minority Report: Evaluating Political Equality in America*. University of Chicago Press.

Grimmer, Justin, Eitan Hersh, Marc Meredith, Jonathan Mummolo, and Clayton Nall. 2017. "Comment on 'Voter Identification Laws and the Suppression of Minority Votes.'" *Journal of Politics* 80 (3): 1045–1051.

Gronke, Paul. 2014a. "Early Voting after *Bush v. Gore*." In *Election Administration in the United States: The State of Reform after Bush v. Gore*, eds. R. Michael Alvarez and Bernard Grofman. New York, NY: Cambridge University Press, 120–143.

Gronke, Paul. 2014b. "Voter Confidence as a Metric of Election Performance." In *The Measure of American Elections*, eds. Barry C. Burden and Charles Stewart III. New York, NY: Cambridge University Press.

Gronke, Paul, Eva Galanes-Rosenbaum, and Peter A. Miller. 2007. "Early Voting and Turnout." *PS: Political Science and Politics* (October): 639–645.

Gronke, Paul, Eva Galanes-Rosenbaum, and Peter A. Miller. 2008a. "Convenience Voting." *Annual Review of Political Science* 11 (February): 437–455.

Gronke, Paul, Eva Galanes-Rosenbaum, and Peter A. Miller. 2008b. "From Ballot Box to Mail Box: Early Voting and Turnout." In *Democracy in the States: Experimentation in Election Reform*. Washington, DC: Brookings Institution Press, 68–81.

Gronke, Paul, and Peter Miller. 2012. "Voting by Mail and Turnout in Oregon: Revisiting Southwell and Burchett." *American Politics Research* 40:976–997.

Gronke, Paul, and Charles Stewart III. 2013, April 11–14. "Early Voting in Florida." Paper presented at the annual meeting of the Midwest Political Science Association, Chicago, IL.

Gusmano, Michael K., Mark Schlesinger, and Tracey Thomas. 2002. "Policy Feedback and Public Opinion: The Role of Employer Responsibility in Social Policy." *Journal of Health Politics, Policy and Law* 27 (5): 731–772.

Hacker, Jacob S., and Paul Pierson. 2011. *Winner-Take-All Politics: How Washington Made the Rich Richer—and Turned Its Back on the Middle Class.* New York, NY: Simon & Schuster Paperbacks.

Hajnal, Zoltan, Nazita Lajevardi, and Lindsey Nielson. 2017. "Voter Identification Laws and the Suppression of Minority Votes." *Journal of Politics* 79 (2): 363–379.

Hall, Thad E., Krysha Gregorowicz, and Leah Alley. 2016. "It's Not Convenient: Absentee Voting and the Federal Write-In." In *Why Don't Americans Vote? Causes and Consequences*, eds. Bridgett A. Kind and Kathleen Hale. Santa Barbara, CA: ABC-CLIO.

Hall, Thad E., and Kathleen Moore. 2014. "Poll Workers and Polling Places." In *Election Administration in the United States: The State of Reform after Bush v. Gore*, eds. R. Michael Alvarez and Bernard Grofman. New York, NY: Cambridge University Press, 175–185.

Hanmer, Michael J. 2009. *Discount Voting: Voter Registration Reforms and Their Effects.* New York, NY: Cambridge University Press.

Hanmer, Michael J., and Paul S. Herrnson. 2014. "Provisional Ballots." In *The Measure of American Elections*, eds. Barry C. Burden and Charles Stewart III. New York, NY: Cambridge University Press.

Hasen, Richard L. 2012. *The Voting Wars: From Florida 2000 to the Next Election Meltdown.* New Haven, CT: Yale University Press.

Hasen, Richard L 2014. "Essay: Race or Party? How Courts Should Think about Republican Efforts to Make It Harder to Vote in North Carolina and Elsewhere." *Harvard Law Review* 127 (1): 58–75.

Help America Vote Act. 2002. Vol. 116, pp. 1666–1730.

Hero, Rodney E. 1992. *Latinos and the U.S. Political System: Two-Tiered Pluralism.* Philadelphia, PA: Temple University Press.

Herrnson, Paul S., Michael J. Hanmer, and Ho Youn Koh. 2018. "Mobilization Around New Convenience Methods: A Field Experiment to Encourage Voting by Mail with a Downloadable Ballot and Early Voting." *Political Behavior* 41:871–895.

Herron, Michael C., and Daniel A. Smith. 2012. "Souls to the Polls: Early Voting in Florida in the Shadow of House Bill 1355." *Election Law Journal* 11 (2): 331–347.

Herron, Michael C., and Daniel A. Smith. 2014. "Race, Party, and the Consequence of Restricting Early Voting in Florida in the 2012 General Election." *Political Research Quarterly* 24 (February): 1–20.

Hersh, Eitan D. 2015. *Hacking the Electorate: How Campaigns Perceive Voters.* New York, NY: Cambridge University Press.

Hersh, Eitan D., and Yair Ghitza. 2018. "Mixed Partisan Households and Electoral Participation in the United States." *PloS One* 13 (10): e0203997.

Hersh, Eitan D., and Clayton Nall. 2016. "The Primacy of Race in the Geography of Income-Based Voting: New Evidence from Public Voting Records." *American Journal of Political Science* 60 (2): 289–303.

Hershey, Marjorie Randon. 2015. *Party Politics in America.* 16th ed. Upper Saddle River, NJ: Pearson Education.

Hetling, Andrea, and Monika L. McDermott. 2008. "Judging a Book by Its Cover: Did Perceptions of the 1996 US Welfare Reforms Affect Public Support for Spending on the Poor?" *Journal of Social Policy* 37 (3): 471–487.

Hicks, William D., Seth C. McKee, Mitchell D. Sellers, and Daniel A. Smith. 2015. "A Principle or a Strategy? Voter Identification Laws and Partisan Competition in the American States." *Political Research Quarterly* 68 (1): 18–33.

Hicks, William D., Seth C. McKee, and Daniel A. Smith. 2016. "The Determinants of State Legislator Support for Restrictive Voter ID Laws." *State Politics and Policy Quarterly* (December): 411–431.

Highton, Benjamin, and Raymond Wolfinger. 1998. "Estimating the Effects of the National Voter Registration Act of 1993." *Political Behavior* 20:79–104.

Hill, Kim Quaile, and Jan E. Leighley. 1992. "The Policy Consequences of Class Bias in State Electorates." *American Journal of Political Science* 36 (2): 351–365.

Hill, Kim Quaile, and Jan E. Leighley. 1994. "Mobilizing Institutions and Class Representation in U.S. State Electorates." *Political Research Quarterly* 47 (1): 137–150.

Hill, Kim Quaile, Jan Leighley, and Angela Hinton-Andersson. 1995. "Lower-Class Mobilization and Policy Linkage in the U.S. States." *American Journal of Political Science* 39 (1): 75–86.

Holbrook, Thomas M., and Scott D. McClurg. 2005. "The Mobilization of Core Supporters: Campaigns, Turnout, and Electoral Composition in the United States." *American Journal of Political Science* 49:689–703.

Huang, Chi, and Todd G. Shields. 2000. "Interpreting the Interaction Effects in Logit and Probit Analyses: Reconsidering the Relationship between Registration Laws, Education, and Voter Turnout." *American Politics Quarterly* 28:80–95.

Hur, Aram, and Christopher H. Achen. 2013. "Coding Voter Turnout Responses in the Current Population Survey." *Public Opinion Quarterly* 77 (4): 985–993.

Igielnik, Ruth, Scott Keeter, Courtney Kennedy, and Bradley Spahn. 2018. "Commercial Voter Files and the Study of U.S. Politics: Demystifying the Digital Databases Widely Used by Political Campaigns." *Pew Research Center* https://www.pewresearch.org/methods/wp-content/uploads/sites/10/2018/12/final-voter-file-report-2.15.18.pdf (accessed June 12, 2019).

Issenberg, Sasha. 2012. *The Victory Lab: The Secret Science of Winning Campaigns.* New York, NY: Crown.

Jackson, Robert A., Robert D. Brown, and Gerald C. Wright. 1998. "Registration, Turnout, and the Electoral Representativeness of U.S. State Elections." *American Politics Quarterly* 26 (3): 259–287.

Johnson, Martin, Paul Brace, and Kevin Arceneaux. 2005. "Public Opinion and Dynamic Representation in the American States: The Case of Environmental Attitudes." *Social Science Quarterly* 86 (1): 87–108.

Karp, Jeffrey A., and Susan A. Banducci. 2000. "Going Postal: How All-Mail Elections Influence Turnout." *Political Behavior* 22:223–239.

Karp, Jeffrey A., and Susan A. Banducci. 2001. "Absentee Voting, Mobilization, and Participation." *American Politics Research* 29:183–195.

Karp, Jeffrey A., and David Brockington. 2005. "Social Desirability and Response Validity: A Comparative Analysis of Overreporting Voter Turnout in Five Countries." *Journal of Politics* 67 (August): 825–840.

Key, V. O. 1949. *Southern Politics: In State and Nation.* New York: Vintage Books.

Keyssar, Alexander. 2009. *The Right to Vote: The Contest History of Democracy in the United States.* New York, NY: Basic Books.

Kim, Jae-On, John R. Petrocik, and Stephen N. Enokson. 1975. "Voter Turnout among the American States: Systematic and Individual Components." *American Political Science Review* 69 (1): 107–123.

Knack, Stephen. 2001. "Election-Day Registration: The Second Wave." *American Politics Research* 29 (January): 65–78.

Knopf, Martha E. 2012. "Does Early Voting Change the Socio-Economic Composition of the Electorate?" *Poverty and Public Policy* 4:1–19.

Kousser, J. Morgan. 1974. *The Shaping of Southern Politics: Suffrage Restriction and the Establishment of the One-Party South, 1880–1910*. New Haven, CT: Yale University Press.

Kousser, Thad, and Megan Mullin. 2007. "Does Voting by Mail Increase Participation? Using Matching to Analyze a Natural Experiment." *Political Analysis* 15:428–445.

Kramer, Gerald. 1973. "The Effects of Precinct-Level Canvassing on Voter Behavior." *Public Opinion Quarterly* 34 (4): 560–572.

Kreitzer, Rebecca J., Allison J. Hamilton, and Caroline Tolbert. 2014. "Does Policy Adoption Change Opinions on Minority Rights? The Effects of Legalizing Same-Sex Marriage." *Policy Research Quarterly* 67 (4): 795–808.

Kropf, Martha. 2014. "The Evolution (or Not) of Ballot Design Ten Years after *Bush v. Gore*." In *Election Administration in the United States: The State of Reform after Bush v. Gore*, eds. R. Michael Alvarez and Bernard Grofman. New York, NY: Cambridge University Press, 157–174.

Laing, Matthew, Narelle Miragliotta, and Paul Thornton-Smith. 2018. *A Review of Convenience Voting in the State of Victoria*. https://law.unimelb.edu.au/__data/assets/pdf_file/0003/2902152/Convenience-Voting-Report-1-October-2018.pdf (accessed February 25, 2020).

Larocca, Roger, and John S. Klemanski. 2011. "Election Reform and Turnout in Presidential Elections." https://files.oakland.edu/users/larocca/web/index.htm (accessed January 15, 2016).

Lazarsfeld, Paul F., Bernard Berelson, and Hazel Gaudet Lazarsfeld. 1944. *The People's Choice: How the Voter Made up His Mind in a Presidential Campaign*. New York, NY: Duell, Sloan, and Pearce.

Leighley, Jan E., and Jonathan Nagler. 2013. *Who Votes Now? Demographics, Issues, Inequality, and Turnout in the United States*. Princeton, NJ: Princeton University Press.

Leip, David. 2015. "United States Presidential Election Results." *Atlas of U.S. Presidential Elections*. http://uselectionatlas.org/ (accessed December 15, 2015).

Li, Quan, Michael J. Pomantell, and Scot Schraufnagel. 2018. "Cost of Voting in the American States." *Election Law Journal* 17 (3): 234–247.

Lijphart, Arend. 1997. "Unequal Participation: Democracy's Unresolved Dilemma." *American Political Science Review* 91 (1): 1–14.

Lowenstein, Daniel Hays, Richard L. Hasen, and Daniel P. Tokaji. 2008. *Election Law: Cases and Materials*, 4th ed. Durham, NC: Carolina Academic Press.

Manza, Jeff, and Christopher Uggen. 2008. *Locked Out: Felon Disenfranchisement and American Democracy*. New York, NY: Oxford University Press.

Masket, Seth. 2009. *No Middle Ground: How Informal Party Organizations Control Nominations and Polarize Legislatures*. Ann Arbor, MI: University of Michigan Press.

Massicotte, Louis, Andre Blais, and Antoine Yoshinaka. 2004. *Establishing the Rules of the Game: Election Laws in Democracies*. Toronto, ON: University of Toronto Press.

Mateyka, Peter J. 2015. "Desire to Move and Residential Mobility: 2010–2011." *American Community Survey*. https://www.census.gov/content/dam/Census/library/publications/2015/demo/p70-140.pdf (accessed May 21, 2017).

McDonald, Michael P. 2010. "American Voter Turnout in Historical Perspective." In *Oxford Handbook of American Elections and Political Behavior*, ed. Jan Leighley. Cambridge, UK: Oxford University Press, 125–143.

McDonald, Michael P. 2016a. "General Election Turnout Rates." *United States Election Project*. http://www.electproject.org/ (accessed January 10, 2016).

McDonald, Michael. 2016b. "Early Vote: Election Ever Predictions." *Huffington Post*. http://www.huffingtonpost.com/michael-p-mcdonald/early-vote-election-eve-p_b_12853864.html (accessed November 14, 2016).

Mettler, Suzanne, and Mallory Sorelle. 2014. "Policy Feedback Theory." In *Theories of the Policy Process*, eds. Paul A. Sabatier and Christopher M. Weible. Boulder, CO: Westview Press.

Miller, Peter, and Neilan S. Chaturvedi. 2018. "Get Out the Early Vote: Co-Ethnic Mobilization and Convenience Voting." *Journal of Elections, Public Opinion and Parties* 28 (4): 399–423.

Miller, Peter, and Sierra Powell. 2016. "Overcoming Voting Obstacles: The Use of Convenience Voting by Voters with Disabilities." *American Politics Research* 44 (1): 28–55.

Minnite, Lorraine C. 2011. *The Myth of Voter Fraud*. Ithaca, NY: Cornell University Press.

Misra, Jordan. 2019. "Voter Turnout Rates among All Voting Age and Major Racial and Ethnic Groups Were Higher than in 2014." United States Census Bureau. https://www.census.gov/library/stories/2019/04/behind-2018-united-states-midterm-election-turnout.html (accessed May 24, 2019).

MIT Election Data and Science Lab. 2016. Election Performance Index. https://electionlab.mit.edu/epi-press-release (accessed May 24, 2019).

Monroe, Nathan W., and Dani E. Sylvester. 2011. "Who Converts to Vote-by-Mail? Evidence from a Field Experiment." *Election Law Journal* 10 (1): 15–35.

Mossberger, Karen, Caroline J. Tolbert, and Ramona S. McNeal. 2008. *Digital Citizenship: The Internet, Society, and Participation*. Cambridge, MA: Cambridge University Press.

Mycoff, Jason, Michael Wagner, and David Wilson. 2009. "The Empirical Effects of Voter-ID Laws: Present or Absent." *PS: Political Science and Politics* 42 (1): 121–126.

National Conference of State Legislatures. 2018a. "Absentee and Early Voting." (http://www.ncsl.org/research/election-and-campaigns/ absentee-and-early voting.aspx (accessed October 1, 2018).

National Conference of State Legislatures. 2018b. "Same Day Registration." (http://www.ncsl.org/research/election-and-campaigns/ same-day-registration.aspx (accessed April 22, 2018).

National Conference of State Legislatures. 2019a. "Voter Identification Requirements." https://www.ncsl.org/research/elections-and-campaigns/voter-id.aspx (accessed March 15, 2019).

National Conference of State Legislatures. 2019b. "Voter ID History." https://www.ncsl.org/research/elections-and-campaigns/voter-id-history.aspx (accessed March 15, 2019).

National Conference of State Legislatures. 2020. "Automatic Voter Registration." https://www.ncsl.org/research/elections-and-campaigns/automatic-voter-registration.aspx (accessed March 1, 2020).

National Voting Rights Act. 1993. *Statutes at Large*. Vol. 107, pp. 77–89.

Neeley, Grant W., and Lilliard E. Richardson, Jr. 2001. "Who Is Early Voting? An Individual Level Examination." *Social Science Journal* 38:381–392.

Neiheisel, Jacob R., and Barry C. Burden. 2012. "The Impact of Election Day Registration on Voter Turnout and Election Outcomes." *American Politics Research* 40:636–664.

Nickerson, David W., and Todd Rogers. 2014. "Political Campaigns and Big Data." *Journal of Economic Perspectives* 28 (2): 51–74.

Niven, David. 2000. "The Limits of Mobilization: Turnout Evidence from State House Primaries." *Political Behavior* 23 (4): 335–350.

Niven, David. 2004. "The Mobilization Solution? Face-to-Face Contact and Voter Turnout in a Municipal Election." *Journal of Politics* 66 (3): 868–884.

North Carolina State Conference of the NAACP v. McCrory. 2017. 831 F.3rd 204, 215.

Oliver, J. Eric. 1996. "The Effects of Eligibility Restrictions and Party Activity on Absentee Voting and Overall Turnout." *American Journal of Political Science* 40:498–513.

Orren, Karen, and Stephen Skowronek. 2004. *The Search for American Political Development.* New York, NY: Cambridge University Press.

Pacek, Alexander, and Benjamin Radcliff. 1995. "The Political Economy of Competitive Elections in the Developing World." *American Journal of Political Science* 39 (3): 745–759.

Pacheco, Julianna. 2013. "Attitudinal Policy Feedback and Public Opinion: The Impact of Smoking Bans on Attitudes toward Smokers, Secondhand Smoke, and Anti-smoking Policies." *Political Research Quarterly* 77 (3): 714–734.

Pacheco, Julianna, and Jason Fletcher. 2015. "Incorporating Health into Studies of Political Behavior: Evidence for Turnout and Partisanship." *Political Research Quarterly* 68 (1): 104–116.

Parry, Janine, Jay Barth, Martha Kropf, and E. Terrence Jones. 2008. "Mobilizing the Seldom Voter: Campaign Contact and Effects of High-Profile Elections." *Political Behavior* 30 (1): 97–113.

Patterson, Samuel C., and Gregory A. Caldeira. 1985. "Mailing in the Vote: Correlates and Consequences of Absentee Voting." *American Journal of Political Science* 29:766–788.

Pew Charitable Trusts. 2016. "Elections Performance Index." http://www.pewtrusts.org/en/multimedia/data-visualizations/2016/elections-performance-index (accessed December 26, 2016).

Pew Research Center. 2016. "Confidence in Election, View of U.S. Democracy." http://www.people-press.org/2016/10/27/5-confidence-in-election-views-of-u-s-democracy/ (accessed May 1, 2018).

Piven, Frances Fox, and Richard Cloward. 1977. *Poor People's Movement: Why They Succeed, How They Fail.* New York, NY: Vintage Books.

Plutzer, Eric. 2002. "Becoming a Habitual Voter: Inertia, Resources, and Growth in Young Adulthood." *American Political Science Review* 96 (1): 41–56.

Plutzer, Eric, and Julianna Sandell Pacheco. 2008. "Political Participation and Cumulative Disadvantage: The Impact of Economic and Social Hardship on Young Citizens." *Journal of Social Issues* 64 (3): 571–593.

Powell, G Bingham Powell, Jr. 1986. "American Voter Turnout in Comparative Perspective." *American Political Science Review* 80 (1): 17–43.

Putnam, Robert D. 1993. *Making Democracy Work: Civic Traditions in Modern Italy.* Princeton University Press.

Rakich, Nathaniel. 2019. "Early-Voting Laws Probably Don't Boost Turnout." *FiveThirtyEight*, January 30. https://fivethirtyeight.com/features/early-voting-laws-probably-dont-boost-turnout/.

Rhine, Staci L. 1995. "Registration Reform and Turnout Change in the American States." *American Politics Quarterly* 23: 397–403.

Rhodes, Jesse H. 2017. *Ballot Blocked: The Political Erosion of the Voting Rights Act.* Stanford, CA: Stanford University Press.

Richey, Sean. 2008. "Voting by Mail: Turnout and Institutional Reform in Oregon." *Social Science Quarterly* 89 (4): 902–915.

Rigby, Elizabeth, and Melanie J. Springer. 2011. "Does Electoral Reform Increases (or Decrease) Political Equality?" *Political Research Quarterly* 64 (2): 420–434.

Rigby, Elizabeth, and Gerald C. Wright. 2013. "Political Parties and Representation of the Poor in the American States." *American Journal of Political Science* 57:552–565.

Riker, William H., and Peter C. Ordeshook. 1968. "A Theory of the Calculus of Voting." *American Political Science Review* 62:25–42.

Robinson, Adia. 2018. "Dramatic Increased in Voters Purged from Voter Rolls between 2014 and 2016: Report." *ABC News*. https://abcnews.go.com/Politics/millions-voters-purged-voter-rolls-2014-2016-report/story?id=56756914 (accessed August 1, 2018).

Rocha, Rene, and Tetsuya Matsubayashi. 2014. "The Politics of Race and Voter ID Laws in the States: The Return of Jim Crow?" *Political Research Quarterly* 67 (3): 666–679.

Rogers, Todd, and Mashahiko Aida. 2014. "Vote Self-Prediction Hardly Predicts Who Will Vote, and Is (Misleadingly) Unbiased." *American Politics Research* 42 (3): 503–528.

Rolfe, Meredith. 2012. *Voter Turnout: A Social Theory of Political Participation.* New York, NY: Cambridge University Press.

Rosenstone, Steven J., and John Mark Hansen. 2002. *Mobilization, Participation, and Democracy in America.* New York, NY: Pearson Education.

Rubin, Jennifer. 2019. "Stacey Abrams Gives a Graduate School Class on Voter Suppression." *Washington Post*, April 8. https://www.washingtonpost.com/opinions/2019/04/08/stacey-abrams-gives-graduate-school-class-voter-suppression/?utm_term=.ecc0bf1bdca5 (accessed April 8, 2019).

Schattschneider, E. E. 1942. *Party Government.* New York, NY: Holt, Rinehart, and Winston.

Schattschneider, E. E. 1960. *The Semi-Sovereign People: A Realist's View of Democracy in America.* New York, NY: Wadsworth Thompson Learning.

Schlozman, Kay Lehman, Sidney Verba, and Henry E. Brady. 2012. *The Unheavenly Chorus: Unequal Political Voice and the Broken Promise of American Democracy.* Princeton, NJ: Princeton University Press.

"Selected Characteristics of People at Specified Levels of Poverty in the Past 12 Months." 2015. *American Community Survey*. https://factfinder.census.gov/faces/tableservices/jsf/pages/productview.xhtml?pid=ACS_ 15_1YR_S1703&prodType=table (accessed May 21, 2017).

Shelby County v. Holder. 2013. 570 U.S. 529.

Sheppard, Jill, and Katrine Beauregard. 2018. "Early Voting in Australia: The Costs and Benefits of Convenience." *Political Science* 70 (2): 117–134.

Sinclair, Betsy. 2012. *The Social Citizen: Peer Networks and Political Behavior.* Chicago, IL: University of Chicago Press.

Smith, Rogers. 1993. "Beyond Tocqueville, Myrdal, and Hartz: The Multiple Traditions in America." *American Political Science Review* 87: 549–566.

Smith, Rogers. 1997. *Civic Ideals: Conflicting Visions of Citizenship in U.S. History.* New Haven, CT: Yale University Press.

Solt, Frederick. 2008. "Economic Inequality and Democratic Political Engagement." *American Journal of Political Science* 52 (1): 48–60.

Solt, Frederick. 2010. "Does Economic Inequality Depress Electoral Participation? Testing the Schattschneider Hypothesis." *Political Behavior* 32 (2): 285–301.

Soss, Joe, and Sanford F. Schram. 2007. "A Public Transformed? Welfare Reform as Policy Feedback." *American Political Science Review* 91 (1): 80–98.

Soss, Joe, and Sanford F. Schram. 2011. *Discipling the Poor: Neoliberal Paternalism and the Persistent Power of Race.* University of Chicago Press.

Southwell, Priscilla L. 2016. "It's Not Convenient: Should Other States Follow the Northwest and Vote by Mail?" In *Why Don't Americans Vote? Causes and Consequences,* eds. Bridgett A. Kind and Kathleen Hale. Santa Barbara, CA: ABC-CLIO.

Southwell, Priscilla L., and Justin Burchett. 2000. "The Effect of All-Mail Turnout Elections on Voter Turnout." *American Politics Quarterly* 28 (January): 72–79.

Springer, Melanie. 2014. *American Electoral Institutions and Voter Turnout, 1920–2000.* Chicago, IL: University of Chicago Press.

Stein, Robert M. 1998. "Introduction: Early Voting." *Public Opinion Quarterly* 62 (Spring): 57–69.

Stein, Robert M., and Patricia A. Garcia-Monet. 1997. "Voting Early, but Not Often." *Social Science Quarterly* 81:657–671.

Stein, Robert M., and Greg Vonnahme. 2014. "Polling Place Practices and the Voting Experience." In *The Measure of American Elections*, eds. Barry C. Burden and Charles Stewart III. New York, NY: Cambridge University Press.

Steinmo, Sven, Kathleen Thelen, and Frank Longstreth. 1992. *Structuring Politics: Historical Institutionalism in Comparative Analysis.* Cambridge, UK: Cambridge University Press.

Stewart, Charles, III. 2006. "Residual Vote in the 2004 Election." *Election Law Journal* 5 (2): 158–169.

Stewart, Charles, III. 2008. "Improving the Measurement of Election System Performance in the United States." In *Designing Democratic Government: Making Institutions Work*, eds. Margaret Levi, James Johnson, and Susan Stokes, 288–312. New York, NY: Russell Sage Foundation.

Stewart, Charles. 2013. "Voter ID: Who Has Them; Who Shows Them." *Oklahoma Law Review* 66:21–52.

Stewart, Charles, III. 2014. "Measuring Elections." In *The Measure of American Elections*, eds. Barry C. Burden and Charles Stewart III. New York, NY: Cambridge University Press.

Timpone, Richard. 2002. "Estimating Aggregate Policy Reform Effects: New Baselines for Registration, Participation, and Representation." *Policy Analysis* 10:154–177.

Tocqueville, Alexis de. 1835. *Democracy in America.* Chicago, IL: University of Chicago Press.

Tolbert, Caroline, Todd Donovan, and Bruce Cain. 2008b. "The Promise of Election Reform." In *Democracy in the States*, eds. Bruce E. Cain, Todd Donovan, and Caroline J. Tolbert, 1–20. Washington, DC: Brookings Institution Press.

Tolbert, Caroline, Todd Donovan, Bridgett King, and Shaun Bowler. 2008a. "Election Day Registration, Competition, and Turnout." In *Democracy in the States: Experimentation in Election Reform*, eds. Bruce E Cain, Todd Donovan, and Caroline J Tolbert. Washington, DC: Brookings Institution Press, 83–98.

.Tolbert, Caroline J., John A. Grummel, and Daniel A. Smith. 2001. "The Effects of Ballot Initiatives on Voter Turnout in the American States." *American Politics Research* 29 (4): 625–648.

Tolbert, Caroline J., Ramona S. McNeal, and Daniel A. Smith. 2003. "Enhancing Civic Engagement: The Effect of Direct Democracy on Political Participation and Knowledge." *State Politics and Policy Quarterly* 3 (1): 23–41.

Tolbert, Caroline J., and Daniel A. Smith. 2005. "The Educative Effects of Ballot Initiatives on Voter Turnout." *American Politics Research* 33 (2): 283–309.

United States Elections Project. 2018b. "National General Election VEP Turnout Rates, 1789-Present." http://www.electproject.org/national-1789-present (accessed June 1, 2018).

United States Elections Project. 2018c. "State Turnout Rates." http://www.electproject. org/home/voter-turnout/voter-turnout-data (accessed June 1, 2018).

U.S. Census Bureau. 2019. "Voter and Registration in the Election of November 2018." https://www.census.gov/data/tables/time-series/demo/voting-and-registration/p20–583.html (accessed May 24, 2019).

U.S. Department of Health and Human Services. 2016. "Poverty Guidelines." https://aspe. hhs.gov/poverty-guidelines (accessed August 12, 2016).

U.S. Election Assistance Commission. 2012. "2012 Election Administration and Voting Survey." https://www.eac.gov/assets/1/Page/990050%20EAC%20VoterSurvey_508Comp liant.pdf (accessed January 31, 2017).

U.S. Elections Project. 2018a. "CPS Vote Over-Report and Non-Response Bias Correction." http://www.electproject.org/home/voter-turnout/cps-methodology (accessed June 1, 2018).

"U.S. Poverty Statistics." 2016. Federal Safety Net. http://federalsafetynet.com/us-poverty-statistics.html (accessed May 23, 2017).

Vandewalker, Ian, and Keith Gunnar Bentele. 2015. "Vulnerability in Numbers: Racial Composition of the Electorate, Voter Suppression, and the Voting Rights Act." *Harvard Latino Law Review* 99 (18): 99–150.

Vercellotti, Timothy, and David Anderson. 2006. "Protecting the Franchise, or Restricting It?" Paper presented at the annual meeting of the American Political Science Association. Philadelphia.

Verba, Sidney, Kay Lehman Schlozman, and Henry Brady. 1995. *Voice and Equality: Civic Voluntarism in American Politics.* Cambridge, MA: Harvard University Press.

Voting Rights Act. 1965. *Statutes at Large.* Vol. 79, pp. 437–446.

Waldman, Michael. 2016. *The Fight to Vote.* New York, NY: Simon and Schuster.

Walker, Hannah, Gabriel Sanchez, Stephen Nuno, and Matt Barreto. 2018. "Race and the Right to Vote: The Modern Barrier of Voter ID Laws." In *Changing How America Votes*, ed. Todd Donovan. Lanham, MD: Rowman and Littlefield Publishers, 26–37.

Walker, Hannah L., Michael C. Herron, and Daniel A. Smith. 2018. "Early Voting Changes and Voter Turnout: North Carolina in the 2016 General Election." *Political Behavior* 41: 841–869.

Wass, Hanna, Mikko Mattila, Lauri Rapeli, and Peter Soderlund. 2017. "Voting while Ailing: The Effect of Voter Facilitation Instruments on Health-Related Differences in Turnout." *Journal of Elections, Public Opinion and Parties* 27 (4): 503–522.

Weaver, Russell. 2015. "The Racial Context of Convenience Voting Cutbacks: Early Voting in Ohio During the 2008 and 2012 U.S. Presidential Elections." *SAGE Open* 5 (3): 2158244015591825. https://doi.org/10.1177/2158244015591825.

Weilhouwer, Peter W. 2000. "Releasing the Fetters and the Mobilization of the African American Electorate." *Journal of Politics* 62 (11): 206–222.

Weiser, Wendy R. 2014, October 1. "Voter Suppression: How Bad? (Pretty Bad)." Brennan Center for Justice at New York University School of Law.

Weister, Wendy R., and Max Feldman. 2018. "The State of Voting 2018." *Brennan Center for Justice.* https://www.brennancenter.org/publication/state-voting-2018 (accessed August 1, 2018).

Wolfinger, Raymond E., and Steven J. Rosenston. 1980. *Who Votes?* New Haven, CT: Yale University Press.

Wolfinger, Raymond E., Benjamin Highton, and Megan Mullin. 2005. "How Postregistration Laws Affect the Turnout of Citizens Registered to Vote." *State Politics and Policy Quarterly* 5 (1): 1–23.

Index

Tables and figures are indicated by *t* and *f* following the page number